DARK THREATS AND WHITE KNIGHTS

The Somalia Affair, Peacekeeping, and the New Imperialism

On 4 March 1993 two Somalis were shot in the back by Canadian peacekeepers, one fatally. Barely two weeks later, sixteen-year-old Shidane Abukar Arone was tortured to death. Dozens of Canadian soldiers looked on or knew of the torture.

The first reports of what became known in Canada as the Somalia Affair challenged national claims to a special expertise in peacekeeping and to a society free of racism. Today, however, despite a national inquiry into the deployment of troops to Somalia, most Canadians are proud of their nation's role as peacekeeper to the world. Incidents of peacekeeping violence are attributed to a few bad apples, bad generals, and a rogue regiment.

In *Dark Threats and White Knights*, Sherene H. Razack explores the racism implicit in the Somalia Affair and what it has to do with modern peacekeeping. Drawing on the records of the military trials and public inquiry, Razack examines, first, the nature of the violence itself, and second, the ways in which peacekeeping violence is largely forgiven and ultimately forgotten. The matter of racism has all but disappeared from public memory and what remains is the myth of an innocent, morally superior middle-power nation obliged to discipline and sort out barbaric Third World nations. Modern peacekeeping, Razack concludes, maintains a colour line between a family of white nations constructed as civilized and a Third World constructed as a dark threat, a world in which violence is not only condoned but seen as necessary.

SHERENE H. RAZACK is a professor in the Department of Sociology and Equity Studies in Education at the Ontario Institute for Studies in Education, University of Toronto.

DARK THREATS AND WHITE KNIGHTS

The Somalia Affair, Peacekeeping, and the New Imperialism

Sherene H. Razack

UNIVERSITY OF TORONTO PRESS
Toronto Buffalo London

ISBN 0-8020-8708-6 (cloth)
ISBN 0-8020-8663-2 (paper)

Printed on acid-free paper

National Library of Canada Cataloguing in Publication

Razack, Sherene
Dark threats and white knights : the Somalia Affair, peacekeeping and the
new imperialism / Sherene H. Razack.

Includes bibliographical references and index.
ISBN 0-8020-8708-6 (bound).   ISBN 0-8020-8663-2 (pbk.)

1. Peacekeeping forces.   2. United Nations – Peacekeeping forces.
3. Peacekeeping forces – Canada.   4. Somalia Affair, 1992–1997.   5. Racism.
6. Imperialism.   I. Title.

JZ6377.C3R39 2004   327.1' 72   C2003-906789-0

The publisher gratefully acknowledges permission to reproduce in revised form articles
from the following: *Hypatia* 18, 1 (2003) (chapter 1); *Cultural Anthropology* 15, 1
(2000) (chapter 2); *University of Missouri–Kansas Law Review* 71, 2 (2002) (chapter 3).

This book has been published with the help of a grant from the Canadian Federation
for the Humanities and Social Sciences, through the Aid to Scholarly Publications
Programme, using funds provided by the Social Sciences and Humanities Research
Council of Canada.

University of Toronto Press acknowledges the financial assistance to its publishing
program of the Canada Council for the Arts and the Ontario Arts Council.

University of Toronto Press acknowledges the financial support for its publishing
activities of the Government of Canada through the Book Publishing Industry
Development Program (BPIDP).

For my father
Ishmile

Contents

Acknowledgments

A friend once asked why I needed a research grant to write this book. A book of this nature requires countless hours spent over documents, many on a CD-ROM and others on-line or in libraries. I could not do this without research assistance and a generous grant for which I thank the Social Sciences and Humanities Research Council. The team of researchers, graduate students from the Department of Sociology and Equity Studies in Education of OISE/UT who worked on this project over the four years it took, provided much more than their stellar research skills. They gave generously of their insight and passion for social justice. For these gifts I thank Sheila Gill, Eve Haque, Gabrielle Hezekiah, Melanie Knight, Teresa Macias, Carmela Murdocca, Hijin Park, and Leslie Thielen Wilson. To Carmela and Leslie, who worked the longest on the project, I owe my heartfelt thanks for believing in this project even more than I did. Their consistent brilliance, competence, and caring highly motivated me to understand peacekeeping violence and to produce work that would matter. Leslie Thielen Wilson was the backbone of the project and I relied on her thoughtful and deeply ethical responses to violence as well as her amazing editing eye and research skills in ways that went well beyond 'research assistance.' Even at the zero hour, Leslie continued to make suggestions that immeasurably improved the book. I am grateful to Godah Barre, Rohan Bansie, Ahmed Hashi, Karen Mock, Isaac Sechere, and Michelle Williams for interviews in which they shared their recollections and related documents of the Inquiry into the Deployment of Canadian Troops to Somalia.

Friends and family steadied me in ways too numerous to mention. My love and thanks go to my cottage writing buddies Honor Ford Smith and Narda Razack for listening to the arguments and providing critical feedback as well as fine meals and friendship. I am deeply grateful for the love and friendship of Ruth Roach Pierson, who shared her vast historical knowledge of Germany and many of her books on the Nazi years, inspiring me to reflect more deeply than I otherwise would on racism and the state. Over the years I presented parts of this work at annual Law and Society meetings and critical race conferences and benefited from friends who shared their own understanding of race. I thank them all. To my mother, my sister, my brothers, and my children, a big hug and thanks. Yes Ben and Ilya, your cheerful inquiries about the status of the book and even your interruptions sustained me more than you will ever know. To Larry Brookwell, whose love and support go well beyond considerable computer help and countless conversations, I can only repeat the standard line and mean it with all my heart: This book could not have been done without you. Finally, this book is dedicated to my father, with whom I shared its early conclusions but who died before it was completed. From the start, this book was a way to tell you that I absorbed all of those dinner-table political arguments you were known for. They shaped me in ways I have only now begun to understand. You taught me that history matters. I miss your keen sense of international justice and the passion of your convictions more than I thought possible.

THE WHITE MAN'S BURDEN

Rudyard Kipling
McClure's Magazine (February 1899)

Take up the White Man's burden –
　　　　Send forth the best ye breed –
Go, bind your sons to exile
　　　　To serve your captives' need;
To wait, in heavy harness,
　　　　On fluttered folk and wild –
Your new-caught sullen peoples,
　　　　Half devil and half child.

Take up the White Man's burden –
　　　　In patience to abide,
To veil the threat of terror
　　　　And check the show of pride;
By open speech and simple,
　　　　An hundred times made plain,
To seek another's profit
　　　　And work another's gain.

Take up the White Man's burden –
　　　　The savage wars of peace –
Fill full the mouth of Famine,
　　　　And bid the sickness cease;
And when your goal is nearest
　　　　(The end for others sought)
Watch sloth and heathen folly
　　　　Bring all your hope to nought.

Take up the White Man's burden –
　　　　No iron rule of kings,
But toil of serf and sweeper –
　　　　The tale of common things.
The ports ye shall not enter,
　　　　The roads ye shall not tread,
Go, make them with your living
　　　　And mark them with your dead.

Take up the White Man's burden,
      And reap his old reward –
The blame of those ye better
      The hate of those ye guard –
The cry of hosts ye humour
      (Ah, slowly!) toward the light: –
'Why brought ye us from bondage,
      Our loved Egyptian night?'

Take up the White Man's burden –
      Ye dare not stoop to less –
Nor call too loud on Freedom
      To cloak your weariness.
By all ye will or whisper,
      By all ye leave or do,
The silent sullen peoples
      Shall weigh your God and you.

Take up the White Man's burden!
      Have done with childish days –
The lightly-proffered laurel,
      The easy ungrudged praise:
Comes now, to search your manhood
      Through all the thankless years,
Cold, edged with dear-bought wisdom,
      The judgment of your peers.

DARK THREATS AND WHITE KNIGHTS

The Somalia Affair, Peacekeeping, and the
New Imperialism

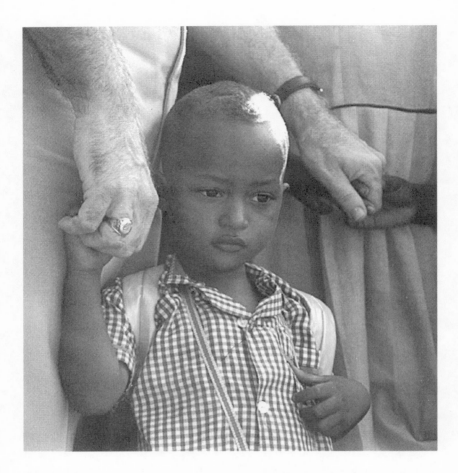

The photo appeared with the following article: Allan Thompson – *Toronto Star*, Sunday, 30 December 2001: B2 – 'Battling to reclaim lost lives Sierra Leone's slim hope of stability depends on its ability to rehabilitate its war-affected children.' The caption read: 'Small Comfort: Roméo Dallaire holds hands with two of the war-affected children he has come to Sierra Leone to help.'

INTRODUCTION

'Savage Wars of Peace'

The problem of the twentieth century is the problem of the color line, – the relation of the darker to the lighter races of men in Asia and Africa, in America and
the islands of the sea.

W.E.B. Du Bois, *The Souls of Black Folk* (1903)[1]

I still think today as yesterday that the color line is a great problem of this century. But today I see more clearly than yesterday that back of the problem of race
and color, lies a greater problem which both obscures and implements it: and that
is the fact that so many civilized persons are willing to live in comfort even if the
price of this is poverty, ignorance and disease of the majority of their fellowmen;
that to maintain this privilege men have waged war until today war tends to
become universal and continuous, and the excuse for this war continues largely to
be color and race.

W.E.B. Du Bois, Preface to new edition of *The Souls of Black Folk* (1953)[2]

Our security will require transforming the military you will lead – a military that
must be ready to strike at a moment's notice in any dark corner of the world.

President George W. Bush, Speech to West Point graduates, 2003[3]

The hands of Canada's most well-known general clasp the hands of two Black
children in war-ravaged Sierra Leone. Almost destroyed from his encounter
with the 'devil' in Rwanda, General Roméo Dallaire, known for his efforts to
stop the genocide in that country, has returned to Africa. He has come to
work with children traumatized by war. They have something in common:
each has seen great brutality and suffered trauma as a result. The general
wants to come to terms with his past, not only with post-traumatic stress but

with the 'ghosts of Rwanda,' the 800,000 people he felt he couldn't save; they were massacred while a skeletal UN peacekeeping force looked helplessly on.[4] This is the story of peacekeeping we want to remember: our mission in the First World to save Africans, our helplessness and vulnerability in the face of so much horror, and our bravery in continuing nonetheless to help. For us, peacekeeping is Rudyard Kipling's white man's burden, barely transformed from its nineteenth-century origins in colonialism, when it provided moral sanction for waging 'savage wars of peace,' wars to 'fill the mouth of famine' and 'bid the sickness cease.' The nineteenth-century poet exhorted white men – Americans on the eve of an imperial war in the Philippines – to take up the thankless burden of meeting the needs of their 'new-caught sullen peoples, / Half devil and half child.'[5]

For a brief moment in national history, modern peacekeeping revealed its sordid colonial origins. In Canada, two incidents stand out amidst the half dozen or more officially acknowledged ones and scores of uncounted others. On 4 March 1993, two Somalis were shot in the back by Canadian soldiers, one fatally. Barely two weeks later, on 16 March, a Somali prisoner, sixteen-year-old Shidane Abukar Arone, was tortured to death by soldiers of the Canadian Airborne Regiment. Dozens of men looked on or knew of the torture. Gruesome photographs of the 16 March event survive; photographs of the bloodied and battered head of a Black man, a baton holding his head in place for the camera as his torturer posed grinning beside him. For a while the photos confirmed that what had gone on during the Canadian peacekeeping mission in Somalia in 1993 could not be easily separated from racism, or indeed from colonialism. Soldiers had acted more like conquerors than humanitarians, and their actions underscored the meaning of Black bodies both here and there, historically and in the present.

As time went on, the racial dimensions of the peacekeeping encounter became even more evident. On 15 January 1995, *CBC Newsworld* announced that it had obtained a videotape of Canadian Airborne Regiment soldiers serving in Somalia. Filmed as a holiday video, the tape showed soldiers uttering a number of racist remarks as they sat around drinking beer under the hot sun. Corporal Matt MacKay, a self-confessed neo-Nazi who said he had quit the white supremacist movement two years earlier, gleefully reported, 'We haven't killed enough n— yet.' Private David Brocklebank (later court-martialled for his role in the murder of Shidane Arone) announced to the camera that the Somalia operation is called 'Operation "Snatch Nig-Nog."' In the background, Private Kyle Brown (also later charged with the torture and murder of Shidane Arone) was silent. Another soldier explained that a stick is used for cracking the heads of Somalis, while another commented that the

Somalis were not starving and that 'they never work, they're lazy, they're slobs, and they stink.'[6] No sooner had the public digested the first videotape than another emerged depicting violent and racist hazing rituals of another unit of the Airborne Regiment during a party in Canada. In this videotape, we see a Black soldier being smeared with faeces spelling out the words 'I love the KKK,' then tied to a tree and sprinkled with white flour. He is later made to crawl on all fours and to suffer a simulated sodomizing.[7]

Still later, trophy photos surfaced of soldiers posing with bound and hooded Somali youth, some of whom appeared to have been beaten. In the photo that appears on the cover of this book, young children sit tied and hooded; they are made to wear signs around their necks with the word 'thief' in Somali and forced to sit in the hot sun in plain view of everyone. This photo, perhaps even more than the ones of a tortured Arone, seemed to leave no room for doubt that something had gone terribly wrong in Somalia, something more wide-spread than a single incident of brutality. The soldier apparently standing guard over the children is Captain Mark Sargent, then the military chaplain. Captain Sargent has never spoken publicly about his role, but the military ombudsman for whom he now works as an investigator, and others, have claimed that he was merely trying to ensure that the children were not further harmed.[8] Others maintain that the chaplain had simply indulged in the com-mon practice of having trophy photos taken whenever there were detainees. As military police investigations revealed, several soldiers had posed for such photos, some sending them home as souvenirs. A copy had even been posted on the refrigerator door in the unit's tent in Belet Huen. It is clear, too, that the soldiers' superiors knew about the practice of the humiliation of children, and also about the taking of trophy photos. Colonel Serge Labbé maintained that when he first witnessed the humiliation of children, he ordered that it be stopped, an order Lieutenant Colonel Carol Mathieu jotted down in his field-message book. If this was indeed the order given, it was not obeyed. In late January 1993, when the photo of the five children and the chaplain was taken, several soldiers recorded the event either by taking trophy photos themselves or writing about it in letters home. Once the killing of Arone came to the media's attention, however, trophy photos were ordered to be destroyed. As General Ernest Beno wrote to Colonel Labbé in April 1993, if the Canadian public ever saw such photos, they would be disturbed.[9]

It is not clear just how routine was the event depicted in the photo. Some soldiers have claimed that they were initially disturbed by the routine practice of the 'bagging and tagging' of detainees.[10] As ex-Captain Michel Rainville (who was himself implicated in the 4 March killing) explained to the media, he shared his misgivings with his superiors and was reassured that the humiliation of the children was the only acceptable way to deter petty thievery.[11] Another soldier, breaching military rules, made the photo available to a national inquiry on the events in Somalia and planned to testify about what he felt was a contravention of the Geneva Convention. (For his actions, Corporal Michel Purnelle was disciplined and charged by the military with a series of infractions, among them leaving his post to appear before the commission of inquiry).[12] The soldier who took the photo, Captain Jeff DeLallo, maintained that the signs around the children's neck were the idea of the Somali interpreter and were 'for their own good.' When he was interviewed by military police in July 1994, Captain DeLallo felt himself to be the target of a government witch-hunt, presumably prompted by the furor over the torture and murder of Shidane Arone.[13]

What should we feel about six- to eight-year-old children being tied up, humiliated, and left to sit in the scorching sun for two hours? It may well be, as one journalist suggested, that Canadian peacekeepers were merely taking the advice of the local population in tying up the children and seeking to deter thievery through humiliation, although this explanation begs the question of whether we would have taken such advice if the children had been our own.[14] Seen alongside the 4 March and 16 March incidents, the videotapes, other incidents that would later come to light in a national inquiry, and subsequent military efforts to cover up what happened, the actions of peacekeepers seem far less benign than a cultural misunderstanding.

The first reports of what became known in Canada as the 'Somalia Affair' briefly highlighted for Canadians the connection between racism, peacekeeping, and the violent events we now know to be an aspect of most if not all peacekeeping ventures. The connection shook our sensibilities to the core, challenging as it did national claims to a special expertise in peacekeeping, and more importantly, to a history without racism. The flare died, however, as quickly as it was born. Today, despite a national inquiry into the deployment of troops to Somalia, what most Canadians are likely to associate with peacekeeping is the nation's glorious role as peacekeeper to the world, and its traumatized heroes such as Roméo Dallaire. Few would now recognize the name of Shidane Arone and many would be outraged at the juxtaposition of the word peacekeeping with racial violence. At most, some would concede that what happened in Somalia was horrible, but they would put it down to a few 'bad apples,' bad generals, and a 'rogue regiment,' the latter now happily disbanded.

Racism has all but disappeared from public memory of the Somalia Affair, despite its early dramatic appearances in the photographs and films. 'Spectacle,' Toni Morrison writes, 'is the best means by which an official story is formed and is a superior mechanism for guaranteeing its longevity. Spectacle offers signs, symbols and images that are more pervasive and persuasive than print which can smoothly parody thought.'[15] The official story that emerged from the spectacle of the Somalia Affair – a spectacle that began with photos of the violent death of a Black man in custody and Black children bound and humiliated – was that of a gentle, peacekeeping nation betrayed by a few unscrupulous men. Violence transformed into gold.

This book explores what racism had to do with the Somalia Affair, what it has to do with modern peacekeeping, and how it disappears in the law and in national memory. These three themes are pursued through an examination of the voluminous records of military trials and the public inquiry into the deployment of Canadian troops to Somalia. They are also pursued in the texts of popular culture where both national and international mythologies about peacekeeping in the post–cold war era can be tracked. I follow two racial stories. One is the story of the violence itself and what would drive men from the North to commit such atrocities against people of the South. This is a story about race and the masculinities that make the nation white. The second story, and in many respects the more significant one, concerns the ways in which peacekeeping violence is largely forgiven and ultimately forgotten, both erased and de-raced, when the story of the violence travels from the South to the North and enters legal arenas such as military trials and a national inquiry. Race disappears from public memory through a variety of tricks, and incidents of racial violence become transformed into something else, something we can live with. In place of racial epithets, humiliated children, and tortured, beaten, and executed bodies, a new story emerges about the heroism of the peacekeepers of Northern countries and the traumas *they* have had to endure as they go about the business of assisting Third World nations into modernity.

Why tell these two stories now? First, the terrorist attacks on the World Trade Center and the Pentagon and the resulting 'war against terrorism' have made us all aware, if we were not before, of the racial underpinnings of the New World Order. In this book, recalling W.E.B. Du Bois's famous observation, I refer to these underpinnings as the colour line. Embedded deep within the conceptual foundations of the Bush administration's notion of a life-and-death struggle against the 'axis of evil' is a thoroughly racial logic. Disciplining, instructing, and keeping in line Third World peoples who irrationally hate and wish to destroy their saviours (as Kipling's poem predicted) derives from the idea that Northern peoples inhabit civilized lands while the South, in Chinua Achebe's words, 'is a metaphysical battlefield devoid of all recognizable humanity into which the wandering European enters at his peril.'[16] On such battlefields, violence occurs with impunity and is often legally authorized. As it was in Somalia in 1991, colour-line thinking was certainly in evidence in the American invasions of both Afghanistan in 2002 and Iraq in 2003, invasions justified on the ground that it was necessary to drop thousands of bombs on Afghanis and Iraqis in order to save them from the excesses of their own society. For Kipling as for President George W. Bush, a savage war of peace 'To veil the threat of terror / And check the show of pride' is the West's burden to bear. Oil, the free market, and the historical support the United States has given to the Taliban and to Saddam Hussein, among other despotic regimes, all disappear under 'smart' bombs. Once the smoke clears, peacekeepers walk in.

Second, the legal transformation of peacekeeping violence into a story of Northern goodness and heroism tells us a great deal about *how* violence directed against bodies of colour becomes normalized as a necessary part of the civilizing process. National and international mythologies of heroic white people obliged to make the world safe for democracy and needing to employ violence to do so flood our airwaves. Saluting Noam Chomsky for having unmasked 'the ugly, manipulative, ruthless universe that exists behind that beautiful, sunny word "freedom,"' Arundhati Roy underlines this key feature of the New World Order: great crimes against humanity are committed in the name of justice and righteousness.[17] Law has an important role to play in this process, for it is in the courtroom and at hearings that a public truth is proclaimed about who we are as a people and as a nation. The explanatory frameworks utilized in the legal context reveal how racial hierarchies are organized through knowledge production. We see, for example, how the notion that Somalis possessed different values from ourselves enabled the court to understand that violence in such a setting was both normal and necessary. Such assumptions, racist in their origin and impact, enable us to know ourselves as superior. Examining legal narratives for the ways in which they organize how we come to know ourselves is a valuable undertaking if we are to dismantle those deeply internalized myths about our civilizing mission.

This book examines the eviction of Third World peoples from the realm of common humanity through a detailed look at one such legal encounter: the military trials and national inquiry into the deployment of Canadian troops to Somalia. Employing a case study such as the Somalia Affair to say something about the larger global story of racism and modern peacekeeping has an important advantage. The case-study approach provides an opportunity to examine up close how individuals perform national and international mythologies. Through a study of these performances we can move beyond the myths and the stories that nations and regions tell about their origins and history. We can begin to understand who people think they are and how this informs what they do. When Canadian peacekeepers went to Somalia, who did they think they were and what did they think they were doing in the hot desert of Belet Huen? By the same token, when a nation announces itself as peace-keeper to the world, and when its national subjects derive from this and related mythologies a sense of self, history, and place, what material structures and practices sustain these beliefs and are, in turn, sustained by them? And what racial hierarchies underpin and are supported by such apparently inno-cent beliefs? The hold that mythologies have should not be underestimated. They have the power to make a nation replace tortured and dead bodies with traumatized soldiers. Mythologies help the nation to forget its bloody past and present. By showing in a context-specific way both how a racially specific national and international subject is performed, produced, and sustained and how such performances keep the global order in place, I hope most of all to reveal that subject's fictive and destructive core and to suggest another, more ethical way of imagining ourselves and of living in the world.

Du Bois, writing fifty years after his prophetic declaration that the colour line would remain the problem of the twentieth century, noted that behind the colour line was the fact that so many people were willing to live with its effects. Du Bois's insight that we are somehow able to live with the pernicious effects of the colour line suggests that it is imperative to understand how our daily participation in a colour-lined world is secured. In this study of peace-keeping violence, what is revealed is that we come to know ourselves in inti-mate ways *through* the colour line. A Canadian today knows herself or himself as someone who comes from the nicest place on earth, as someone from a peacekeeping nation, and as a modest, self-deprecating individual who is able to gently teach Third World Others about civility. So deep is this sense of self that it becomes inconceivable to imagine that Third World Others have any sort of personhood. Race, as Anthony Farley has written, drawing on Frantz Fanon and others, is a form of bodily pleasure and 'legal expressions of the colorline are, similarly, sensations that people have both in and about their bodies. The master and his slave may both come to see and feel themselves through the law that defines, commands, and is their expression of their situa-tion.'[18] To unmake the colour line is to unmake ourselves. It is to give up race pleasure.

The colour line and the race pleasure on which it depends have a long his-tory. As Kipling describes in his poem, 'savage wars of peace' were exactly how nineteenth-century colonial projects were characterized. When New World Order mythologies refer to the obligation of the First World, and the United States in particular, to teach the Third World about democracy, the underlying logic is the same as nineteenth-century colonialism and imperialism's notion of a civilizing mission. As Edward Said has often pointed out, imperialism is not just about accumulation but about the *idea* of empire. What distinguishes imperialist projects of the nineteenth century and of today from earlier empires is the idea that certain territories beseech and require domination. Empire is a structure of feeling, a deeply held belief in the need to and the right to dominate others *for their own good*, others who are expected to be grateful. The imperial past lives on in contemporary American proclamations of 'we are number one, we are bound to lead, we stand for freedom and order, and so on.'[19] Individuals come to define themselves within these scripts, believing deeply in 'the illusion of benevolence'[20] and requiring, as before, grateful natives.

In the chapters that follow, I show how modern peacekeeping is constructed as a colour line with civilized white nations standing on one side and uncivilized Third World nations standing on the other. In chapter 1, this line is revealed in the peacekeeper as a figure who is entrusted with the task of sorting out the tribalisms and the warlords that have mysteriously sprung up in regions of the world where great evil dwells. Confronted with such savagery, peacekeepers can 'lose it,' either by descending into violence themselves or descending into madness. The traumatized peacekeeper, an important Canadian icon, is a man who bears witness to the savagery and who is overcome by it. I locate his story in both an older national narrative about the special qualities of a middle-power peacekeeping nation and a global one about a family of civilized nations forced to stand together to confront 'absolute evil.' Such narratives, I argue, achieve coherence only if we imagine the world to be divided between the civilized and the uncivilized.

In chapter 2, I show what happens when men from the First World go to Africa to assist Africans into modernity. Men who understand themselves to be on colonial terrain, as some Western peacekeepers seem to have done, have humiliated, raped, tortured, and killed the local population they came to help. Many incidents involve children and are collective, openly accomplished events, remarkable indicators of how much the violence is driven by an impulse to teach the natives a lesson, and how much it is considered to be ordinary. In this chapter, I show the pervasive character of the violence in Somalia – that is, its everydayness. In answering the question, 'What did the soldiers think they were doing?' I suggest that acts of violence helped to convince the men of their own masculine and racial superiority. I emphasize that the men who committed the most egregious acts of violence shared with those who watched, condoned, or encouraged it a belief that in Somalia they had an obligation to discipline and instruct the natives, a duty that was clearly patriotic.

What is the relationship of soldiers of colour to the colour line? The question arises in the Somalia Affair because two of the key perpetrators of violence, at least the two so identified in legal processes, were of Aboriginal origin. In chapter 3, I explore their participation in the violence, a participation some have tried to explain as an attempt to 'outwhite the white guys' in order to gain acceptance. I reject this compensatory line of argument, one that suggests that men of colour compensate for their low status by seeking the prestige that engaging in violence provides. I show that although men from subordinate groups (working-class white soldiers and the two Aboriginal soldiers) ended up bearing almost exclusive responsibility for the crimes committed in Somalia, their acts of violence sprang from the pursuit of racial dominance that intimately structured the peacekeeping encounter. All soldiers were invited to 'act white' – that is, to come to know themselves as men from the land of clean snow whose presence in the hot desert of Belet Huen was a civilizing one. For some men, the civilizing endeavour required violence.

There is no question that the Somalia Affair shocked the nation. It prompted us to disband the Canadian Airborne Regiment and to establish a Commission of Inquiry, one that was shut down by the Canadian government, however, before it could investigate fully the events of 4 and 16 March 1993, and particularly before it could probe the role of military leaders. Chapter 4 discusses the public truth we ended up with once the Inquiry had submitted its final report. Race could hardly be ignored in the Inquiry but its role was considered to be largely limited to white supremacist activity among the soldiers. Beyond noticing the use of racial slurs, the Inquiry did not view the encounter as one that race overdetermined. The result, I argue, while a courageous naming of the duplicity and irresponsibility of the leadership, nevertheless exonerated the troops who were thought to have been pushed to the brink by the savagery of Africans and Africa itself and who were abandoned by their leaders. The Inquiry also exonerated the nation, reinstalling our innocence through the trope of a nation betrayed. Officially, we remember ourselves as the principal victims of the Somalia Affair, a remembrance that keeps the colour line intact. We believe we were duped by our own, and that it was our very niceness and national naïveté that led to the debacle in Somalia. We still have not abandoned our sense of the world as a place where we sally forth, often as the 'hero's friend,' to help those less fortunate than ourselves. We cannot imagine that we are implicated in the crises we set out to solve.

I end this book with reflections on what it means to act morally in the New World Order. Morality seems besides the point, superfluous, as Hannah Arendt observed of the totalitarian regime of Adolf Hitler, in a world transformed by U.S. determination to consolidate itself as an empire. Amidst the war cries of the American administration, first against Iraq and now moving relentlessly on towards Syria and Iran, it feels foolish even to attempt to grapple with the issue of morality. How, Arundhati Roy asks in her book *War*

Talk,[21] can we resist empire? This study of peacekeeping has provided some signposts. In the conclusion, I consider the features of the moral universe in which both warmongers and peacekeepers locate themselves – a universe of white knights fighting for peace in the 'dark corners of the earth,' as George W. Bush characterized it. I argue for a rejection of this moral universe and its colour line, urging instead that we put ourselves back into history, rendering 'evil' thinkable and finding out how we have produced it. Only then, can we find ways of acting morally.

The story of racial violence at the heart of peacekeeping is clearly not a Canadian one alone. In this post–cold war and apparently largely decolonized New World Order, violence of the kind evident in the Canadian example has occurred elsewhere. From Somalia to Bosnia, it is hard to find a peacekeeping venture that has not included incidents where peacekeepers tortured, raped, and killed, as well as racially degraded the population they came to assist. The violence of peacekeepers has often been ignored or, more often, justified by the tense, warlike circumstances in which it occurs. More often than not, when it is acknowledged, peacekeeping violence is exceptionalized. Outrage and condemnation, not to mention accountability, have been particularly lacking in legal inquiries. Concern centres on military inefficiency and on the failure of the United Nations to properly plan and execute peacekeeping missions. It is rare to find an acknowledgment that peacekeeping violence occurs, and rarer still to encounter explanations that pay attention to the racial features of the peacekeeping encounter. Legal inquiries seem to contain the violence, functioning as a kind of 'narrative shield' that dissolves the horror in 'a storm of words.'[22]

Although it makes several references to them, this study does not fully explore peacekeeping violence in other countries. Instead, what it provides is a framework for understanding such violence principally as colonial violence enacted in the name of nation. We cannot fully appreciate how peacekeeping violence occurs and is forgiven without understanding its connection to specific national projects. When American, Italian, and Belgian troops committed heinous acts of peacekeeping violence, their nation's specific colonial histories and mythologies profoundly shaped who the perpetrators thought they were, what they thought they were doing, and, ultimately, what the home country thought of their activities. What remains true for all examples of peacekeeping violence, however, is their overtly race-based nature.

On the question of the importance of acknowledging the context in which we write, anthropologist Renato Rosaldo gives an example of how personal history might influence scholarship: 'Has, for example the writer of an ethnography on death suffered a serious personal loss?'[23] Rosaldo uses this question to make his point that we are neither partial nor impartial, innocent nor complicit; we are simply involved. Rosaldo's question prompts me to examine my own relationship to the issues of racial violence and peacekeeping and to the Somalia Affair. I hasten to add that this relationship was not informed by a serious personal loss, although the last stages of the book's completion occurred in the months following my father's death and was surely deeply inspired by his relentless questioning of the 'international' and of the place of Muslim and Black bodies within it. Neither was this work driven by a sense that what happened to individual Somalis was deeply personal. I am not Somali and I have not suffered the kind of grief that the parents of Shidane Arone have endured. Where the personal connection is, however, is in the relationship I bear towards those everyday national mythologies about Canada as a kinder, gentler nation – mythologies enacted in peacekeeping.

This national mythology has always depended on race. It is informed by the notion that 'we' know about democracy and 'they' do not; 'we' have values of integrity, honesty, and compassion that 'they' do not; that 'we' are a law-abiding, orderly, and modest people while 'they' are not. As an immigrant to Canada from the Third World, I have long understood that the 'we' is a white category and that it refers to people who imagine themselves to be the original citizens (Aboriginal peoples are considered dead or dying and people of colour are considered recently arrived). Again, the fault line is a racial one. In the national fantasy, the 'we' are of Anglo-Saxon origin, descendants of a Northern people who consider themselves innately given to civility.[24] The instruction of the natives that is so central to peacekeeping is also central to the everyday experiences of immigrants of colour in the North. It is a civilizing process that is deeply familiar and utterly dehumanizing. My impulse to name the colour line in peacekeeping springs from this everyday experience of eviction from the national, an eviction that swiftly occurs whenever racism is named.

Civilizing missions have wrought terrible damage. There is, as Homi Bhabha observes, a profound emergency in the lives of racialized peoples.[25] The people of Iraq, and the people of Palestine are only two examples of those who have not only borne the brunt of civilizing missions but who have in the bargain been accused of causing their own destruction. On the home front, Aboriginal peoples are driven by the police to the outskirts of the city and left to freeze to death. Black men die in police custody, as Shidane Arone did. Dozens of Aboriginal women working as prostitutes were murdered before anyone official took serious notice. And all the while we insist that there is no racism here, or that racism is worse elsewhere. Internationally, while we bask in the warm glow of being a peacekeeping country, a profound emergency goes on that we have had a hand in creating. It will not do to stand above it all proclaiming our innocence and vulnerability and at the same time our willingness to help.

What the Somalia Affair has to teach us is that the dehumanization of others is more easily accomplished and condoned when we understand those others to be different and when we understand ourselves to be standing outside of the world's crises as impartial and compassionate observers. In the Somalia Affair, we see some of the everyday common-sense notions that blunt the responses of the average person to violence – notions about saving people from themselves, about their mysterious descent into evil and into the thrall of warlords, and about a belief in our own equally mysterious capacity to do good. We see how it happens that we care less and see less about the human rights of others, even while paradoxically we assert our special responsibilities towards them. This study demonstrates that the essence of racism, a dehumanizing of the Other, is accompanied by a profound belief in our own superiority, a superiority conveyed in the thousand ordinary phrases we use to express national character and belonging, and to expel so many Others from the nation. We may not be able to give up these patriotic and exclusionary impulses altogether, but we *can* learn to 'love a *land* instead of just patrolling a territory,' as Roy poetically insists.[26] The profound emergency in the lives of racialized peoples requires no less. It requires that we divest ourselves of the fantasy of the white man and his burden at both the national and international level and begin to acknowledge how we are implicated in the crises of our time. Only then can peacekeeping transcend the racial scripts in which it is so deeply mired.

CHAPTER 1

Those Who 'Witness the Evil': Peacekeeping as Trauma

States like these, and their terrorist allies, constitute an axis of evil, arming to threaten the peace of the world.

President George W. Bush referring to North Korea, Iran, and Iraq, State of the Union Address, 2002[1]

We came into contact with absolute evil.

Canadian peacekeeper and witness of ethnic cleansing and other atrocities in the Croatian wars[2]

It is said that a Canadian speech-writer in the Bush administration coined the phrase 'axis of evil,' which has been so much a part of American political vocabulary since the 11 September 2001 terrorist attacks on the World Trade Center and the Pentagon.[3] If this is true, it is fitting. For the better part of the 1990s, Canadian peacekeepers have described their activities in Somalia, Rwanda, Haiti, Bosnia, Kosovo, and Croatia as encounters with 'absolute evil.' The American president and the Canadian peacekeeper quoted above both imagine the international as a space where civilized peoples from the North go to the South to do battle with evil. So great is the evil that (mysteriously) dwells in the South that it defies description.

Without a specific history, 'absolute evil' is nonetheless understood *through* history. The biblical overtones of the phrase takes us back to Indian or 'savage' wars fought long ago against 'heathens,' and to an even more distant memory of crusades starting in the eleventh century, when Christian knights battled Muslim armies, and the future of Europe itself was believed to be at stake. Providing the 'resurrected togetherness and enabling of "religion,"'[4] the encounter between good and evil promises a *racial* togetherness. An 'axis of evil' reassures

people of the North that, as in a colonial era, they belong to a family of civilized
nations, a family forced to confront the savagery of the nether regions of
Africa, the Middle East, and Eastern Europe. Whether in peacekeeping or in
George W. Bush's (and his father's) apocalyptical encounters with Saddam
Hussein, colour gives the phrase 'axis of evil' its currency, and it is colour, too,
through a call to join the family of civilized nations, that gives peacekeeping its
allure. Citizens of nations who join the alliance against evil come to know
themselves as members of a more advanced race whose values of democracy
and peace are simply not shared by others.

An apocalyptical encounter between good and evil is hard to resist. Myths
evoke 'a complex system of historical association by a single image or phrase.'[5]
John F. Kennedy, for example, relied on the idea of the frontier to mark himself as a president ready and able to fight communism abroad, recalling in a
single word cowboys and Indians, the undeniable civilization (and victory) of
the one and the savagery of the other.[6] The remembered past evoked by the
phrase 'axis of evil,' a past of the internal colonization of Aboriginal peoples
and external colonizing ventures across the South, culminates in a contemporary encounter. As this latest instalment goes, the West's historic burden to
fight against evil must be taken up again with the end of the cold war and the
birth of what has come to be widely described as the New World Order. We
thought we could rest. We hoped that with the collapse of the Soviet Union,
'a new order of free nations' would begin to take shape. Michael Ignatieff
describes 'our' state of mind: 'With blithe lightness of mind, we assumed that
the world was moving irrevocably beyond nationalism, beyond tribalism,
beyond the provincial confines of identities inscribed in our passports, towards
a global market culture which was to be our new home.'[7] Impossibly naive, we
became victims of our own innocence. Instead of our hoped-for global fraternity, the New World Order is 'the disintegration of nation states into ethnic
civil war; the key architects of that order are warlords; and the key language of
our age is ethnic nationalism.'[8]

In these New World Order stories, warlords and ethnic nationalism, indisputable scourges of our age, are often pictured as though they have risen up
from the landscape itself and not out of histories in which the West has featured as a colonizing power. No longer anchored in a history, nationalisms
and the violence that accompany them seem to be properties of certain people
and certain regions. Following the media story of ethnic violence, for instance,
leads to three inescapable conclusions, observes Jan Pieterse: '(1) the perpetrators are mad, (2) the West and onlookers are sane, and (3) humanitarian intervention under these crazy circumstances, although messy, is the best we can
do.'[9] We are easily tempted into believing that, no sooner had they ended, col-

onism and the 'savage wars of peace' described by Kipling are strangely upon us again. Myth, in this instance of an inexplicable rise in savagery, 'disarms critical analysis' because it appeals to a deeply racially inflected memory: for North Americans, the golden age of cowboys and Indians, and for Europeans, African and Asian colonial adventures.[10] It is not surprising that North American soldiers in Vietnam and peacekeepers in Somalia both described where they were as 'Indian country.'[11] When racial chords are struck it becomes difficult, as I will show, to think beyond the simple storylines of mythology.

Peacekeeping has a starring role to play in the mythologies of the New World Order. Under the auspices of a United Nations dominated by the United States, peacekeepers are entrusted with the task of sorting out the tribalisms and the warlords, protecting the people of the South from the internal evil that threatens them. The evil, however, is powerful and the international a realm fraught with danger. Human rights violations mark the Third World 'as a region of aberrant violence.'[12] Confronted with such savagery, First World peacekeepers sometimes 'lose it,' descending into savagery themselves, as some are seen to have done in Somalia and upon their return home, or else they can become traumatized from too close a brush with 'absolute evil.' Increasingly, and this is perhaps true more of middle powers like Canada than it is for the United States,[13] peacekeeping encounters are narrated as captivity narratives once were a century ago, although the hero of the peacekeeping-trauma narrative is most likely to be a man, and the 'capture' by the 'Indians' is no more than an encounter.

> The hero of the captivity narrative is a White woman (or minister) captured by the Indians during a 'savage war.' The captive symbolizes the values of Christianity and civilization that are imperilled in the wilderness war. Her captivity is figuratively a descent into Hell and a spiritual darkness which is akin to 'madness.' By resisting the physical threats and spiritual temptations of the Indians, the captive vindicates both her own moral character and the power of the values she symbolizes. But the scenario of historical action developed by the captivity narrative is a passive one that emphasizes the weakness of colonial power and ends not with a victorious conquest but with a grateful and somewhat chastened return home.[14]

The stories of peacekeepers who are overwhelmed by the inherent evil of the land and its peoples are narrated in documentary films and news features as stories about traumatized white men (and only a few white women) in Africa and Eastern Europe. Upon their return these peacekeepers bear witness to an alien world, a world so savage that only a powerful alliance of civilized nations can intervene to stop the carnage. Like the narrative about an axis of evil, the story of traumatized peacekeepers depends for its coherency on the logic of rational men and women from white nations who encounter people and things in the south that are beyond rationality, things that can literally drive them mad.

To speak of the racial logic of peacekeeping trauma is to speak about the work that is done by narratives. A narrative is different from a personal story and it is important to hold the difference in mind. Peacekeepers do experience trauma, and the rotting bodies, snipers, and child soldiers are real enough, but the events of trauma, Kali Tal notes, are codified in narrative form until they become a signifier for something else.[15] It is the codified story, and not the individual experiences, that I refer to when I consider trauma. Deconstructing narratives – that is, looking for the way in which they are about something else – means separating the experiences of individuals from the way their stories are assembled for our consumption.

Attending to the work that narratives do, Renato Rosaldo suggests, is less about demystification than it is about dismantling. As he does with the narrative of imperialist nostalgia, where people mourn the passing of what they themselves have destroyed, Rosaldo suggests that while demystification is useful, such as revealing the connection between nostalgia and guilt or demonstrating how little about imperialism there actually is to be mourned, it is more important to dismantle narrative by probing its productive function.[16] Imperialist nostalgia, the yearning for the glorious days of the Raj, for instance, transforms colonial agents into innocent bystanders harmlessly sipping tea in old palaces in much the same way that witnessing the evil and becoming traumatized by it transforms peacekeepers and their nations into hapless victims of a timeless evil, rather than agents implicated in complex histories of colonialism and neo-colonialism. In probing what is produced by stories of traumatized peacekeepers, we might ask, as Kali Tal suggests for narratives of the trauma of the holocaust and of sexual violence, what 'is the connection between individual psychic trauma and cultural representations of the traumatic event?'[17] Focusing on cultural representations of peacekeeping in the 1990s, stories about trauma, the special qualities of middle-power nations, and the burden to be borne by the family of civilized nations in the New World Order, I explore in this chapter what it means for us in the North to cast ourselves as traumatized in both a national and an international story about the West's confrontation with absolute evil.

I. Those Who 'Witness the Evil'

It is worth noting at the outset what is at stake in dismantling peacekeeping stories of trauma. Reflecting on the embracing of traumatized figures in national U.S. culture (in Berlant's example the figure is the child worker traumatized by exploitation), Lauren Berlant asks about 'the place of painful feeling in the making of political worlds.'[18] What the frame of trauma accomplishes is the installation of 'the feeling self as the true self, the self that must be protected from pain or from history.'[19] Traumatized subjectivity replaces rational subjectivity 'as the essential index of value for personhood and thus for society.'[20] One important consequence is that we can no longer talk about injustice and how it is organized. Instead, we talk about pain and how to heal. When 'feeling bad becomes evidence of a structural condition of injustice' and 'feeling good becomes evidence of justice's triumph,' then both the problem and the solution are removed from their material and historical contexts.[21]

In the case of peacekeeping, the television documentaries and news features of traumatized soldiers that are considered here visually draw us to dead and mutilated African and Eastern European bodies, but mostly so that we might feel the horror of what it was like for Northern men and women to witness such atrocities. With their experiences at the core of what we feel, it becomes difficult to contest the story. To challenge such pain, Berlant reminds us, is to inflict violence on already damaged persons.[22] How, in the face of the enormous personal pain of witnesses (we do not talk much about the actual survivors of these atrocities), do we talk about our complicity in the production of the atrocities? And how do we move towards responsibility? Keeping in mind what the trauma narrative dislodges and renders unspeakable, and in particular the way that it traps us in a story about a civilized West in a primeval encounter with evil, I begin the task of dismantling.

Roméo Dallaire: The Making of an Icon

The Rwandan genocide in 1994, in which over 800,000 people were slaughtered while a skeletal UN peacekeeping force watched helplessly, remains one of the century's enduring images of evil. Not surprisingly, Rwanda (and not Somalia) is the context most often referred to in Canadian trauma narratives. It is not difficult to understand why any peacekeeper who confronted the thousands of corpses, most displaying signs of brutal violence, would be traumatized by the sight. Canadian peacekeepers found themselves in the middle of the Rwandan genocide. Early in 1994, the commander of the UN peacekeeping mission, Canadian General Roméo Dallaire had gathered evidence of an approaching and well-planned Hutu massacre of Tutsis. He appealed to his Canadian superior at the UN for help. Remembered for his now famous telex of 11 January 1994 to General Maurice Baril in which he inserted a personal plea for intervention, 'where there's a will, there's a way, let's go,' Dallaire has since been described as a 'voice in the wilderness of horror.'[23] When no help was forthcoming, and the genocide ensued, Dallaire returned to Canada a traumatized man – suicidal and unable to put the horrors behind him.

Dallaire is not without his critics, but they have been remarkably few for so controversial a mission. Only one journalist has suggested that Dallaire's inexperience and infatuation with the idea of the ideal peacekeeper as someone without a gun who simply tries to talk people out of things, might have cost the lives of at least the ten unarmed Belgian paratroopers whom the Hutus killed, and perhaps the lives of many more.[24] Another newspaper, renowned for its conservative and anti-feminist stance, dismissed Dallaire's trauma narrative as a fabrication, just as it dismissed women who accused their fathers of childhood sexual violence.[25] A senate committee of the Belgian government criticized Dallaire for having failed to come to the aid of the Belgian peacekeepers he assigned to guard Rwanda's interim president.[26] For the most part, however, although opinion is divided on whether Dallaire could have done more, most concede, as does Alison Des Forges of Human Rights Watch, that he is a tragic hero, a man who faced impossible odds.[27]

What Dallaire actually did or did not do has long ago ceased to matter. The narrative, a nationally specific, cultural story, has taken over. By 1998, with Dallaire as its iconic figure, there were a series of documentaries made by the Canadian Broadcasting Corporation (CBC), and a succession of newspaper and magazine articles that conveyed to the public the figure of the traumatized peacekeeper. Sometimes joined in these stories by journalists and NGO workers who describe 'the physical and emotional scars that will never heal,' traumatized soldiers share the pain of being witness to 'unspeakable evil.'[28] In 1998, the Canadian military produced *Witness the Evil*, a documentary on post-traumatic stress disorder (PTSD) suffered by peacekeepers. Intended for use within the military and also for the media, the film became the subject of the CBC documentary *The Unseen Scars*, shown several times on Canadian television in recent years. It is in *Witness the Evil* and *The Unseen Scars* that we see the full emergence of the traumatized peacekeeper and his function in national mythology.

Witness the Evil ensures that viewers also bear witness to the Rwandan genocide. Images of mutilated bodies, fields filled with corpses, and large piles of machetes dramatically convey a brutality that is frequently described as an apocalypse. In an opening scene, a Canadian soldier makes the sign of the cross in his tent and we know that we are watching a story unfolding in an unholy place. The soldiers give their testimony, breaking down in tears when they describe the smell of rotting bodies, the packs of dogs fighting over corpses, and, most of all, the hundreds of beheaded and mutilated children. They narrate their utter helplessness and vulnerability when confronted with the barbarism and irrationality of Rwanda Patriotic Army (RPA) soldiers. Medical units describe being watched by RPA soldiers from the bushes, others tell of dangerous roadblock encounters in which the Rwandan troops slap a Canadian soldier and try to buy a female medical officer for the price of a chicken. Soldiers describe their duties searching for mass graves and the surreal experience of accidentally stepping into a hole that turns out to be the chest cavity of a corpse, the first of several layers of corpses. We are easily convinced by these scenes that nothing is left of Rwanda but bodies piled upon bodies.

Corporal Daines reveals that his encounters with the bodies of massacred children have deeply affected his own family life. Corporal Cassavoy describes how certain smells and sights (roasted meats, newborn children, rusted out vehicles) trigger his flashbacks. Dallaire himself, deeply sad, confirms that he too is haunted by smells and sounds, and often wishes he had lost a leg instead of his 'marbles.' The soldiers all report their terrible frustration that wearing the blue helmet of the United Nations meant very little. Major Lancaster found himself in the middle of a massacre, able to grab babies off their mothers' backs but unable to do much else. Village elders stopped the killing in this instance. The following day, Lancaster recounts that he was unable to get out of bed, overwhelmed by feelings of helplessness. The images of the genocide give way at the end of the documentary to images of Canadian soldiers bathing African children as a voice-over lists the clinical symptoms and chemistry of post-traumatic stress disorder, suggesting that it is a physical condition that can affect behaviour both during and after active duty. 'Helpless witnesses to evil' and immobilized by the overwhelming knowledge that 'all the best thinking in the world went into the UN' and yet the West still could not prevent a genocide, the soldiers return home. We, the television viewers understand that even the best institution the West had to offer was no match for the evil of Africa. A voice-over reassures us that at least we made things a little bit better. Tearfully, the soldiers conclude that while they have enormous pride in the good they did, the price was often too high.

'Wars re-circulate as trauma,' writes Patricia Zimmerman, referring to the trauma of women raped in Bosnia, mothers of the disappeared in Latin America, survivors and their descendants of the internment of Japanese Canadians and Japanese Americans during the Second World War, and, archetypically, the survivors of the Holocaust. For these trauma victims, documentaries heal.[29] They enable victims to move beyond their pain by speaking out and rejecting 'victimization, isolation, individualism, and silence.' Trauma narratives in documentaries are 'productive, performative acts' enabling victims to survive.[30] Zimmerman observes that the trauma victims of the documentaries she reviews refuse 'to speak only in pain.' They speak of injustice. War is depicted not only as an image but 'as an act of aggression against women, scarring bodies, psyches, family histories, memories.'[31] How are peacekeeping trauma narratives productive performative acts? Certainly peacekeepers who speak of their trauma attest that speaking out is the beginning of healing. But their speaking out is not about genocide they have directly experienced.

Witness the Evil and *The Unseen Scars* depict a genocide whose victims are first and foremost the peacekeepers who witness it, most of them after the killing had stopped. It is their pain and not the Rwandans' that we are invited to listen to, and it is injustice directed against them that we must consider. Injustice revolves around the inefficacy of the military for not paying attention to peacekeeping traumas, the UN for producing the helplessness of the peacekeepers, and, for Dallaire at least, other Western governments who had no interest in stopping the genocide. If we are to fix the trauma, the films suggest, we must offer counselling to peacekeepers and either refuse to send our soldiers into situations where they can do very little, or prepare them better for the little they can do, an argument that anticipates those who call for increased military spending.[32] It is as though the Germans who watched Jews dragged off to concentration camps, or the Canadians who saw their Japanese neighbours forcibly removed to internment camps have become the primary victims.

The trauma of peacekeepers is of a different order than other trauma victims and the biggest difference is what they are traumatized by. Mapped on to the nation, peacekeeping trauma narratives produce a biblical narrative of a First World overwhelmed by the evil of the Third World. As Dallaire himself describes, his trauma was born out of an encounter with the devil and what followed was a slow descent into hell. 'Je suis couvert de sang' ('I am covered in blood') he told journalists, describing vividly his nightmares upon return to Canada,[33] a direct connection between the hacked up bodies and ourselves that is made clear in the only display case in Canada's national war museum devoted to peacekeeping missions in the 1990s. The display case shows Dallaire's bulletproof vest worn in Rwanda, his UN blue helmet and beret, and two Hutu machetes. The machetes were aimed at us, the display implies; the invisibility of the Rwandans is more or less complete.

As Liisa Malkii has suggested, the erasure of the experience of Rwandans themselves and their 'speechlessness' in the stories that are told of the genocide should greatly concern us. It signals our investment in understanding ourselves outside of history. We come to know of the Rwandan genocide as a horror that is unknowable and unthinkable. The 'flood of terrifying images' tells us all we need to know, and in place of history and context, the very information needed to consider the future,[34] we install 'absolute evil' and the good soldiers overwhelmed by it. If time 'must be given to the tasks of witnessing and testimony of Rwandans,'[35] then this is a bearing witness that is fundamentally different from the peacekeepers' witnessing of the evil. Whereas the one requires us to pursue accountability (ours as well as theirs), the other invites us only to consider genocide as timeless and unchangeable, a feature of the landscape. Throughout *Witness the Evil*, the act of aggression that is the source of trauma remains amorphous, overwhelming, and African. Visually, it is hacked up Black bodies on an African landscape. These images do not only 'displace narrative testimony' of the Rwandans themselves but also actively silence and dehumanize Africans by presenting them as a 'mere, bare, naked, or minimal humanity.'[36]

As witness, the peacekeeper is not personally implicated in what has traumatized him. He stands in the place Dana Nelson has described as the 'objective and disembodied space of the universalist standpoint.' From this vantage point, he is witness to a depravity that can be named but is no less mystical. His is an 'occulted standpoint,' the viewpoint of the observer who is not himself of the landscape yet who is able to understand hidden things (the presence of the devil) that the Rwandans themselves presumably cannot see.[37] For Mary Louise Pratt, 'a fantasy of dominance and appropriation' is built into this 'otherwise passive, open stance,' a position she notes of imperial naturalists and scientific observers who thought themselves unconnected to imperial conquest but whose assumption of the right to define and name what they saw and to encode the landscape as empty and awaiting European improvement was a cornerstone of imperialism.[38] 'The improving eye' of Pratt's 'anti-conquest man' (her term for the naturalists and scientists who saw themselves as different from conquerors) is clearly in evidence in refugee experts and relief officials, as Malkii has pointed out for Rwanda, standing 'surrounded by milling crowds of black people peering into the camera, and benevolently, efficiently, giving a rundown on their numbers, their diseases, their nutritional needs, their crops, and their birth and mortality rates.'[39] And it is in evidence when the camera scans the mounds of bodies, and we let it tell us all we ever need to know about Rwanda.

The story of an encounter with unfathomable evil is only intelligible through race. It is perhaps no accident that so many writers of Dallaire's story compare Rwanda with Joseph Conrad's Congo in his 1901 novel *Heart of Darkness*, and Dallaire to Marlowe, the narrator of Conrad's novel. Journalist Carol Off, for instance, writing of Dallaire, begins her chapter 'Into Africa' with an epigraph from Conrad. For her, Dallaire is like Marlowe who sees the folly of colonial greed in Africa (in Dallaire's case the folly of the UN) as well as the 'lusty red-eyed devils' lurking in the jungle.[40] For those caught between 'two strains of the truly sinister,'[41] there is only madness, either as trauma or as violence. When peacekeepers are violent, as they were in Somalia, we are easily able to forgive it and even to expect it, understanding that it is the cruelties of Africa and Africans who push Western men to violence. Edward Said, in discussing Conrad's understanding of imperialism in *Heart of Darkness*, points out that Conrad is largely unable to think outside of imperialism. For him there are no subjects who inhabit Africa.[42] Chinua Achebe put it more forcefully: Africa, for Conrad, 'is a metaphysical battlefield devoid of all recognizable humanity, into which the wandering European enters at his peril.'[43]

Witness the Evil and the news features on Dallaire invite us to understand ourselves racially as well as nationally – that is, as good people forced to stand helplessly by as evil unfolds and as more powerful nations refuse to help. To be invited, as these documentaries do, into the 'abstracted space of universalizing authority over others' is to join a fraternity, the fraternity of those who are nei- ther of the hacked bodies on an African landscape nor of the unscrupulous United States or incompetent UN. Before long, we begin to feel the bond that comes from sharing such high moral ground.[44] An international thus consti- tuted is an 'affective space,' a place where middle-power nations can experience belonging.[45] Dallaire himself has made explicit the affective space of the mid- dle-power nation. Upon his return from Rwanda, he spoke passionately of Canada's noble calling. As he put it in an interview, 'To be that intermediary between the superpowers – who don't give a s– anyways [*sic*] – and the Third World Countries who know they need the presence of our capabilities ... tab- ernacle,[46] you've got a hard time to find a more noble concept.'[47] Canadians have a unique destiny to fulfil as a middle power. Our nobility lies in 'keeping the big boys out of it.'[48]

We look to Dallaire to narrate in his person the moral responsibility of a middle-power nation. In the words of American Broadcasting Corporation (ABC) newscaster Ted Koppel, he is simply 'a soldier who was caught in the middle, trapped between what he knew he ought to do and what he was being ordered to do,' a man 'caught between the madness of genocide' and 'a world largely indifferent to it.'[49] He is unmistakably on high moral ground, a place, to paraphrase Dallaire himself, where moral values, ethical values, and religious beliefs come up against the UN's rules of engagement and its prohibition against the use of force. Profiled on the national news in a segment entitled 'Death and Duty,' Dallaire was nonetheless careful not to dispense with the UN as an institution altogether:

> However, you can't crucify the UN when ultimately people wanted it to be inef- fective. And I mean I had people come on the ground and tell me that they were

doing an estimate because under their parameters, it would take about 85,000 dead Rwandans to risk one white or black Western soldier's life. I mean some of them actually had mathematics on this stuff. So when I'm asked, you know, why did you stay; why didn't you pack it in? I said if we can save one Rwandan, at least morally we've attempted to stymie the debacle that was going on.[50]

As the *National Post* concluded, Dallaire has become a symbol of 'the level of impotence that Canadian soldiers have experienced during recent peace-keeping missions.'[51] His plight is the plight of the nation, a nation destined to be sidelined by the United States (most recently through peacekeeping activities in Afghanistan in 2003) and by an inefficient UN. While his return to Africa (Sierra Leone) in 2001 as Canada's special adviser on child victims of war reassured us that we still had people to save, and that we could still do the saving, Dallaire continues to personify our fragility in encounters with absolute evil, our hesitant but deeply moral stance, and, above all, our non-involvement in the horrors. As one writer rendered Dallaire in a fictionalized account, in Rwanda, the Canadian commander of UN troops was 'a miracle of mimesis, a perfect incarnation of his country and his employer too ...: Unassuming, apprehensive, ineloquent and naive, like Canada.'[52] Dallaire is also 'The Last Just Man,' which is the title of an award-winning 2002 documentary in which he is once again the living embodiment of what it means to go into the heart of darkness and to find oneself as the only moral being.[53] So much do we identify with his plight that in 2000, when Dallaire was found drunk and passed out in a park near Ottawa, the news cameraman who found him did not take photos. As he later explained, 'I didn't shoot it because I was depressed to imagine a man like that could be here and didn't have help.'[54] As a nation, our responsibility is clear: We must go 'to General Dallaire's rescue.'[55] In saving him, we save ourselves.

Canadians have turned with alacrity to the vision of ourselves as a good nation overwhelmed by the brutalities of the New World Order. Recent Canadian novels have been written, journalist Graham Fraser approvingly observed, 'in support of Canada's role on the world stage.'[56] In Alan Cumyn's 1998 novel *Man of Bone*, a fictional Canadian diplomat Bill Burridge is taken hostage. Described by Fraser as 'a trauma-damaged idealist,' Bill Burridge is captured and tortured by guerrillas in a fictional Third World country whose history he barely knows. Burridge does not even know where Santa Irene is when he is first told of his posting there. In Cumyn's second novel, Burridge appears before a UN Human Rights Committee, and like Dallaire who broke down when he took the stand, Burridge is humiliated by losing control of his bowels. 'This is a risky time for Canada,' Fraser writes sympathetically of Cumyn's hero, reading the novel as a story of the plight of a middle-power nation in the New World Order. Conservatives insist that we stay home and avoid the risks, even abandoning our historic role of peacekeeping. However, as Fraser reassures us, Liberals know that politics is not only about the local. Most 'Canadians want their country to be engaged with the world.'[57]

Our engagement with the world is everywhere depicted as the engagement of the compassionate but uninvolved observer. In November 2002, Toronto artist Gertrude Kearns held an exhibition of paintings entitled 'Undone: Dallaire/Rwanda.' The exhibition included large canvases of earth-coloured, military-camouflage markings within which figures were discernable: Dallaire with his hands covering his face; Dallaire showing horror and helplessness; a landscape of corpses and machetes; and a UN jeep sitting uselessly atop a mound of bodies. Only the blue of Dallaire's eyes and the blue of the UN helmet relieve the unrelenting brown of the camouflage landscape. For the artist, the camouflage signals the jungle, the land itself. It also reflects Dallaire being deceived by the Hutus, by the UN, and by his own mind. The title 'Undone' suggests the UN's responsibility, its failure to complete its mandate, and Dallaire's own state of coming apart. As the show's curator explains:

> Gertrude Kearns uses camouflage as a metaphor for psychological deception. Its pattern thinly veils the hard silhouette of what we deeply know. We hide our vulnerability, sometimes to the point of unfeeling. Better to conceal the truth and shun what we cannot change than admit our fallibility. Dallaire's voice and stories advance and recede in the fabric of Kearn's canvasses. She pulls his guilt and frustration through the camouflage screen. We are left with the prospect of our collective impotency.[58]

Impotent, moved, undone: this is our fate. Viewers of the exhibition congratulated Kearns in the gallery's book of comments for her depiction of what it is to be 'powerless in the face of colossal evil.' Both Dallaire and the artist are saluted for their courage in revealing to us 'man's inhumanity,' an inhumanity that leaves us stunned and overwhelmed. Trauma narratives help to organize our place in the world in just the way the novels and art exhibitions illustrate. We come to know ourselves as a compassionate people; indeed, trauma suggests that it is our very vulnerability to pain that marks us as Canadians. From our position as witness, we help to mark out the terrain of what is good and what is evil. Possessed of unique sensibilities, sensibilities that take us to the depths of grief and trauma, we can diagnose the trouble and act as the advance scout and the go-between. In this way, trauma narratives furnish middle-power nations such as Canada with a home-made, that is to say a specifically *national*, version of the politics of rescue. What can be so wrong with this? Again, Malkii elucidates the problem:

> It is difficult to see what might be so problematic in seeing the suffering of people with the eyes of 'humanitarian concern' and 'human compassion.' It is surely better than having no compassion or simply looking the other way. But this is not the issue. The issue is that the established practices of humanitarian representation and intervention are not timeless, unchangeable, or in any way absolute. On the contrary, these practices are embedded in long and complicated histories of their own – histories of charity and philanthropy, histories of international law, peacekeeping and diplomacy, histories of banishment and legal protection, histories of empires and colonial rule, histories of civilizational and emancipatory discourses and missionary work, histories of the World Bank and other development initiatives in Africa, and much more.[59]

When we produce narratives of 'anonymous corporeality and speechlessness,' when we hide our own implication and stand outside of history, preoccupied with our own pain, we stake out the colour line, producing ourselves as individuals and as a nation on the civilized side of things.[60] In this we have not been alone, although the position of 'trauma damaged idealist' has suited our middle-power aspirations to a T.

Ungrateful Natives and Helpless Soldiers

Since the early 1990s, the Canadian Armed Forces have opened five Operational Trauma and Stress Support Centres across the country. A Canadian study conducted in 1995 found a post-traumatic stress disorder (PTSD) prevalence above 20 per cent six months after peacekeepers came home.[61] In 2002, the Armed Forces published a report on the systemic treatment of soldiers with PTSD, in response to the complaint of Christian McEachern (a soldier who had driven a vehicle into the doors of army headquarters in Edmonton) that he had been poorly treated in the army once he had been diagnosed with PTSD.[62] Canadian activity on PTSD is matched elsewhere. As Ben Shepherd documents, since the 1980s – with the 're-discovery' of trauma and the publication of a check-list of symptoms for it in the *Diagnostic and Statistical Manual III* (DSM III) and the establishment of such organizations as the International Society for Traumatic Stress Studies – trauma has become a household word, a universal condition shared by survivors of rape, holocausts, war, football riots. and personal tragedy. Treatable through drugs as well as therapy, by the 1990s, trauma had nonetheless become a timeless and hopeless condition, unconnected to factors in individual patient biographies.[63] For peacekeepers, trauma is seen to develop more out of the everyday stressors of their missions than from battle. For Christian McEachern, for example, one source of trauma was the discrimination he experienced as a reservist, at the hands of soldiers who were 'regular army; another was his frustration that he was unable to stop the rape of a woman whose cries he heard outside the Canadian camp.'[64] The twenty-five soldiers who filed suits claiming that they suffered PTSD, which the Canadian military ignored, maintain that they were psychologically scarred because of inadequate military funding. Unable to help wounded civilians dying in the street, the soldiers say that they experienced considerable duty-related stress.[65]

Offering the controversial thesis that the proliferation of trauma cases and the 'therapy culture' that surrounds them reflect a 'feminization of public life' and a shift in values away from Protestant restraint and towards 'self-indulgence and sentimentality,' Shepherd laments that the link between masculinity and war has now been severed. War is no longer a test of manhood and men today are 'too vulnerable.'[66] An examination of clinical studies of peacekeeping trauma reveals, however, not the passing of the glorious age when men were men, but rather a moment in history when soldiers describe (and clinicians interpret) their breakdowns as originating in the helplessness they feel when they are unable to stop atrocities. Just as peacekeepers and presidents see themselves as embroiled in encounters with 'absolute evil,' so too clinicians plot the etiology of an illness born out of encounters between aggressive natives and soldiers unnaturally restrained by the UN. In this way, clinical studies repeat, without interrogation, threads of the same narrative line discernable in television documentaries and newspaper articles about trauma. That is to say, trauma occurs when men from civilized nations are pushed to the brink by the intolerable conditions under which they are obliged to keep the peace. A race shadow haunts the pages of these seemingly objective and scientific studies in both the explanations given and those omitted. Researchers rarely seek to historically and socially contextualize their explanations, preferring to describe them merely as conditions of the New World Order. It is commonplace, Linda Polman shows, for governments, aid workers, journalists, and, I would add, clinicians, to describe the UN as though it were an organization that had nothing to do with its member countries.[67] Equally, peacekeepers are often described as helpless victims of the UN's excesses, as though they too bear no responsibility for their actions.

In 1994, shortly after the American-led UN peacekeeping mission in Somalia ended, a Norwegian scholar Lars Weisaeth, who had been studying soldiers trauma for some time, coined the phrase 'UN Soldiers Stress Syndrome.'[68]

What was thought to distinguish this form of stress from earlier forms (for example, in Congo in the 1950s where a Swedish study determined that soldiers under twenty-one were more vulnerable to stress than were others) was the changed nature of peacekeeping. In a UN-sponsored book on international responses to traumatic stress, published in 1996 and introduced by the then secretary-general of the United Nations, Boutros Boutros-Ghali, Weisaeth and two military analysts elaborated on the new form of peacekeepers' stress. Peacekeepers were now more likely to be involved in peace enforcement, a situation that differed from traditional peacekeeping in that there was not always consent from all the conflicting parties. Peacekeepers thus found themselves in warlike conditions, surrounded by populations who did not always welcome their presence. The new stressor was 'fear of losing control over one's aggression,' a stance of neutrality required by the UN (retaliation is only permitted in self-defence) but made difficult in practice by conditions of 'physical danger, provocations, and humiliations, and being a passive witness to helpless victims of violence attacked by the feuding factions.'[69]

Importantly, as a 1996 study by Brent Litz explained, '[p]eacekeepers who suppress their frustration, fear, resentment and anger are at risk of acting-out their feelings both during a mission (e.g. unnecessary acts of violence, callousness, dehumanization of one or more parties), and/or upon their return home (e.g. reduced empathy towards significant others, quick temper).'[70] Prefiguring in an alarming way the explanations that surfaced when Canadian peacekeepers tortured and executed Somalis, and when Gulf War veterans killed their wives,[71] the new etiology of trauma naturalized the peacekeeping encounter as one between peacekeepers struggling for restraint and civility in an environment where even the most civilized man, confronted with ungrateful natives and dangerous warring factions, could fail.

With Somalia and not Rwanda as the focus, clinical PTSD studies began to identify in greater detail the unique aspects of the encounter between Somalis and peacekeepers that contributed to trauma. Peacekeepers in Somalia were hypervigilant, and experienced a general sense of fear, a situation Litz hypothesizes may have been due to the close proximity of the Somalis and the frustration of soldiers trained for combat but charged with providing humanitarian aid. Hostility and anger were predictable (and by implication legitimate) responses. More than one-quarter of U.S. soldiers qualified for a diagnosis of PTSD after service in Somalia.[72] The events that were described as most stressful include: rocks thrown at unit (76 per cent), unit fired upon (65 per cent), and rejection by Somalis when trying to help (56 per cent). If the best peacekeepers were warriors, as both scholars and journalists proclaimed about the era of peace enforcement rather than peacemaking, then the international environment exposed them to three new perilous conditions: ingratitude, often expressed aggressively; the stress of not being able to respond as warriors should, that is, with force; and the 'malevolence of the environment.' Faced with these, peacekeepers increasingly could not find meaning in their activities, and, as a consequence, coped less well with its stresses, experiencing trauma and/or resorting to violence.[73]

In clinical studies, peacekeeping violence is reconstituted as an illness and what remains unexamined, as Tracy Karner noted of PTSD and Vietnam veterans, is social and military socialization that influences how soldiers respond to stressors. There is a 'medicalization of masculinity' at work in the explanations of PTSD, Karner hypothesizes. Loss of control of one's aggression and the hardships of practising an unaccustomed restraint are both naturalized in trauma studies as qualities that emerge from the environment itself and not from hegemonic notions of who the ideal man/soldier is.[74] If notions of hegemonic masculinity invade the texts of trauma research, a racial masculinity is also present. Soldiers who imagine themselves in a primeval confrontation with evil, a showdown between the civilized and the uncivilized world, are unlikely to respond constructively to what are undoubtedly situations of great danger and stress. They may well be enacting a racism that clinicians have rarely considered.

Racial socialization can profoundly affect what soldiers are likely to find meaningful. Possessing little understanding of either their own or the history of the population they have come to help, and steeped in the racism prevalent in their countries of origin, Northern peacekeepers can easily subscribe to a simplistic and colonial understanding of their role as being about helping those less fortunate, a charitable act that requires properly grateful recipients who must be seen as deserving. Certainly the emphasis that is placed on grateful natives calls to mind a very old colonial trope that Toni Morrison has described as 'the plight of the rescued.' Discussing Friday, the 'savage' saved by Robinson Crusoe, Morrison notes that the price of rescue for Friday is that he must offer his master his services, loyalty, and even his language. The rescuer 'wants to hear his name, not mimicked but adored.' Friday's dilemma is that he owes too much.[75]

Two further studies of peacekeeping stress done by Litz and his co-authors[76] have begun to denaturalize the peacekeeping relationship, suggesting some of the factors that complicate what is otherwise too easily a colonial narrative. In an empirical study in which 3,310 American peacekeepers who served in the Somalia mission responded to questionnaires, the researchers evaluated four factors: peacekeepers exposure to combat-like events and circumstances (for example, the number of times peacekeepers went out on dangerous patrols);

exposure to everyday circumstances that disheartened or frustrated soldiers (for example, the harshness of the climate and the looting of camp supplies); the pressure to uphold restraint; and the presence of positive factors such as the provision of humanitarian aid. These factors were then correlated to the presence of PTSD, measured by such indicators as the presence of suicidal feelings. Perhaps the most significant finding is that while peacekeepers who experienced combat-like events as well as everyday stressors were most likely to experience PTSD (a finding similar to trauma studies conducted with Vietnam veterans), the key factor likely to produce trauma were the everyday stresses of the mission. Thus, 'although one might surmise that a degree of life threat that a peacekeeper encounters would produce greater frustration when forced to restrain from action, it appears that the *lower magnitude, daily discomforts of peacekeeping* are more strongly implicated.'[77] The pressure to uphold restraint was *not* a factor in PTSD. Finally, the researchers conclude: 'Identifying strongly with the population served in a peacekeeping mission may obviate the ameliorative influence of rewarding elements on PTSD symptoms.'[78] Peacekeepers who believed in the merits of their humanitarian work were less likely to experience trauma. In one of the few studies to control for race, Litz and his co-authors observed an important pattern:

> When male and female soldiers were compared on these various dimensions, differences were negligible. When comparisons were made among Caucasian, Hispanic, and African American soldiers, a salient effect was that African Americans were more gratified by the humanitarian aspects of the mission than were both Caucasians and Hispanics.[79]

An encounter that is conceptualized broadly as one between vulnerable, imperilled peacekeepers and a dangerous, alien population seems likely to produce trauma. In contrast, peacekeepers who experience their environments as something other than one in which they are in danger from out-of-control natives may in fact fare better. Mythologies that constitute the international simply, and racially, as a space of warring tribes, ungrateful natives, and unpredictable dangers abstract both the peacekeepers and the parties of the conflict from their interconnected histories and invite soldiers into a drama of mythic proportions.

It is clear that peacekeeping and humanitarian work *are* immensely dangerous and challenging. In 2002, *Sharing the Front Line and the Back Hills*, another UN-sponsored book on the traumas of peacekeepers and humanitarian aid workers, was published and introduced by the secretary-general of the United Nations, Kofi Annan. The editors begin with the heart rending last e-mail of UN worker Carlos Caceres shortly before he and his co-workers were murdered in East Timor. They also begin with Roméo Dallaire's story. As the collection of testimonials by peacekeepers, humanitarian workers, and scholars proceeds, we learn about 'mission stress' caused by the tremendous danger of UN missions, the frustration of not being able to help everyone, the lack of mission amenities, and the often intolerable geographical conditions. After reading the deeply moving stories of trauma in this collection, it is difficult indeed to challenge such pain, particularly when the stories are not those of violent peacekeepers but of murdered humanitarian workers. Yet we *must* challenge the pain not by denying that it is real but by socially and historically contextualizing the event in which peacekeeping trauma emerges.

Complicating the narrative lines of the peacekeeping and humanitarian experience is necessary if we are to escape the snare of the colour line – the belief that peacekeeping is primarily about civilized nations sorting out, at our great peril, the tribal antagonisms and ethnic nationalism of the South. Restricted to this narrative, we do not see the historical, social, political, and economic contexts in which atrocities, as well as the tragedy of trauma for those who witness and are unable to stop them, occur. To go beyond our pain and our helplessness, to take responsibility, we must begin with our invest-ments – investments that trauma narratives have revealed to be deeply national.

II. On Being the Hero's Friend:
Canadian Investments in Peacekeeping

If Canada can be considered a model middle power, then peacekeeping has been for Canadians a classic middle-power activity.[80]

Canadians have generally (but not always) liked peacekeeping and often stub-bornly claim that it, like the telephone, is their own invention. Peacekeeping has reinforced the values Canadians hold dear. Canadians like to see themselves as friendly, commonsense folk, who would rather mediate than fight. In so large a country with so few people, with no common geography, language or religion, peacekeeping seems to be one of the few symbols – along with hockey and the Mounties – to which Canadians can look to define their identity in the world. But the world has changed in recent years and so seemingly has the nature of peacekeeping.

Geoffrey Hayes, 'Canada as a Middle Power'[81]

In a remarkably candid and unusual paper presented at the Third Annual Banff Conference on World Development in 1965, Donald Gordon assessed what he deemed to be the Canadian tendency, 'on an ever-increasing scale, to worship the myth of middle powermanship.'[82] Canadians, Gordon felt, perhaps realizing that they could have no major power pretensions, often tried to make a virtue out of their limited powers by claiming to possess the special qualities of the go-between – 'a link between east and west, between haves and have-nots, and between whites and non-whites.'[83] Peacekeeping is an important part of this claim, since it provides Canada with a definitive space in the international arena. Since peacekeeping 'has overtones of romance, adventure and intrigue,' it inspires domestic unity. (Peacekeeping is the one national activity that has the support of both French and English Canadians.)[84] Since 'there isn't as much obsessive attention [on Canada] as we would like to believe,'[85] Gordon pointed out, peacekeeping mythology goes far in convincing Canadians that they are in fact noticed internationally.

Beyond appreciating why countries like Canada are so drawn to peacekeeping, Gordon's short article is also open about the racial context in which peacekeeping takes place. Canadians are 'members of a white, "have," North American complex.'[86] When they enter peacekeeping situations in Africa, for instance, they are going to end up firing at non-whites and a racial incident will ensue. More to the point, in such peacekeeping encounters it is likely to be their alliances with other white Northern nations that will prevail unless Canadians want to risk those alliances. Belgium, for example, was an ally, a relationship that was likely to be compromised in peacekeeping operations in Congo (which Gordon, writing in 1965 or earlier, naturally had in mind). Neutrality, he warned, was seldom an option since silence on an issue, again in the Congo example, simply contributed to prolonging the conflict. There was in fact very little glory to be had in peacekeeping. Either one got caught in the problem of alliances or one became a laughing stock because UN operations were often so ineffective. Added to this was the fact that peacekeeping cost a great deal.

Gordon's early realism about peacekeeping as practice and mythology is unique. That peacekeeping has a racial context and that it is an activity related to how white Northern states secure their identities and positions are ideas mostly absent from contemporary national peacekeeping discourses. In its place, one sees a vigorous national mythology that attempts to secure both national and international status for Canada through the articulation of Canada as a middle-power nation that is nicer and less aggressive than the United States. Never having been a colonial power or engaged in aggressive occupations (internal colonialism is once again ignored) Canadians are content to see themselves as playing a secondary, more innocent role in world affairs, a position that is the basis for the national role of a traumatized and helpless people, as explored in the first part of this chapter.

The national role of helper to larger Western nations in their colonial activities in the Third World is readily in evidence in Canadian history and frequently romanticized by Canadian historians. Africa has long occupied the space of degeneracy in the European imagination and thus the space in which white nations and their national subjects come to know themselves as dominant. Canada has been no exception in this respect, although early Canadian activities in Africa were under the shadow of Great Britain. During the 1880s, for example, Canadian 'voyageurs' known for their skill as boatmen were called upon to rescue the British Governor General in Sudan from the Mahdists. The Metis, Aboriginal, and white boatmen who sailed up the Nile are recorded in the history books as brave men who helped the fledgeling nation of Canada to come to know itself, a nation without colonial possessions that nevertheless became sufficiently grown up to fight the Boers in South Africa and, ultimately, to help to defeat the Germans in two world wars.[87] Then, as now, nationhood and manhood required testing in war.

For Canadians, of course, as for Americans and other white settler nations, manhood and nationhood were first achieved through the suppression of Aboriginal nations. The suppression of the Riel Rebellion (the struggle of the Metis peoples in Western Canada for recognition as a people) in the latter half of the nineteenth century provided the newly formed nation of Canada with its first sense of 'maturity,' or, as two well-known Canadian military historians put it, the first sense that the new nation 'could hold its own.'[88] When there were few internal wars left to fight, and decolonization dramatically limited colonial terrain outside Canada, peacekeeping became the 'best guarantee that Canada's military would not go the way of the dodo.'[89] Not surprisingly, given the connection between military activities and the making of Canada as a white settler society, Canada's role as peacekeeper to the world easily replicated a colonial model.

Historically, peacekeeping is seen as enabling Canada to grow up outside the shadow of both Great Britain and the United States. Carving out this space, Canadian history texts describe the natural advantage Canada possessed as a peacekeeper as 'a disinterested, non-colonial power without military commitments' in the trouble spots of the world.[90] Canadians are therefore ideal to sort out the 'tribal and economic antagonisms' that erupt in the newly decolonized regions of the world. Giving full rein to the imperial fantasy, historians Jack Granatstein and David Bercuson describe Canadian peacekeeping activities in the Congo: 'At Leopoldville night clubs, Canadian soldiers can be seen escorting Congolese damsels and creating inter-racial harmony.'[91] Without a trace of irony, these historians point out that the unique skills possessed by Canadian peacekeepers, skills in resisting provocation, in handling hostile crowds, and in carrying out their mandate 'without loss of face or, more important, loss of life,' are honed while subduing Canada's native populations, most recently at the siege of Oka in 1990.[92] Acknowledging that the Mohawks and their supporters might not agree, they nonetheless state with confidence that the Canadian army's actions in putting an end to Aboriginal protests at Oka (actions involving hundreds of armed troops and a handful of protesters) is a classic example of peacekeeping.[93]

Canadian scholars refer to peacekeeping as Canada's 'calling' and claim the nation's special relationship with the United Nations. In the words of Gregory Wirick, the 'United Nations has been Canada's avocation: a calling more than a duty, an inclination no less than an interest. Beginning with the creative engagement of such well-known figures as Lester Pearson, Escott Reid and John Holmes, the gallery of Canadian politicians and diplomats who have sought to improve the United Nations (UN) system and enhance Canada's standing in it has been long and impressive.'[94] From this perspective, Canadians are 'instinctively committed to the UN and a multilateral approach; anxious to be involved and helpful; fearful that non-involvement might lead to penalties of some kind or, what would be almost as hurtful to the Canadian psyche, might simply cause the country to be ignored; and finally, stretching diplomatic and military resources to the utmost.'[95]

As a national vocation, and as the dream of a middle power who exists next door to the United States, peacekeeping neatly enables Canadians to tell a story of national goodness and to mark ourselves as distinct from Americans. Peacekeeping makes it possible to proclaim a history of 'doing good' and 'maintaining order among the fractious nations and peoples of the world.'[96] While Canadian peacekeeping has often served U.S. interests, Granatstein and others insist that it has also had 'an aura of independence and the implicit sense that it served higher interests than simply those of the United States, or even the West.'[97] Ironically, the only thing wrong with Canadian peacekeeping, in the view of military historians, is that Canadians sometimes fail to see when war and not peace is required: we should have been there in the Gulf, for example, despite the opposition of Canadians to the war with Saddam Hussein.[98]

Woven into the mythology of a nation of peacekeepers is the idea of climate. As public policy professor Seymour Lipset put it, 'Canadians are defined by their weather. The climate forces you to believe in co-operation and putting others' welfare first,' he says, noting the massive outpouring of relief during the Quebec ice storm and Manitoba floods.'[99] We can blame our world famous 'do goodism,' writes Professor Lipset, 'on those Canadian cold fronts.'[100] As I have shown elsewhere,[101] the Canadian national story is a characteristic settler one in this respect with its rhetoric and imagery of enterprising and hardy citizens

of a cold land who through their hard work have forged a nation out of nothing. In this compressed narrative, white people become the original inhabitants
since it is only they who are cast as capable of making the country what it is.
They bring order and civilization where previously there was none, a logic that
survives intact in the responses of Canadian courts to Aboriginal land claims
and immigrant rights. Canadian nationalism has relied on the notion that
stronger and superior Northern peoples also have a superior capacity for governing themselves and a correspondingly greater commitment to liberty.[102]

The self-effacing, cooperative, peace-loving Canadian is the heart of the
national mythology. Robertson Davies, a pre-eminent Canadian novelist,
summing up the Canadian national character in 'The Canada of Myth and
Reality' (1980), describes Canadians as possessors of a voice but one that is not
forceful and self-centred. The Canadian voice is that of a 'secondary character,
the hero's friend, the confidant; but the opportunity and heart ... is that of one
who may be a hero, and a new kind of a hero, a hero of conscience and spirit,
in the great drama of modern man.'[103] Canadians evidently share Davies's sentiments. As public opinion polls repeatedly confirm, peacekeeping provides
Canadians with an identity that distinguishes them from Americans and that
provides sufficient glory to enable Canadians to think of themselves as part of
a global order.[104] The hero's friend, however, encountered new moral dilemmas in the New World Order where military aggression is required to keep the
natives in line. For some, Canada has simply opted to 'sleep' through the
dilemma and has ended up losing its place in the world. We failed to act even
when our friends, the Americans, were threatened, refusing to participate in
the war against Iraq in 2003 and condemning ourselves to mediocrity.[105] For
those who argue along these lines, what Canada risks in failing to increase military spending and in limiting its participation in George W. Bush's 'War on
Terror' is its very place in the international community, a community of Western Nations that sees itself as a family of civilized nations.

The Hero's Friend in the New World Order

The hero's friend is not a warrior. To keep his place in the family, he has had
to make several adjustments in an era of what is often called muscular peacekeeping. Writers in the *Canadian Defence Quarterly* make some of these deli-
cate adjustments to the national mythology. Keith Krause describes three
types of peacekeeping actions: actions to restore stability to a region threatened from outside, for example, the Gulf War; the maintenance of order in
weak states, for example, Somalia; and the promotion of justice in states where
there are massive human rights violations such as ethnic cleansing, for exam-

ple Bosnia. Canada, Krause argues, should concentrate on the-maintenance-of-order type of peacekeeping since Canadians often do not support stability operations such as the Gulf War and Canada, by virtue of its 'professionalism' and history as a peacekeeping nation, is best at 'order creation' rather than the more aggressive 'be bloodied' activities of the stability efforts.[106] 'It is not Canada's job to articulate an overarching vision of a "New World Order," Krause concludes. Rather, the more modest role of participating in multilateral commitments is best for the nation.[107] The apparently lesser role in the global story that is outlined in national mythology enables Canada to participate in peacekeeping encounters as an entirely innocent party without troublesome histories or ethical dilemmas. Canadians unabashedly claim this higher moral ground, but in the 1990s and particularly since the Somalia Affair, they have had to work hard to keep it. As Canadian scholars, journalists and military analysts struggled with the story of peacekeeping as an inherently noble calling, peacekeepers as victims begin to appear alongside of peacekeepers as violent men. The traumatized peacekeeper handily resolved the contradiction inherent in Kipling's 'savage wars of peace.'

No picture conveyed to the world the peacekeeper as victim more than *Toronto Star* photographer Paul Watson's Pulitzer Prize-winning photo of a dead U.S. Marine's body being dragged through the streets of Mogadishu by an angry mob. The photograph conveys in unmistakable colour the perils white bodies encounter from Black mobs when they attempt to keep the peace. When an account of the Somalia Affair and Canadian peacekeeping violence is published with this photo as the cover page, the implication is clear: Canadian peacekeepers also encountered mob violence and their own violence towards Somalis is therefore more understandable. Indeed, Dan Loomis's private publication of an account of the Somalia Affair,[108] with just such a front cover, assists readers who are unable to make the connection. 'His picture clearly depicts the kind of problems Canadians faced in Somalia. One picture is worth a thousand words.'[109] Canadians, of course, were stationed in the village of Belet Huen, far from Mogadishu. No Canadian died at the hands of a Somali. Further, even the U.S. experience must be analysed critically. The claim that American peacekeepers were irrationally targeted by savage mobs must be put alongside of American bombing of Mogadishu and the thousands of Somali lives lost as a result.

While Loomis is writing an openly pro-military book, other scholars who make a greater claim to objectivity also juxtapose peacekeeping violence with the dangers faced by peacekeepers, the dangers serving to ameliorate if not annul the violence of peacekeepers. For instance, Geoffrey Hayes writes about the disturbing events in Somalia and moves, within one paragraph, to the dif-

ficulties Canadian soldiers faced in Bosnia and ultimately to the suicide of a
Canadian reservist upon his return home from Bosnia. Similarly, Pierre Martin and Michel Fortmann describe the crisis of peacekeeping as far as the
media is concerned and illustrate in the process how peacekeeping violence
and dangers faced by peacekeepers are juxtaposed:

> Two events exemplify the profound crisis as far as the media are concerned,
> namely the death of a young Somali at the hands of Canadian soldiers in March
> of 1993, and the incident in which Canadian soldiers were taken hostage and
> shot at by drunken Bosnians in December of the same year. In the first case, the
> Canadian image of fundamental goodness was called into question. In the sec-
> ond, the powerlessness and danger experienced by Canadian peacekeepers in the
> line of fire was starkly revealed.[110]

In the contest between peacekeeping violence and peacekeeping trauma,
trauma has won hands down. Martin and Fortmann report that Somalia notwithstanding, Canadians have continued to show massive support for peacekeeping. In a poll taken in March 1993, it was Bosnia and not Somalia that
touched the hearts of most Canadians, and the slight dip in support for peacekeeping in 1993 was restored in polls of 1994.[111] The authors conclude their
analysis of Canadian public opinion by making three points about peacekeeping in the New World Order: peacekeeping 'is becoming more complex and
difficult to comprehend'; peacekeeping goals are becoming more 'confusing';
and significantly, peacekeepers cannot be perceived as heroes but rather as
'weak and fallible human beings.'[112]

Evidently, in a world of angry Black mobs and weak and fallible human
beings, 'war in defence of human rights' can go badly wrong. Canadians,
Michael Ignatieff counsels, would do well to exercise caution.[113] Canada
should return to the old days when intervention required that nations consent.
If peace enforcement is undertaken, Canadian historian Jack Granatstein
advises that the UN should not be ambitious; it should recognize the perils of
using force and note that it is easier to minimize the use of force if the United
States is not involved.[114] Canada and its 'friends' should nonetheless continue
to develop rapid-reaction forces. Cautious and aware of the perils, the hero's
friend is still nonetheless anxious to participate in the clean up of the New
World Order, for this is the very meaning of civility. In the end, the trepida-
tions of our scholars notwithstanding, Canadians find our place in the action,
and like other Northern nations, negotiate the tension between democracy
and military intervention through the colour line itself. That is, we are able to
participate in aggressive interventions on the strength of the argument that

the natives will understand little else but force. Our middle-power narratives about being the conscience of the world, and of being especially good at 'order creation,' flow easily into the global story about an out-of-control Third World that increasingly requires the firm hand of the First World.

III. Sending in the Warriors:
'The Spread of Non-Democratic Regimes and Human Rights Abuses'

In her book *Manliness and Civilization*, Gail Bederman explores the way in which whiteness became a manly ideal in nineteenth-century America. Male power, she theorized, was linked to the notion of civilization. Civilized white men were thought to have 'a racial genius for self-government' and, in the words of President Theodore Roosevelt, 'a manly duty to "destroy and uplift" lesser, primitive men for their own good and the good of civilization,' a duty that had required the conquest of native peoples, the Philippines and the annexation of Hawaii. As Bederman reminds us, it was in order to 'exhort American men to conquer and rule the Philippines' that Rudyard Kipling coined the phrase the white man's burden.[115] Writing of the same period in American history, Dana Nelson uses the notion of white manhood to discuss how a white ideal of masculinity came to stand in for the nation. For Nelson, 'white male power was negotiated through imaginary and actual relationships to "Indians."' Men's longing 'to be part of a civic brotherhood' and to 'an imagined fraternity of white men' required perpetual engagement with the racial other.[116] The civic brotherhood and fraternity that is enabled through the civilizing mission is also evident in New World Order mythologies about rogue states and the civilizing initiatives they require, a world in which Canada is anxious to participate.

For the United States, David Savran remarks, the end of the cold war provoked a massive identity crisis. Anti-communism was replaced by the idea of a terrorist or rogue state – both an internal and external threat against which the state must defend itself.[117] The threat comes from governments that are 'inimical to democracy' and human rights as well as from drug traffickers. In the early 1990s, as Savran notes, in George Bush's vision, the U.S. was the 'freest,' 'strongest nation on earth' and 'the beacon of freedom in a searching world'[118] which was obliged to step in and save the world in Somalia. These or similar lines would be used several times over throughout the nineties in peacekeeping missions from Bosnia to Haiti, and they would be heard a great deal after 11 September 2001 and the terrorist attacks on the Pentagon and the World Trade Center.

The literal meaning of rogue state is a state that does not regard itself as bound by international norms. Since rogue states have no respect for human rights and the rule of law, they must be kept in line by states that do. Thus, the United States, 'hailed as the leader of "enlightenment states"' that are entitled to resort to violence as they see fit, 'engages in a number of activities designed to stop rogue states, activities ranging from peacekeeping, economic sanctions, military aid to opposition parties in rogue states, to outright military aggression.'[119] Relying on this logic, Noam Chomsky argues, the United States launched missile attacks against Iraq in 1991, despite lacking a UN Security Council resolution authorizing such force, and did so again in 2003. It invaded Panama, announcing its right to do so as one of self-defence against a state that was allegedly being used as a base to smuggle drugs to the United States. It shipped arms to Indonesia after the UN required Indonesia to withdraw from East Timor, and it has continued to back Israel after the UN ordered Israel to withdraw from its occupation of Lebanon and parts of Palestine. In both Turkey and Colombia, repressive regimes have been also covertly backed by the United States. Importantly, the use of force in contravention of the UN and international law is defended both as self-defence, as in many of the cases above, and as necessary in order to stop human rights abuses. Thus, the U.S.-led NATO bombings of Yugoslavia were intended to stop ethnic cleansing in spite of clear indications that the bombings would escalate the violence and increase the numbers of refugees.

Military intervention into the affairs of states is not an easy action to defend if one remains within the liberal paradigm of freedom, autonomy, and state sovereignty. However, as John Stuart Mill himself took care to clarify, sovereignty and autonomy, cornerstones of the liberal paradigm, are not concepts to be applied to 'barbarians.'[120] Violations of state sovereignty, therefore, have long been defensible practices when dealing with barbarians. For Winston Churchill, the use of force was justified against 'uncivilised tribes and recalcitrant Arabs'; for David Lloyd George, it was defensible against 'niggers.'[121] The paradox of humanitarian goals accomplished by force directly mirrors the paradox of liberalism itself where all human beings are equal and are entitled to equal treatment; those that are not entitled to equality are simply evicted from the category human and exiled to 'the other side of universality,' both a symbolic and material domain, the place where lesser humans reside.[122] It is this logic that enables peace enforcement to replace peacekeeping, with a minimum of fuss.

In government and scholarly publications and in the media, peace enforcement is generally introduced as follows: Everyone hoped that the end of the cold-war era meant a world of cooperation among former enemies. Unfortunately, this peace did not happen. States are disintegrating due to assertive nationalism, environmental degradation, and 'the erosion of state sovereignty.' Most of all, there is a spread of non-democratic regimes in the Third World. (The disease metaphor is not, I believe, coincidental.) 'In other parts of the Third World, the combination of economic, social, environmental, demographic, and ethnic problems are undermining already weak power structures in which democracy – as it is understood and practised in the developed world – had never seriously taken root.'[123]

Large scale civil wars prevail, or, as in Somalia, a more 'primitive style, a kind of "high tech" gang warfare along road warrior lines that bear a greater resemblance to random mass criminal activity than to modern conventional or insurgent war.'[124] Western nations are called upon to do something about the chaos, the descent into tribalism, and the massive human rights violations that accompany these conflicts. (This project of cleaning up the gangs at the international level matches the rhetoric and practices at the national level.) Indeed, the chaos is such that peacekeeping nations have to abandon the traditional condition of peacekeeping, which is that the nation concerned has to consent to the intervention. There must now be what is often described as 'peacekeeping with teeth' or 'muscular peacekeeping' where Northern nations go in uninvited to sort out the mess.[125] The new peacekeepers are 'warriors of the New World Order.'[126]

Africa, as the place where democracy has simply failed to thrive, is often the focus of New World Order stories. Kofi Annan, secretary-general of the UN, for example, partially acknowledges Western complicity but describes Africa's inevitable descent into chaos in the New World Order:

> During the cold war the ideological confrontation between East and West placed a premium on maintaining order and stability among friendly States and allies, though super-Power rivalries in Angola and elsewhere also fuelled some of Africa's longest and most deadly conflicts. Across Africa, undemocratic and oppressive regimes were supported and sustained by the competing super-Powers in the name of their broader goals but, when the cold war ended, Africa was suddenly left to fend for itself. Without external economic and political support, few African regimes could sustain the economic lifestyles to which they had become accustomed, or maintain the permanent hold on political power which they had come to expect. As a growing number of States found themselves internally beset by unrest and violent conflict, the world searched for a new global security framework.[127]

'A new global security framework,' sufficiently vague, nonetheless opens the door for aggressive intervention. Annan's position has been taken on by Canadians wholeheartedly. First, the Canadian response to Annan's 'Agenda for Peace' is to adjust the concept of peacekeeping until it can bear the contradiction of muscular peacekeeping. Wrestling with muscular peacekeeping, the Canadians have settled for 'Peacebuilding,' which centres on building stability and civilization but leaves sufficient room for the idea of a standing force that can strike quickly.[128] When the minister of foreign affairs described the Canadian peacebuilding initiative, he used Annan's analytical framework step by step. He began with the idea that this was a new kind of war, moved to the observation that traditional peacekeeping no longer suffices, and dramatically concluded that we must re-think the whole concept of security if what we are involved in are activities like intervening to stop ethnic cleansing.[129] Peacebuilding is 'providing a lifeline to foundering societies struggling to end the cycle of violence.'[130] Making peacebuilding sound like a development initiative, Lloyd Axworthy is careful nonetheless to leave the door open for more aggressive actions.

The perfect justification for a more aggressive peacekeeping is quite simply that the natives will understand nothing else and that the crises are so dire that no civilized nation would fail to aggressively intervene. The Canadian prime minister of the early 1990s, Brian Mulroney, put the new interventionist approach best when he stated in an address at Stanford University, 'Quite frankly, such invocations of the principle of national sovereignty are as out of date and as offensive to me as the police declining to stop family violence simply because a man's home is supposed to be his castle.'[131] Some authors proposing UN-sponsored peacekeeping even candidly suggest that peacekeepers may well be obliged to revive colonialism, in the interests of world security. Paul Johnson, for example, writes:

> We are witnessing today a revival of colonialism, albeit in a new form. It is a trend that should be encouraged, it seems to me, on practical as well as moral grounds. There simply is no alternative in nations where governments have crumbled and the most basic conditions for civilized life have disappeared, as is now the case in a great many third-world countries.[132]

'Happily,' he continues, 'the civilized powers need not get stuck in the old colonial quagmire, because they have the example of the trusteeship system before them. The Security Council could commit a territory where authority has irretrievably broken down to one or more trustees. These would be empowered not merely to impose order by force but to assume political functions. They would in effect be possessed of sovereign powers.'[133]

For peacekeeping countries, of course, from whom 'labor and expense will be needed, as well as brains, leadership and infinite patience,' '[t]he only satis-faction will be the unspoken gratitude of millions of misgoverned or ungov-erned people who will find in this altruistic revival of colonialism the only way out of their present intractable miseries.'[134] Significantly, as Johnson and other writers are careful to elaborate, the

> appeals for help come not so much from Africa's political elites, who are anxious to cling to the trappings of power, as from ordinary desperate citizens, who carry the burden of misrule. Recently in Liberia, where rival bands of heavily armed thugs have been struggling for mastery, a humble inhabitant of the capital, Mon-rovia, named after the fifth president of the United States, approached a marine guarding the United States Embassy and said, 'For God's sake come and govern us!'[135]

Remarkable for what the story leaves out more than for what it includes, the images of grateful natives confirm Westerners' sense of superiority, discourag-ing critique and mobilizing support for peacekeeping activities. Such images of beseeching and grateful natives, however, were in short supply as the nine-ties wore on.

Beginning with the UN peacekeeping mission in Somalia, the fairy tale of peacekeeping began to have bad endings. Peacekeeping was apparently failing, leaving in its wake ungrateful natives and increased violence. *New York Times* journalist Barbara Crossette, writing in 1999, illustrates what became the slightly revised New World Order storyline, written virtually without varia-tion in all mainstream newspapers in the West by the end of the 1990s. 'The World Expected Peace. It Found a New Brutality,' reads the headline, begin-ning the now familiar descent into chaos.[136] The crises have piled up in the 1990s: Kosovo, Sierra Leone, Angola, Iraq, Haiti, and Serbia and all the while, the United Nations 'drift helplessly by.' Nobody is in charge and humanitarian interventions go hopelessly awry, as they did in Somalia. Wash-ington, Crosette writes, seems to have retreated and grown soft, the rogues have grown more brutal and now kill more civilians: 'In this ugly new order, brutalizers act with impunity and prove daily that a peaceful, humane world is not going to be built with good governance programs. Force, or a credible threat of force may be necessary.'[137] To anyone believing the dominant media story during the 1990s, the terrorist attack on the World Trade Center in 2001, in which 3,000 people lost their lives, confirmed both their worst fears and the solution: apply greater force.

For the most part, Western scholars have shared the journalistic paradigm evident in Crossette's column. The UN should abandon peacekeeping, opines

Canadian scholar Michael Ignatieff in the *New York Times*, because it cannot
cope with 'new forms of ethnic tyranny.'[138] Instead, 'what's required are combat capable warriors under robust rules of enforcement, with armor, ammunition and intelligence capability and a single line of command to a national
government or regional alliance.'[139] Others argue in more guarded tones,
maintaining that the UN and the United States in particular must continue to
participate in peacekeeping because 'the ability to project power for humanitarian purposes over long distances is the singular mark of a world power.'[140]
However, it must be established that peacekeeping in this era, or more accurately peace enforcement, requires the highest level of 'political-military
skills.'[141] Neutrality and passivity can no longer be the hallmarks of peacekeeping in 'failed state' situations where lawlessness prevails.[142]

Entire corpuses of new concepts are deployed to explain both the urgency to
intervene and more aggressive interventions. Peacekeeping becomes peacebuilding, as in the Canadian state's response, or peace maintenance according
to some scholars.[143] Reviewing new terms and conceptual shifts in peacekeeping literature, Jonathan Goodhand and David Hulme note the importance of
two terms in particular: peacebuilding or conflict handling, referring to interventions in contexts where warlike circumstances prevail and where peacekeepers may be operating before, during, and after conflicts;[144] and complex
political emergencies (CPE), referring to contexts in which there is 'prolonged
and violent struggle by communal groups,' often 'ethno-nationalist in nature'
where 'criminality becomes the political norm.'[145] Both terms organize the
reality of contemporary peacekeeping in ways that reify the intervention of
Western states into non-Western states largely through the idea that conflicts
today lie outside civilization and require extraordinary measures. There is here
very little interrogation either into what might have caused such descents into
barbarism in the Third World or of the West's right, indeed moral obligation,
to intervene or not intervene, for that matter. Instead, scholars have devoted
their efforts to codifying the new violence and suggesting how it differs from
violence of the cold war period.

The new terms and constructs legitimating aggressive Western intervention
often depend upon the language of human rights. For example, French governments of the late 1980s and early 1990s attempted to promote a new norm
of international law called a 'right to interfere.' As Phillipe Guillot has argued
for the French context, the right to interfere emerged in a context in which
the French intelligentsia demanded the right to enforce human rights in the
Third World.[146] Replacing proletarian internationalism with a new cosmo-
politanism, the French public shifted to what Gerard Prunier[147] and others[148]
suggest is a new white man's burden, a burden the public felt particularly

called upon to assume since France was understood to be the birthplace of human rights. When more conservative governments replaced the socialist ones that had initially endorsed the right to interfere, and when the failures of peacekeeping in Somalia began to emerge, 'humanitarian diplomacy' gave way to calls for withdrawal from conflicts and occasionally support for a more aggressive peacekeeping. In either an interventionist or non-interventionist climate, what remains constant is the making of Western nations through the positioning of themselves as more civilized than non-Western nations, an identity that Western politicians deploy to great advantage domestically and internationally.

Peacekeeping particularly provides middle powers with a role in international governance. In France's case, participation in UN peacekeeping helped to consolidate France's position as a permanent member of the Security Council.[149] In the case of Italy, Paolo Tripodi writes that Italy sought to improve its international status, damaged by years of failed development activities, by participating in UN peacekeeping efforts in Somalia.[150] In sum, peacekeeping provides a way for both settler colonies and ex-colonial powers to perform themselves as members of an international brotherhood of civilized states. The international epitomized by the United Nations becomes a space where there is no outright aggression or colonial domination. There is only Third World barbarisms. Tautologically, some scholars therefore argue that peace-maintenance cannot be a colonial enterprise in which the colonial power plays the role of master and the colonized plays the role of servant. Instead, peace-maintenance occurs under international authority, an authority that is 'the servant of both an international and locally supported rule of law and order.'[151]

Television cameras facilitate such opportunities for state-making and demonstrations of membership in the family of civilized nations. Third World nations descending into chaos and ethnic tyranny, First World nations trying their best to sort them out and to stop the bloodshed but finding that civility is not the most effective approach: this is a script that requires tyrants, heroes, and grateful populations. The international so constituted has to be *performed*. As Francois Debrix suggests, the only difference between peacekeeping initiatives in Somalia and previous colonialist enterprises is that peacekeeping 'had to be put on display by and for the media.'[152] Peacekeeping, he argues, 'depicts a fantasy space or dream land of international affairs (where peacekeeping is realized, etc.) inside which claims to neo-liberalism on a global scale can be made.'[153] Debrix considers peacekeeping as virtual in the sense that 'the vision of global unity or governance that peacekeeping is designed to mobilize is a matter of visual illusion.'[154] Perhaps most provocative is his contention that strategies such as peacekeeping are sometimes deployed in the absence of real threats and the presence of a simulated danger.[155] (Here we might recall the United States' claim in 2003 that Iraq possessed weapons of mass destruction, weapons that were never found.)

Rogue states, drug trafficking, and so on enable the international to be imagined as besieged by unruly Third World peoples, a situation that the UN can address through peacekeeping: 'Through the UN, the international comes to represent a single international territory, the territory of the "universal social contract."'[156] As the first post–cold war peacekeeping encounter, Somalia was one of the first examples of peacekeeping as a staged event. Debrix concludes:

> Reinvested by George Bush's post–Gulf War vision of a New World Order, the United Nations has been given in Somalia a chance to perform as an indisputable 'international actor,' as a symbolic and legitimate power to be reckoned with as the century draws to an end. In Somalia, the UN's task is not simply to mobilize strategies of visual surveillance and panopticism (as was the case in North Korea and Iraq). It is rather to show the international community that it can actively construct and organize the neoliberal world order through its peacekeeping interventions. Somalia, in fact, inaugurates a series of panopticism in order to achieve global governance in practice in certain regions of the globe where, as will be argued, a more forceful intervention is required. Unlike panopticism, the strategies of visual simulation relied upon by the UN to achieve its ideological objectives are now intended to be highly visible. To put it bluntly, the UN will have to act, and it will have to be seen.[157]

To look at peacekeeping as a performance, and to consider what the performance secures, an international sphere that positions some actors as more civilized than others, and some states as having the right to intervene and discipline others, is not to deny that the conflicts of the post–cold war period have been bloody and terribly violent and do require intervention. What the hegemonic peacekeeping story accomplishes is to turn these conflicts into attributes of Third World states and Third world peoples, qualities that are somehow innate and unconnected either to colonial histories or to contemporary Western dominance. What is obscured, Jan Pieterse suggests, is that 'the cold war left behind a legacy of authoritarianism, the supremacy of security in politics, surplus armaments, and a tradition of politics of polarization – in many cases overlaid upon the earlier authoritarian legacy of colonialism.'[158] In Somalia for example, 'local wars over resources are fought out with cold war weaponry.'[159] The tribalism and hatreds of conflicts such as Somalia and Rwanda did not come out of thin air. Humanitarian intervention may well be 'the military corollary of neo-liberal globalization.'[160] That is to say, it pro-vides 'a smokescreen for a new politics of containment in peripheralized regions.'[161]

Arguing in the same vein, Mel McNulty suggests how colonial histories affected conflict and peacekeeping in Rwanda in 1990–4. By far the most prevalent analysis of the Rwandan civil war and the ensuing genocide is that the crisis was ethnically driven. McNulty shows how France's Rwandan inter-ventions were a primary cause of the prolongation of the conflict, resulting in the ironic situation where a powerful external actor with a direct hand in the conflict then became a peacekeeper. France has long had a colonial hand in the region first by ensuring that no real decolonization took place in its ex-colonies and that patron-client relationships replaced colonial regimes. France drafted military agreements with the states of francophone Africa, agreements to provide military technical assistance and support and used such agreements, for instance, to protect the dictatorship of Mobutu in Zaire.

In Rwanda, similar agreements were also made and in 1990, invoking this agreement, France intervened when civil war broke out, ostensibly to protect its nationals. The French stayed in Kigali for three years, however, actively training the Rwandan army and maintaining checkpoints and patrols. They actively backed President Hanyarimana even though his record on human rights was a weak one. (In particular, the Hanyarimana regime refused to grant refugees the right of return, a key demand from well-financed, educated, and organized exiles; French support for him scuttled any fledgling peace efforts). In April 1994, when President Hanyarimana was assassinated, France evacu-ated its own nationals as well as members of the government's inner circle, thereby preserving what McNulty describes as the chief ideologues of the genocide. As peacekeepers in 1994, France was not surprisingly seen as the regime's supporters. With little knowledge of internal conflicts in Rwanda, French peacekeepers made a number of decisions that prolonged and exacer-bated the conflict.[162]

It is these kinds of histories that are taken out of the story of peacekeeping and humanitarian intervention, leaving the much simpler and more powerful story of a civilized West faced with the disintegration of African states and their descent into barbarism. As Mahmood Mamdani has written of Rwanda, many write as though genocide has no history and cannot be understood as rational. Showing how the Rwandan genocide 'needs to be thought through within the logic of colonialism,'[163] that is through the production of Hutu and Tutsi as political identities of native and settler respectively, Mamdani's work suggests what peacekeeping mythologies leave out: the historical, social, and political contexts that bring us to the terrible place of genocide.

The manifestly racial theme of the international story of peacekeeping invites Northern nations to participate in what might be accurately described as a brotherhood or family of civilized nations. Middle-power states, such as France, Canada, Belgium, Italy, and Australia have practically no other means to prove their membership in the club. A powerful and seductive story of the West bringing human rights and democracy to non-Western countries, the story of the New World Order is also a dangerous one with murderous consequences. When General Roméo Dallaire took up command of UN peacekeeping forces in Rwanda, he had, by his own admission, no knowledge of the African context. Unaware of Rwanda's colonial histories, it took the General some time to begin to appreciate Rwanda's contemporary power arrangements. He underestimated, for example, the sophistication of Rwandan elites, all schooled in Western universities, including Canada, and remained unaware for the longest time of the Rwandan government's human rights violations and of French power in the country. Dallaire, Carol Off writes, went to Africa 'full of wide-eyed innocence.'[164] Canadian peacekeepers went to Somalia sharing much the same sentiments. Impressed with their own nobility and superiority, and not at all equipped to understand the West's implication in the civil war in Somalia, peacekeepers were surprised and outraged when they found ungrateful natives and a complicated conflict. In such an environment, violence directed at Somalis enabled some peacekeepers to manage their own fears and ignorance and to see themselves as men in control.

Conclusion

'What the Afghans Need Is Colonizing,' read a headline in the Canadian newspaper the *National Post*, only one month after the terrorist attack on the World Trade Center and barely two weeks after the subsequent invasion of Afghanistan by the United States. America needs to take up 'the white man's burden' and 'civilize' the Afghans, wrote reporter Mark Steyn.[165] Too easily dismissed as ranting of the far right, this call for a revival of colonialism has in fact been a feature of the New World Order for most of the post–cold war period. The natives have descended into barbarism and will understand nothing else but force. They are in dire need of civilizing. They consistently mess up their lives and their states, and after 11 September (for those in the North), *our* lives and *our* states. As 'failed states,' comments journalist Pepe Escobar in the *Asia Times*, what is conveniently omitted is how they got to be that way in the first place.'[166] History is evacuated and the simplest of storylines remains: more civilized states have to keep less civilized states in line. In this sense, the story of the New World Order continues a much older theme captured so succinctly in Kipling's phrase 'the white man's burden.' Peacekeeping plays an important role in this new civilizing mission.

In examining the making of men and nations through both international and national mythologies about peacekeeping, what is most evident is that a racial hierarchy structures both. Civilized First World peoples and nations must discipline and instruct uncivilized Third World peoples in human rights and democracy. The storyline requires that the international be imagined as a space of a universal social contract. The UN oversees the contract and member states who do not respect the rules are disciplined by those that do. Like disembodied liberal subjects who have no prior history, so too states in this international order have no histories. That the histories of colonialism might have anything to do with how it comes to be that white men are in Africa teaching Africans about democracy (a lesson taught with guns) is resolutely struck from the story. The international racial epic is told again on the domestic front when the refugees and migrants of the Third World begin to make their way to the countries of the North. Here, too, a besieged and betrayed Northern peoples (like the traumatized peacekeepers) must force themselves to be uncharacteristically stern and impose strict border-policing measures.[167] Both are stories of white innocence.

The power of the story of good and evil enacted globally, whether in peacekeeping trauma narratives or in President Bush's speeches, should give us pause. For while it is its very refusal to consider history and context that gives the story its power, its psychic appeal surely comes, paradoxically, from the mythology that informs our history. In 1973 in *Regeneration through Violence*, Richard Slotkin advised us to remember the power of mythology and its constitutive role in the making of the nation. The real founding fathers, he argued, are not the politicians who drafted the constitution but rather

> those who (to paraphrase Faulkner's *Absalom, Absalom!* [1951]) tore violently a nation from the implacable and opulent wilderness – the rogues, adventurers, and land boomers; the Indian fighters, traders, missionaries, explorers, and hunters who killed and were killed until they had mastered the wilderness; the settlers who came after, suffering hardship and Indian warfare for the sake of a sacred mission or a simple desire for land; and the Indians themselves, both as they were and as they appeared to settlers, for whom they were the special demonic personification of the American wilderness. Their concerns, their hopes, their terrors, their violence, and their justifications of themselves as expressed in literature, are the foundation stones of the mythology that informs our history.[168]

Remarkably prescient, Slotkin anticipates that writers and critics who fail to reckon with these mythological figures will be unable to see when they take over national politics. Slotkin discusses such American moments in the nineteenth century, moments when the national aspiration became defined as 'so many bears destroyed, so much land pre-empted, so many trees hacked down, so many Indians and Mexicans dead in the dust.'[169] In the twentieth century, national politics is dominated by intrepid men who confront evil itself and who, on slow days, bring order and civility to savage lands. These men are kin to Slotkin's Indian fighters, traders, missionaries, explorers, and hunters. They regenerate or reinvent themselves through violence, to borrow Slotkin's argument. If we are to think beyond these mythologies, we first have to identify how they operate and recognize their power, the project I have pursued in this chapter.

It *is* difficult to dismantle mythology and to begin to render things like genocide and ethnic cleansing 'thinkable.'[170] Even when we are able to dismantle mythologies and to consider the historical, social, and political contexts of the countries we set out to 'help,' a formula for responsible intervention does not come easily to mind. Categorically refusing to intervene is as irresponsible a position as intervening because 'they' will only understand force. What is at least clear, however, is that our only chance to assume a more responsible role lies in rejecting the simple and deeply raced storylines of traumatized nations, middle-power countries and their special capabilities, and showdowns with 'absolute evil.' As subsequent chapters explore, peacekeepers caught in these kinds of civilizing narratives of instruction and discipline of the Third World by the First World carry around in their heads those ideas Edward Said analyzes in the novels Europeans wrote about the Third World in the nineteenth century, 'notions about bringing civilization to primitive or barbaric peoples, the disturbingly familiar ideas about flogging or death or extended punishment being required when "they" misbehaved or became rebellious, because "they" mainly understood force or violence best; "they" were not like "us," and for that reason deserve to be ruled.'[171]

Such notions encase the violence of individual peacekeepers and white Northern states, sheathing them in a skin of civility. Only occasionally do the contents spill out, revealing blood, bone, sinew and gore, and even then, it remains seductive to believe that 'they' asked for it. Such is the power of mythology.

CHAPTER 2

Men from the
'Clean Snows of Petawawa'

There must have been times when the heat and dust made them long for the clean snows of Petawawa.

Peter Desbarats, *Somalia Cover-Up*[1]

War, and especially race war, leads to brutalization, which leads to atrocity.

Christopher Browning, *Ordinary Men*[2]

A soldier writing in his diary just one month into the Canadian peacekeeping mission in Somalia noted the frustration of his fellow soldiers, their 'racism and closed-mindedness,' and wondered whether he would be able to prevent 'what I know is wrong.'[3] The killing of an unarmed Somali and the wounding of another on 4 March, the torture and murder of Shidane Arone on 16 March, child detainees inhumanely treated, and scores of incidents of the humiliation and violence of the local population all tell a story of a peacekeeping encounter overdetermined by race.

The casual brutality that some peacekeepers brought to their encounters with Somalis is evident in the incidents of violence involving American, Italian, and Belgian troops, the latter two also the subject of their own national inquiries. Perhaps due to the absence of a national inquiry and thus to the privacy surrounding reported incidents, very little is known of the American encounter. Specialist James Morris was convicted of negligent homicide for shooting a Somali in the back and killing him on 14 February 1993.[4] Gunnery Sergeant Harry Conde was convicted of assault of two Somali teenagers, one of whom reportedly tried to take Sergeant Conde's sunglasses off his face. Firing his M-79 grenade launcher, Sergeant Conde hit the fleeing youth as well as a bystander. Convicted and fined, a military court believed his explanation that American troops in Somalia faced the same kind of mental stress as they did in Vietnam where they feared that ordinary civilians were armed.[5] Several U.S. soldiers have been court-martialed for being too aggressive but, as one journalist has speculated, the American public paid little notice, especially when there was a picture of an American soldier being dragged through the streets by Somalis.[6]

Italian incidents acknowledged by the Gallo Commission of Inquiry[7] include the torture of a detained Somali man by two soldiers applying electric shocks to his genitals; the gang rape of Somali women, including an incident of a rape with a pistol flare involving several men and onlookers; routine mistreatment, hooding, and binding of detainees, including children; and what the commission called 'student-parties' type of coarse behaviour. Photographs survive of these incidents, as they do in the Canadian cases. There were also allegations that a thirteen-year-old Somali boy had been sodomized and tortured to death by an army major inside the former Italian embassy compound in Mogadishu. It is perhaps especially revealing that when medical officer Lucca Cierro visited the military camp at Johar and noticed the burns from cigarettes and the bruises on the bodies of Somalis, he was reassured by Marshal Valerio Ercole, – one of his fellow sodiers who was later convicted of abuse of authority by an Italian court – not to worry because bruises don't show on Black bodies.[8]

The everydayness of peacekeeping violence emerges from the interviews given to *Panorama*, an Italian magazine, by Italian troops who participated in some of the incidents, took photos of them, and observed them. Michele Patruno, a twenty-six-year-old called to compulsory military service in Somalia, described the routine destruction of Somali property and homes as well as the everyday mistreatment of detainees who were deprived of food and water, given bread with hot pepper, and tortured with electric shock, cigarette burns, and razor wire cuts. Patruno confirmed the torture incident with the electric shocks, as well as gang rapes and the killing of two women and a baby, and opined that many more Somalis had either died in detention or were shot than had been officially acknowledged.[9] In his diary, Francesco Aloi kept a log of the exact number of Somali prisoners killed, raped, and tortured. His girlfriend, seeking to bring the diary to the attention of military authorities, described the log as 'an avalanche of murdered Somalis.'[10]

Incidents involving Belgian troops appear to be the most numerous (270 files were opened by the government),[11] many of which involved children. A former Belgian paratrooper came forward with pictures showing two soldiers swinging a Somali child over an open fire, a practice he claimed was a regular one at his base camp near Mogadishu. His photos also accompanied the allegation that a child had been force-fed salt water and pork and then made to eat his own vomit. Children caught stealing were frequently bound and held captive without food or water in the stifling heat. A child held in this way in a metal container cried for help for two days and was eventually found dead. Many soldiers heard his cries, as well as witnessing other events. Children were tied to trucks that were then driven at high speed; they were forced to dig graves they were told were their own. Belgian troops also routinely detained and tortured adult men. One photo shows a soldier urinating on the body of an apparently dead Somali man.

No peacekeeping mission involving Western peacekeepers seems to have been without violence directed at the local population. On many missions, soldiers have been disciplined for getting drunk and firing their rifles, sometimes at crowds.[12] In 1997, Canadian troops, frustrated by the infiltration of their camp by Haitian teenagers, abused detainees in an apparent effort to deter them. As in Somalia, the peacekeeping force appeared not to know what to do about petty thievery and overestimated the seriousness of the threat they posed. Some soldiers considered that the intimidation of infiltrators through beating, blindfolded interrogations, and shouting were justified measures, which they understood to be a part of their orders.[13] In Bosnia, forty-seven Canadian soldiers were accused of drinking while on duty, having sexual relations with nurses, and abusing mental patients.[14] In Kosovo, in one of the few cases carrying a conviction and a stiff sentence, an American peacekeeper, Staff Sergeant Frank Ronghi, raped, sodomized, and murdered eleven-year-old Merita Shabiu. Sergeant Ronghi confided in a member of his unit who drove with him to bury the body in an isolated spot, 'It's easy to get away with this in a third world country – he knew because he had done it in the desert [Kuwait, where Ronghi served during the Gulf War].'[15]

Although peacekeeping violence ranges from racial slurs and small assaults to outright torture and murder, the most egregious acts of peacekeeping violence share certain characteristics. For one, it is mostly openly practised with several witnesses and participants. Second, the soldiers document many of the violent incidents by taking a number of videotapes and trophy photos to visually record the violence they enact and by writing descriptions of it in their diaries. A third feature is that the victims of the violence are often children and youth. Fourth, the violence is sexualized with rape and sodomy occurring. These features make it difficult to consider peacekeeping violence, as journalist Matthew Fisher does of incidents in Somalia, for example, as soldiers pushed to the brink by 'an extremely aggressive and unwelcoming local population.'[16]

African Rights, investigating cases of peacekeeping violence among soldiers who were part of the UN peacekeeping mission led by the United States

(UNOSOM) in Somalia in 1993, was struck by the fact that while numerous extremely violent incidents were verified as having taken place between American, Canadian, Italian, and Belgian troops and the local population, not a single incident of violence was reported between Botswanan soldiers and Somalis. Indeed, the investigative team did not even hear a single shot being fired during their seven days spent in the region:

> In contrast to the great majority of the other soldiers serving with UNOSOM, the Botswanan soldiers were consistently courteous and considerate to the local population. They travelled everywhere with interpreters. They mixed socially with the Somali townspeople. They drove slowly and carefully, especially in town. They worked hard escorting humanitarian convoys: the relief agencies in Bardere estimated that the Botswanans on average escorted twice as many convoys as the US marines they had replaced – despite the fact that there were three times as many marines, with far more equipment, including air support ... The view put forward by some Western journalists and some UNOSOM military commanders that Somali people are inherently aggressive and respect only superior force, is shown to be nonsense by the Botswanans' remarkable demonstration of the possibility of conducting a 'hearts and mind' campaign.[17]

How might we explain the peacekeeping violence of Western troops?

First World soldiers' perception of peacekeeping ventures as taking place on colonial terrain – 'the uncivilized world' in which the natives are clearly not of the same legal and moral order as the peacekeepers, seems to pervade their encounters with the local population. Those whom the peacekeepers have come to help are sometimes shocked to realize their subordinate legal, moral, and *racial* status. The father of Merita Shabiu repeatedly commented of his murdered daughter to an American reporter: 'She was so white, like an American. She had yellow hair. She was like an American.'[18] If the victims and their families are shocked to find themselves treated as the colonized, the soldiers, for their part, are often surprisingly direct about their own sense of no longer being bound by the norms of the 'civilized' world. As one Italian soldier related to *Panorama* magazine:

> One time in Mogadishu, I was on guard. A Somali baby pointed a water pistol at a marine truck. Three shots were fired from the truck. There was nothing left of that baby. I would like people to understand that the dirty stuff that you see in the photos, the torture, the beatings, the kicks and punches they gave each other, not only the parachutists. But they did everything for a very simple reason: In Somalia we were no longer ourselves. We were no longer the people we were before. You

could pass from a civilized world to an uncivilized world: you could no longer find
Saturday and Sunday, you no longer eat meals, you no longer sleep.[19]

Perusing accounts of peacekeeping violence such as these, it is easy to find
parallels between the European soldier in Somalia who can no longer find
Saturday and Sunday and who descends into barbarism, and the character
Kurtz of Joseph Conrad's *Heart of Darkness*, the white man in Congo who
loses his bearings and himself in the 'savagery' of the Dark Continent. For
Conrad, as for the Italian soldier, Africa and Africans drive Europeans beyond
the boundaries of civility.

Peacekeeping, as chapter 1 showed, enables individual Western nations to
constitute themselves as part of a family of civilized nations and Western
peacekeepers often understand themselves as part of a global civilizing mission. In this chapter, I suggest how the civilizing narratives of the New World
Order are *enacted* by individual men. Using the evidence from various Canadian legal processes, I suggest that the very concrete practices of violence
against Somalis enabled individual soldiers to imagine themselves as men
from the land of clean snow, men of Northern nations whose duties in bringing order to Somalis *required* violence. Somalis were constituted as the mass
that threatened to engulf innocent soldiers, a threat that only violence could
dissolve. I propose that the beatings, torture, humiliations, rape, and killings
of Somalis by Western peacekeepers are best understood as colonial violence.
That is to say, the violent practices in which peacekeepers engaged in Africa
are practices intended to establish Northern nations as powerful and superior,
nations in full control of the natives they have come to keep in line. Canadians
were hardly exceptional in this respect, although this chapter will be devoted
almost exclusively to their activities.

To call peacekeeping violence colonial violence is to put considerable
emphasis on the racial aspects of the encounter between Somalis and peacekeepers. The encounters described here are between white armies (even when
individual soldiers are Brown or Black, they remain regulated by the civilizing
mission that they went to Africa to undertake) and a Black population, in an
ex-colony that for the North has long symbolized barbarism. In wishing to
underscore the colonial histories that Northern men brought to their peacekeeping efforts in Africa, I reject explanations for peacekeeping violence that
make exceptions of the men who participate in it either by considering the soldier as a unique figure, strangely prone to violence, misogyny, and racism or
driven to excessive violence by the conditions of military life. While such conditions and soldiers do exist – and we may even identify among the troops in
Somalia a military masculinity, a hegemonic ideal in which physical violence

against women and racial minorities is overvalorized – to sever both the ideal and the acts of violence from their historical and national roots is to miss how white men and states secure their power, and just how much violence it takes to do so.

In my emphasis on the relationship between a racial masculinity and the making of the nation, I argue against those who attribute the violence to the warlike conditions that are said to prevail in modern peacekeeping. Apart from the fact that warlike conditions do not always prevail, to see such violence as an outcome of war is to naturalize it. Not every soldier engaged in racist violence or condoned it, but those that *did* enable us to plot the connections between widely accepted ideas about the moral superiority of the West and the violence that is enacted in the name of nation-building. They afford us, in other words, a closer look at the connections between race, nation, and violence and at the material consequences of where we position ourselves in national and international mythologies.

There is always a gap between mythology and how it is enacted, between the nation as imagined and the individual who achieves national belonging through entering this imaginary. We can perhaps see how 'keeping the natives in line' through violence produces feelings of racial and national superiority, but it is harder to imagine the superiority an individual soldier might feel guarding six-year-old children under the hot sun. In the case of prolonged torture, it is harder still to understand what propelled the man who delivered the blows and the kicks to the head, the man who took the pictures, the man who came to watch. It is perhaps easier to rationalize the actions of men shooting at 'intruders' in the camp, but even here the deliberateness of the shooting gives pause. *What did the soldiers think they were doing?*

To attempt to explore the mind-set of the soldiers is not to indulge in mere speculation, although few direct means are available to document the soldiers' inner worlds. In this chapter, I begin with those scholars who explore the masculinities involved in the making of racial states and who shed light on the psychic worlds of fascists, colonizers, and soldiers or 'soldier males.'[20] While a good case can be made for the uniqueness of these groups of men and the prevalence and significance of violence against subordinate groups in their lives, the case is equally strong that their activities are done in the name of a broader notion of racial superiority. Ordinary people, that is people who can hardly imagine themselves as given to violence of the kind discussed here, come to be linked to peacekeeper violence through a shared understanding of the North's right and obligation to discipline and instruct the natives of the South. It is this shared understanding that is traced here largely through the records available from military trials and the commission of inquiry into the deployment of Canadian troops to Somalia. My aim is to suggest how people are educated to participate in the social, how they are interpellated into practices that leave these trails of violence in their wake. Peacekeeping violence, as I observe at the end of this chapter, is violence that is done in our name and whether we participate directly in it, observe it, condone it, or simply fail to name it for what it is, we are each accountable.

I. Masculinities That Make the White Nation

Violence that arises in military or quasi-military situations, including peacekeeping and policing, is often considered to be violence born of exceptional circumstances. The violence of military men is naturalized as an inevitable by-product of war and of place, that is, as a response to a *legitimate* external threat, and as a response to a cruel environment. Tracy Karner, for example, examining the oral histories of Vietnam War veterans suffering from post-traumatic stress disorders, notes how killing gave the men a sense of power and control, but she presents this as natural, if not inevitable, in the chaos and danger of war.[21] The men's tremendous anger and rage against the Vietnamese and their extraordinary acts of violence become 'a useful response to the horror and the bewilderment of warfare in Vietnam,' and reasonable in light of the fear of death and loss of friends.'[22] Although Karner acknowledges that the men seek to perform a traditional masculinity, one characterized by strength and aggression, and clearly predating Vietnam, she nonetheless views their excessive violence as normal under the circumstances. That the particular gender identity the men seek to perform in Vietnam is only actualized through excessive violence directed at racial minorities and women remains, in the end, simply a function of *where* they are (a brutal place) and *what* they are up against (a brutal people). In the same way, some scholars argue that violent peacekeepers are merely soldiers engaging in the violence that is endemic to militaries. Peacekeepers participate in military culture that is inherently racist, sexist, and homophobic. Their violence is therefore 'a necessary if unfortunate feature of an organization whose existence is premised on valuing aggression and violence.'[23]

To denaturalize what has been taken for granted in these explanations, it is important to consider where Western peacekeepers thought they were, and most of all *who* they thought they were. Here we might profit from scholars who consider how masculinity is performed in colonial contexts. Colonial novels, reflective of the preoccupations of the time and written to appeal to the audiences of their day, offer interesting insights, not because characters in a novel may be directly compared with peacekeepers who imagine themselves to be colonizers today, but because the structure and process of the fictional narratives reveal something about the making of self within racial hierarchies.[24] They reveal, in other words, the range of fears, insecurities, and possible motivations of men who felt obliged to commit acts of violence against Somalis.

In *Images of Imperial Rule*, Hugh Ridley examines a body of fiction that portrays French, German and English colonial activity and outlines the kind of masculine colonial subject who inhabits these fictional worlds. Drawing on Mannoni's 1964 novel *Prospero and Caliban*, Ridley begins, as others have done, with Robinson Crusoe. For Crusoe, the island on which he finds himself inspires a pathological fear of its cannibals, a fear that bears little relationship to reality. Crusoe projects onto the landscape a private vision, one Mannoni calls 'a massive misanthropic neurosis' in which he is the civilized man who must confirm his own superiority or descend into the primitive.[25] Any actual native whom Crusoe encounters has the burden of proof that he is not a cannibal. Friday achieves this by being able to fawn and grovel at Crusoe's feet, thereby confirming Crusoe's superiority. Thus, 'Friday and Crusoe have no actual relationship, no more do the colonial and the "Native" ... their meeting is the encounter of the European imagination with supposed equivalents in reality on which it has projected its trauma.'[26] The self/psychic identity of the colonizing subject, Crusoe, is only made possible through the otherness/alterity of the colonized. For Daniel Defoe's readers, Crusoe represented that which most threatened them: the instability of their own claim to civilization.[27]

Like Crusoe, Northern peacekeepers, even before they go to Africa, have constituted themselves (and they are constituted) as men of superior morality whose task it is to instruct and sort out the natives. While such subject positions may not be available in the same way to women as they are to men, or to racial minority men as they are to white men, the overriding frame of the encounter is one of the civilized North and the barbaric South. Some individuals inhabit this frame as confident colonizers, others simply begin unself-consciously as people who have set out to 'do good.' Either way, a racial hierarchy is installed. In considering the encounter in Somalia between Canadian troops and Somalis, an encounter revealingly described by one of the commissioners of the national inquiry into the deployment of Canadian troops as one between men of clean snow and men of the hot desert, it is particularly relevant to recall the meaning of landscape in colonial fantasies of dominance. In colonial novels of Africa, the landscape represents 'the evil of Africa herself rather than the inherent brutality of imperialism,' a hell, to paraphrase Ridley, in which few men can be saints. The colonies are often depicted as the 'proving ground for national manhood,'[28] a place where real men must resort to violence in order to establish their own potency and the potency of their nations.[29]

In a very useful set of definitions, Ridley distinguishes between the two kinds of violence discernable in the novels: functional violence, the 'teach the natives a lesson' violence, and self-justifying violence, 'meted out [by the colonizer] in order to prove something about himself.'[30] Intended to quell internal fears and insecurities, self-justifying violence is 'relished in situations which involve no threat to whites.'[31] Very often, these two forms of violence must be defended as virtue in the metropolis. Those safely at home are prone to underestimating what it takes to survive in the colonies.[32] In Somalia, it is not always easy to tell which forms of violence were being enacted. I suggest, however, that for men who believed themselves to be in a hostile and alien territory, and who saw themselves as defending their own manhood and the manhood of their nation, the violence affirmed Canadian soldiers as whole and intact, as it did Ridley's literary heroes.

Men whose sense of self and whose nation both crucially depend on establishing dominance over racial Others, undertake what I have elsewhere called 'racial journeys to personhood,'[33] the coming to know oneself as whole and in control through surviving encounters with what is most feared. German scholar Klaus Theweleit's two-volume work, *Male Fantasies*, considers some of the psychic dimensions of this making of self we see in colonial novels, but in this case not in fiction but through a study of men reared in a society that was deeply racially structured. Theweleit's subjects are German fascists of the 1920s and 1930s, members of the Freikorps (private armies of former imperial soldiers who were anti-communist), some of whom went on to become well-known Nazis (for example, Rudolf Hoess, the commandant of Auschwitz). Exploring the extraordinary number of novels written by and the personal memoirs left by the Freikorps, Theweleit describes fascist violence of the 1920s as born of the internal fears of 'soldier males' whose identity is predicated on 'flight from the feminine, a fear of ego dissolution.'[34] For Theweleit, fear of the feminine (the mass) encompasses fear of the racial other; racial domination is simply 'patriarchal domination in its most intense form.'[35] The alien race is 'the most intense embodiment of the terror represented by the mass.' When the Freikorps wanted to eliminate Jews, they imagined themselves eliminating the feminine. The first volume of *Male Fantasies*, entitled *Women, Flood, Bodies, History*, maps how images of women function in the collective unconscious of the fascist warrior as a flood, a mass that threatens to drown the male ego, while the second volume shows how the body becomes a mechanism that protects itself from being engulfed by it.

Theweleit's fascists long for the softness, warmth, sensuality, and pleasure of the feminine but experience a profound terror that to give in to 'the woman within' is to lose control, and literally to lose one's self. The fascist mentality keeps fear of the feminine at bay through 'the armoured organization of the male self in a world that constantly threatens it with disintegration.'[36] The 'hard, organised, phallic body,' the mechanized body eternally subjected to drills, keeps the woman and the Jew from engulfing the male subject. Military academies and later military routines produce the mechanized body, the body that does not think as an individual. 'Attitudes of ascetism, renunciation, and self-control are effective defences' against disintegration.[37] Violence has a central role to play in the making of a self as hard and organized because it dissolves the threat of engulfment: 'Theweleit's men are killers, not out of a simple lust for blood or romantic dreams of glory, but because they want to remain whole.'[38]

As Theweleit concludes of the fascists he studies, '[I]t is only from a position of dominance that the ego can endure life and avoid breakdown.'[39] Thus the soldier male 'escapes by mashing others to the pulp he threatens to become.' He needs the 'immediate perception that "not I, but others" are miasma.' The 'soldier male' engages in what Theweleit calls 'civilian forms' of the violence, – searing critique, instruction, name calling as well as beatings and torture: 'Beating shows him his proper place and his limits. By degrading his opponent, the soldier maintains himself; and he places the impudent who challenges him in the most humiliating of childlike positions.' As with the self justifying violence of the colonizer, through beating, the soldier male feels both relief and pleasure that he is no longer the child being beaten. Fascist torture is a public display of both the victim and the tormentor, and it represents an attempt by the soldier male to maintain his own body as a body that is not of the mass.[40]

The soldier who walks around with a generalized sense of fear that he is at risk, that he is menaced by mysterious, duplicitous 'savages' against whom he must protect himself is experiencing his body in specific ways. The significance of Theweleit's work is his attempt to describe how the body organizes and expresses race, gender, and class hierarchies. As Anson Rabinbach and Jessica Benjamin comment in their foreword to volume two of *Male Fantasies*, in Theweleit's texts,

> the body constructs the external world in its own image. Fear of the inner body with its inchoate 'mass' of viscera and entrails, its 'soft' genitalia, its 'lower half,' is translated into the threat of the 'masses' in the social sense of classes or – especially in those chaotically mixed groups with women and children in the forefront – mass demonstrations. The mass is diametrically opposed to the need for a rigidly, hierarchically structured whole. The 'front' is not simply the place of battle, the locale of violence, but also the site of the body's boundary against self-disintegration.[41]

The body becomes a mechanism for containing 'the soldier's own fear of the desiring production of his own unconscious.' Its cohesion can only be maintained 'through direct action on their own and others' bodies.' In war, civilians and the masses are associated with the pleasures of the body; the soldier constitutes himself as the man of steel who must erect a wall between himself and anything that threatens to transform him into body, emotions, humanity.

Men who experience their bodies as Theweleit describes understand themselves as a race, an 'organizational form' that is in opposition to the mass:

> It follows from this that the man who assigns himself a place in the Aryan, or any other 'higher' race, is aligning himself in opposition to the lower classes, the mass, the proletarian, the woman, the animal. What he is saying is, 'as a man, I am an upstanding individual, a formation, one of your kind, the upper echelons, always on the side of domination and the army.'[42]

They also understand themselves as a nation, not in the sense of government or national borders. Instead, nationalism is an expression of maleness and the nation is a male community of soldiers: 'The nation was seen to have arisen more or less of its own accord in the trenches.'[43] For Theweleit's fascists, 'the battle for nation resembles the men's own battle to become men.'[44]

Theweleit and Ridley are both speaking of a violence born of specific *internal* fears about women and racial Others, fears that grow greater when engulfment seems imminent. There need not be any actual threat to activate the kind of fragmentation that precedes the violence. Crusoe does not require encounters with actual cannibals to believe himself surrounded by them, nor do the Freikorps need actual menacing Jews. Applied to Northern troops in Somalia, it would mean that Africa and Africans themselves represent savagery, a savagery that confirms the civility and the very existence of white men. Ironically, in this racial fantasy of superiority, it is only through the savagery of Europeans themselves that the hierarchical relationship can be confirmed; only then can Crusoe, the Freikorps, or the soldier know who is truly in control. A curious inversion thus underpins the relationship between the stereotypical representation and material practices. While Black men are said to be cannibals, it is white peacekeepers who must roast Black children over an open flame to convince themselves that they are indeed in control.[45] The inversion is itself key to understanding the encounter as racially overdetermined. It is striking how much peacekeeper violence in Africa mimics colonial practices of violence, a correspondence very much in evidence in photos of peacekeeping violence of children bound with hands painted white, of soldiers urinating on the body of a dead Somali, and so on.

Violence Makes the Man and the Nation

The identity-making processes at work in acts of violence reveal prior views of the racial inferiority of those who are the targets of aggression, views that are individual and national. As Dana Nelson has argued for the nineteenth-century American context, a stabilizing of both personal *and* national identity is achieved through racial domination. The oppression of Indians thus became a resource for national manhood, a manhood understood to be white.[46] Similarly, Joanne Nagel argues that hegemonic masculinity (by which is meant the normative demeanour, thinking, and action, the standard 'whether reviled or revered-against which other masculinities compete or define themselves') gives substance to the militaristic nationalism of the United States.[47] In her discussion of Theodore Roosevelt, Nagel concludes that the westward expansion of American settlers and their broader nationalist imperialist projects depended on a racialized, imperial masculinity 'where adventurous, but civilized white men tame or defeat savage men of color, be they American, Indians, Africans, Spaniards, or Filipinos.'[48] Importantly, Nagel also suggests that the connection between masculinity and nationalism sheds light on why the entrance of Blacks, women, and homosexuals into the military has been so much of an issue: 'This unseemly, sometimes hysterical resistance to a diversity that clearly exists outside military boundaries, makes more sense when it is understood that these [military] men are not only defending tradition but are defending a particular racial, gendered and sexual conception of self: a white, male, heterosexual notion of masculine identity loaded with all the burdens and privileges that go along with hegemonic masculinity.'[49]

White, middle-class English masculinity was inextricably tied to the imperial projects and anxieties of Britain at the end of the nineteenth and beginning of the twentieth century and remains so today. Agreeing with Theweleit, that the hegemonic male subject flees from the feminine principle in pursuit of the 'culture of death' that is imperial manliness, Jonathan Rutherford suggests that when we consider the sensibilities of men drawn into hegemonic masculinity, we must understand them as 'sensibilities related to women and to race, which were shaped by the history of empire, family life, class and ethnicity.'[50] Showing how boys brought up to deny feeling and become hardened imperial warriors are estranged from their own bodies, and are preoccupied with the objectification and fetishizing of the bodies of women and people of colour, Rutherford is careful to note the connection between individual family history (a history similar to Theweleit's fascists, of emotionally absent fathers and overbearing mothers) and empire. Colonial hegemonic masculinities were, as Graham Dawson shows, 'necessarily constituted in the encounter with cultural difference: in relation to other, subordinated "non-white" masculinities (as well as in complex and variable relations to femininities which were themselves also in part the product of difference marked by colonial power).'[51]

In imperial Britain, 'the image of a lone, dashing Englishman dispensing justice, wisdom and righteous retribution on his brown subjects,'[52] was one that acquired particular saliency when Britain's imperial power was on the wane. For this imperial figure, 'flogging, imprisonment and summary executions were endowed with a moral and religious virtue'; they were what Englishmen could 'do for the people of India.'[53] Other scholars have noted that imperial manliness often required violence as necessary for the natives' own good, that is to say, an imperial mix of violence, governance and compassion. John Nauright discusses, for example, the cult of Christian manhood at the end of the nineteenth century with its military and nationalistic focus mixed with compassion and concern.[54] As a masculinity forged so intimately in relation to bodies of colour, the anxieties of imperial subjects and imperial nations are easily projected on the bodies of the colonized. Such racial masculinities, described by James Messerschmidt in reference to the period of reconstruction in the American South, require violence at moments of intense anxiety. Messerschmidt describes the rise in lynching after the Civil War as white men's response to a perceived erosion of their power: 'white-male mob violence emerged as an attempt to reestablish the old meanings and hierarchy,' that were lost with the emancipation of slaves.[55] The practice of lynching and castration feminized the African-American male body and 'provided a resource for the physical enactment of white masculine hegemony.'[56]

Contemporary Racial Masculinities

The making of racially dominant masculinities and nations through violence directed at bodies of colour is also evident in contemporary contexts. Euan Hague, for example, examines the genocidal rapes in Bosnia-Herzegovina enacted by Serbs on Muslim men, women, and children, and proposes that we understand this violence as intrinsic to the assertion of the soldier's '*heteronationality* – a different nationality from the rape victim: By raping and impregnating women and girls, watching men rape each other in prison camps, and assuming the power position of "masculine" in all rapes, the Bosnia Serb military and its allied irregulars proved to themselves their own identities as powerful, manly and *crucially Serbs*.'[57] While Hague supports the notion of a 'soldierly masculinity' characterized by sexual aggression, he is nonetheless clear that such masculinities operate in service of a national project, in this case Serbian dominance in Bosnia-Herzegovina. Importantly, while violence enables each soldier to know himself as a particular kind of man, it also facilitates 'a community of males' required in nationalistic and militaristic politics.[58]

The humanitarian or the peacekeeper of First World nations hopes to exert a civilizing influence on the people of the Third World, saving them from dictators and communism, and assisting them into modernity. For the American context, Steve Niva has written, one version of this new man in the 1990s is 'slightly feminized,' distanced from a tough, aggressive masculinity by his talk of the United States as 'the upholder of international law and normality *and* the model for gender relations.'[59] There is, however, an important tension between contemporary civilizing practices and the enactment of violence 'for their own good.' In his study of violence and manhood in post-Vietnam America, James Gibson suggests that the Vietnam War produced another figure for whom humanitarian talk and diplomacy merely inhibits true justice.[60] Written before the peacekeeping ventures of the early 1990s, Gibson's study nonetheless reveals the contours of the masculine subject we often see in peacekeeping, the man attracted to units such as the Airborne Regiment. Sharing the thesis that the Vietnam War ushered in a period of the discredited warrior hero, Gibson argues that the warrior hero returned in the 1970s and 1980s as the paramilitary Rambo of popular culture. Rambo fights and wins endless battles against bad men, often men of colour of the inner cities or men from communist-infested Third World countries. Locating Rambo in material conditions, Gibson argues that many white men experienced a profound racial and gender decentering with civil rights, feminism, and massive immigration. Faced with 'the declining power of their identities and organizations,' he argues, many 'American men jumped psychically' into the fantasy of retaking the world on the new warrior's terms.[61]

Gibson's work is particularly useful when he explores the 'mythic universe' of the new warriors, the symbols that exert a powerful pull on the unconscious.[62] Researching films, magazines such as *Soldier of Fortune*, and the immensely popular paramilitary games, Gibson finds a masculine figure drawn to tremendous savagery against racial Others, a savagery understood as a defence of an imperilled home and nation. Finding correspondences between his own work and Theweleit's, Gibson speculates that the violence keeps the men's fears at bay, enabling them to feel in control. Their's is an all male grouping; paramilitary culture views organizations such as NATO as a confederation of tribes. Tribes, it goes without saying, of civilized white men.[63] The fantasy world of the paramilitary figure is made up of elite commando groups (very much as the Airborne Regiment was to see itself in Somalia) whose members may include racial minorities valued for their specific military expertise (Asians for Ninja fighting, Indians for knife wielding, and so on). Nonetheless, the paramilitary warrior's fight is in defence of whiteness and white nations. His fights always take place in 'Indian country,' 'rugged terrain [that is] infested with Communist guerrillas, swarming gnats, tall grass and choking heat.'[64] A profound racism structures 'Indian country' as the warriors set out to cleanse the world of peoples who are imagined to contaminate a white and civilized world.

Gibson marshals an impressive array of research to show not only the vitality of the paramilitary figure in popular culture but also the impact of the fantasy on real men's lives. From the men who attend the war-game exercises to those who become U.S. presidents, Gibson shows the consequences of the fantasy when it is acted out. Ronald Reagan ran his presidency as though he was in one of the Rambo films Gibson explores, and the racist right's new war – including such events as the shooting of five Communist Party activists in Greensboro, North Carolina, by the Ku Klux Klan in 1979 – reveals that the fantasy of white men taking over the world has deadly consequences.

What happens when men like this go to Africa to secure the world for democracy? As I show below, what might have been extreme at home becomes officially sanctioned in peacekeeping: keeping the natives in line through violence. Moreover, as Jesse Daniels has shown in her study of white supremacists and what Gibson confirms in his study of paramilitary men, what is an extreme masculinity is nonetheless premised on a particular sense of race and nation that is more widely shared.[65] Daniels concludes: 'The racial warrior of the white supremacist movement perceives himself to be a noble freedom fighter waging a just war against the "non-white" hordes, much like the Vietnam soldier/veteran depicted in recent films, as well as the embattled Everyman typified by Michael Douglas's character in the film *Falling Down*.'[66] Indeed, the overlap between white supremacist discourse and that of more mainstream representations of white men is neither a coincidence nor simply the appropriation of these images by white supremacists.[67] Similarly, it might be said of peacekeepers that they perceive themselves as civilized men obliged to help, discipline, and teach less advanced civilizations. Peacekeepers who are themselves racialized are no less drawn to this fantasy, although they must negotiate the fact that their own positions as morally superior men (indeed, as men) are never as secure as white men's.

We can see the dimensions of the fantasy of racial masculinity among peacekeepers in the highly popular book and movie *Black Hawk Down*, a rendition of the American peacekeeping experience in Somalia.[68] As the dust jacket of the book relates, on 3 October 1993,

> about a hundred elite U.S. soldiers were dropped by helicopters into the teeming market in the heart of Mogadishu, Somalia. Their mission was to abduct two top lieutenants of a Somali warlord and return to base. It was supposed to take an hour. Instead they found themselves pinned through a long and terrible night

fighting against thousands of heavily armed Somalis. The following morning, eighteen Americans were dead and more than seventy badly injured.

The men of this epic battle are like brothers:

> They'd been drunk together, gotten into fights, slept on forest floors, jumped out of air planes, climbed mountains, shot down foaming rivers with their hearts in their throats, baked and frozen and starved together, passed countless bored hours, teased one another endlessly about girlfriends or lack of same, driven out in the middle of the night from Fort Benning to retrieve each other from some diner or strip club on Victory Drive after getting drunk and falling asleep or pissing off some barkeep.[69]

In Mogadishu, this 'nearly all white' 'formidable sum of men and machines,' the 'cocked fist of America's military might,' are up against a 'ragged clan' of Somalis, whom they called 'Skinnies' or Sammies.'[70] The battlefield is at once deeply foreign yet lodged somewhere in historical memory: 'Hundreds of thousands of clan members lived in this labyrinth of irregular dirt streets and cactus-lined paths. There were no decent maps. Pure Indian country.'[71]

As Indian country, little has to be known of Somalia. Bowden concludes his description of the soldiers with the boast that 'none of the men in these helicopters knew enough to write a high school paper about Somalia.' They didn't have to know, he explains. They had the army's line on it:

> Warlords had so ravaged the nation battling among themselves that their people were starving to death. When the world sent food, the evil warlords hoarded it and killed those who tried to stop them. So the civilized world had decided to lower the hammer, invite the baddest boys on the planet over to clean things up. 'Nuff said. Little the Rangers had seen since arriving at the end of August had altered that perception. Mogadishu was like the post apocalyptic world of Mel Gibson's *Mad Max* movies, a world ruled by the roving gangs of armed thugs. They were here to rout the worst of the warlords and restore sanity and civilization.[72]

Force is the only thing the natives understand: 'Civilized states had nonviolent ways of resolving disputes, but that depended on the willingness of everyone involved to *back down*. Here in the raw Third World, people hadn't learned to back down, at least not until after a lot of blood flowed.'[73] The civilizing mission sometimes seemed hardly worth the trouble. The soldiers had only contempt for Somalis whom they saw as men who didn't work and who spent the day chewing *khat*. It was hard for them to imagine, Bowden relates, 'what interest the United States of America had in such a place.'[74] If the fantasy of *Black Hawk Down* was shared by other peacekeeping troops in Somalia, it is little wonder that violence directed at Somalis should have been the result.

II. Operation Deliverance

We were perpetually exposed to risks, the risks of riots. Just the regular patrols were a risk. It was a very unpredictable environment where danger literally lurked outside the wire.

Anonymous Canadian solider quoted in Donna Winslow,
The Canadian Airborne Regiment in Somalia[75]

Given the global impact of Hollywood, Canadian soldiers as well as Americans (and indeed Italians and Belgians, too) can equally aspire to be Rambo. There is, however, a specifically Canadian dilemma that affects the soldiers' and the nation's racial fantasy of dominance: the paradoxical figure of the anti-conquest man who is more modest, kinder, and gentler than Americans. Americans are seen to fight wars, the commission into the deployment of Canadian troops to Somalia noted, 'but Canadians pictured themselves as working for peace.'[76] Men from the land of the clean snows are peacekeepers, anti-conquest men, to use Mary Louise Pratt's term for imperial botanists, naturalists and map makers,[77] whose mediation talents paradoxically condemn them to a less than manly role on the sidelines.

Like Theweleit's German subjects for whom there was no colonial theatre in which to enact their fantasies of superiority,[78] Canadians have often found colonial terrain already occupied by Americans, leaving them only with Canada's Aboriginal peoples and people of colour as the less glamourous 'alien race within.' In the Canadian national vocation of peacekeeping, no less than in early colonizing ventures, the glorious dream of being a kinder, gentler version of the United States can easily slide into the distinctly unheroic and less masculine role of younger brother playing second fiddle. As a U.S.-led United Nations mission in Somalia, Operation UNOSOM brought to the surface this national anxiety. Within a few hours of UNOSOM's establishment, Canadian generals were lobbying the United States for a prominent role in Somalia. As the Inquiry reported, Canadian General John de Chastelain immediately telephoned U.S. General Colin Powell and explained that, having been left out of the Gulf War, 'a role that was seen to be secondary would not sit well with the troops, with me, with the Government, or with Canadians.'[79] The leadership of the Armed Forces feared that if they did not assert themselves at the start of the mission, they would see little action, and according to Colonel Serge

Labbé, the Canadians would probably be left with 'guarding the perimeter of an airfield.'[80] In the same way, members of the Airborne Regiment deployed to Somalia also felt anxious (in the words of an unidentified soldier) 'to get over there and show the rest of the world ... what we're made of.'[81] Trained but never exposed to combat, the Regiment felt, as one scholar put it, 'like Olympians when there were no games.'[82] Arguably, whatever the mission was called, soldiers would probably understand it as going off to war.

True to form as the eldest brother, U.S. military planners were more or less indifferent to the predicament of the younger brother. Canadian Armed Forces found themselves having little or no information about or involvement in the planning of the mission.[83] Reliant on CNN to learn what they could, Canadian Armed Forces believed that they would arrive in Somalia to find an enemy ready for battle.[84] The image of Canadian soldiers with their rifles ready and battle positions assumed, landing at the airport in Belet Huen (which had already been secured by U.S. soldiers), must have struck the welcoming crowds of Somali men, women, and children looking on as bizarre, an impression probably strengthened by the sight of the soldiers attempting a six-hour march in heat of forty-five degree Celsius with insufficient water and loaded down with 45 kilograms (100 pounds) of equipment.[85]

There is little doubt that the Forces shared the view of the Somalia Inquiry commissioners that Canada's role in Somalia principally involved saving the Somalis from the excesses of their own tribal society. Somalia, existing in Northern imaginations in anachronistic space and time,[86] is described by one of the commissioners in this way:

> An ancient land that had survived colonialism and the Cold War was now the victim of its own tribal warlords. Hundreds of thousands of Somalis were starving before the television cameras. Prodded by news media, the rich communities of the West underwent one of their periodic spasms of generosity. Under the leadership of the United States, Canada and other United Nations member states rushed into Somalia to deliver these people from disaster.[87]

As Catherine Besteman shows, the story of Somalia as a 'country unable to rid itself of ancient rivalries'[88] became an American media story that had profound repercussions for how the interventions in Somalia were understood. U.S. interventions in Somalia were viewed as civilizing missions, a storyline requiring the erasure of the complexities of Somali history and the 'dynamic hierarchies of status, class, race, and language that were central to the patterning of violence in post-1991 southern Somalia.'[89] In the media story, Somalis became 'savages who got ahead of themselves technologically; ... tribesmen still out there wandering around the primordial landscape, bound by ancient ties and animosities, dutifully following the factional footsteps of their forefathers.'[90] Demonstrating the absurdity of this portrait, Besteman shows how it obscures such underlying factors as the 'heightened competition for resources, capital and opportunities for enrichment nourished by the U.S.-backed development boom.'[91] And, as she concludes, 'Viewing Somalis as caught in a destructive spiral of "tradition" allows us to imagine them as very different kinds of human beings, to pity them, and to feel safe.'[92] Paradoxically, to be surrounded by such primitive peoples can also activate Crusoe-like fears, an effect clearly evident among Canadian troops.

Aptly named Operation Deliverance (the U.S. mission was named Operation Restore Hope), Canadian participation in Somalia was officially described as both military and humanitarian. When the incidents of violence came to light, it became a fact of considerable importance that the mission was characterized not as one of peacekeeping, per se, but of peace enforcement. What this meant to those making the distinction was that the troops operated within a warlike and dangerous context in which their tasks would involve both traditional military operations like securing an area, as well as humanitarian activities like ensuring the deliverance of aid.[93] In practice, the lines between such activities are difficult to draw and both can be undertaken within a colonial framework. Indeed, the Canadian military understood its role as 'putting that region of Somalia back on the path to a normal lifestyle.'[94] Or, in the more direct language of the troops, their task was to 'look after' Somalis who, as it turns out, were neither properly grateful nor deserving, a source of considerable aggravation for them. The soldiers' interviews with anthropologist Donna Winslow are replete with comments such as 'I never saw a starving Somali. I never saw a grateful Somali'; 'We were sent there to help them, and they did nothing to help us'; 'They weren't even appreciative of the work we were doing for them. They just kept destroying everything we were building and I think that was the turning point really, for me anyhow. It was one of the big turning points against the Somalis, around mid-February. I went from feeling sorry for them down to being fed up, thinking, "Let's get out." They brought it all on themselves.'[95] In this atmosphere of ungrateful natives throwing rocks at Canadian troops, Canadians soon found themselves deep in imperial fantasies, fantasies shaped from the start by the vitality of the peacekeeper myth and by the strong sense that Canadians were in Africa to save Somalis from themselves. In the actual encounter with Somali bodies, Black and Muslim bodies clothed in sarong-like garments can be seen as both Africa and Orient. For Western subjects to feel whole and to understand their presence in that space as necessary and justified, Black savagery had to exist.

The Encounter

Who, then, were the men of Operation Deliverance? In her interviews with fifty of the soldiers of the Canadian Airborne Regiment, for a study commissioned by the Inquiry, anthropologist Donna Winslow documented the warrior image that was so central to the troops' perceptions of themselves. Winslow's soldier subjects were mostly convinced that human rights legislation, requiring the Armed Forces to stop discriminating against women and against racial and sexual minorities, weakened the military and contributed to its acceptance of unqualified soldiers (perhaps an allusion to the Cree soldiers most implicated in the killing of Shidane Arone). They vehemently opposed homosexuality and saw efforts to discipline soldiers who harassed women and minorities as limiting the military's capacity to produce effective soldiers. As one soldier explained, men who spend a great deal of time together feel a need to prove they are not homosexuals by going out and 'getting themselves a woman': 'When we go out the woman becomes a machine, an object that we'd use as much as possible, and talk about as much as possible because afterwards there won't be any women around.'[96]

Some soldiers held the view that Canadian society penalized them for violent acts in Somalia that it would condone or treat less severely if committed in Canada. In a revealing moment when violated Black bodies in Canada are linked to violated Black bodies in Somalia, one soldier comments that if 'civilians beat a guy to death, it would probably pass as normal' or if 'five White guys beat up a black guy, Ya so what? It happens.'[97] While such views lead Winslow to conclude that at least the members of the Airborne were 'hyperinvested' in a warrior identity, little connection is made between their perceptions and the perceptions of a racist national culture.[98] Put another way, while it is acknowledged that the men learn to be men through the practices of Othering women, homosexuals, and racial minorities, Winslow fails to see that they learn to be *white* men, a gendered and raced identity enacted in Africa within an official mission to save Somalis from the excesses of their own culture and society. She does not interrogate what James Messerschmidt terms 'the social construction of white-supremacist masculinity'; there is, then, little chance that the racial dimensions of the violence in Somalia could be uncovered.[99] The Airborne Regiment remains exceptionalized and, as I show in chapter 4, racist violence remains confined to it and naturalized as an innate and necessary feature of military life.

Prior to going to Somalia, members of the Airborne Regiment had a 'rash of disciplinary incidents, the unbounded hazing rituals, and the presence of right-wing extremists and racist incidents and paraphernalia.'[100] Over forty-seven members of the Regiment had received some form of criminal or disciplinary charge prior to Somalia and there were many incidents of a racial nature.[101] The televised hazing initiation rituals, in particular video footage depicting among other things the letters KKK written on the shoulder of a Black corporal who was then tied to a tree, sprinkled with flour (referred to as Michael Jackson's secret), symbolically anally raped, and required to crawl on all fours, all seem to confirm the entrenchment of racist, sexist, and homophobic attitudes.

Although the Black corporal in the hazing ritual denied that he found these rituals racist, and others noted that the rituals did not involve a majority of troops, it is useful (when considering the forms of torture used on Shidane Arone, and specifically the allegation that Arone was anally raped with pipes and a stick) to keep in mind Theweleit's analysis of the meaning of anal intercourse among the fiercely heterosexual Freikorps. For Theweleit, anal intercourse in this context is an act of maintenance of the boundaries between the subject and engulfment. The anus is a site of aggression because it represents forbidden territory to a heterosexual man and the ever present possibility that men engaged in homosocial bonding can too easily cross the line into homosexuality: 'Its threat must be defused or it will indeed rip him to pieces.'[102] Less boldly stated, Jonathan Rutherford (citing Eve Kosofsky Sedgewick's contention that homophobia helps to create the boundary between sexual and non-sexual male behaviour) also identifies the homoerotic tension so present among middle-class Englishmen, a tension marking their relations with other Englishmen as well as with colonized men, and their continual need to reassure themselves through violence, that they had not in fact crossed the line.[103]

We might also consider the misogyny that is expressed by rendering a man passive, penetrated, and dependent, as Arone is alleged to have been. Richard Trexler, commenting on the prevalence of sexual punishments for thieves, and in particular the anal rapes between Aboriginal peoples and their Iberian conquerors in pre-seventeenth-century North America, describes the racial and gendered logic of the punishment: '[H]omosexual rape was viewed in this part of the world as the violation of an outsider, like a foreigner, like an animal, and, indeed, like a woman. The notion that passive homosexual behaviour was "against nature" was a subset of the larger view that one could butcher other, less "natural' natures.'''[104]

To violate a man through anal rape, and particularly to do so using a spear or a lance in place of the penis, was the clearest way to assert the power of one group of men over another. It indicated first to the victim, and then to his community, that they had been conclusively changed into dependents.[105] Trexler notes that not more than thirty years ago, gang leaders in France had anal sex with gang members in order to establish the hierarchy. The practice of anal rape to assert dominance also recalls a New York policeman's 1998 beating, sodomizing, and insertion of a broomstick into the rectum of Haitian immigrant Abner Louima.[106] Anal rape, either as symbol or practice, captured succinctly in the phrase 'Bend Over Saddam' written on U.S. missiles bombing Iraq,[107] accomplishes racial and sexual domination. Canadian soldiers clearly shared the view that anal rape was an expression of domination. They demonstrated this in the hazing video and continued to engage in such practices long after the Somalia Affair ended.[108]

Soldiers filmed the incriminating hazing activities in Canada, and while in Somalia took 'trophy photos' and videos of degraded, tortured Somalis, recording their views and activities in diaries. (Military courts and the Inquiry made use of many of these documents.) The taking of such photos is not in itself unusual for soldiers; Canadian soldiers were photographed clowning around with the corpse of an Iraqi civilian blown up by a mine in the Gulf War.[109] However, Theweleit's observation that fascist men wrote an unusual number of autobiographies and diaries as a means of avoiding feelings and degradation, writing 'to keep the man living' presumably in the moment when chaos is kept at bay, seems relevant.[110] Photos, Patricia Vettel-Becker comments, drawing on Theweleit to analyse the combat photography of the Second World War, 'are hard items that will not fail; they hold out the promise of continual erection.'[111] While I cannot conclude that most of the soldiers who went to Somalia were men with an extreme fear of engulfment by the Other, there is some basis for the speculation that men who exhibit aspects of the hegemonic masculinity Theweleit describes, *and who find themselves constituted as colonizers*, such as peacekeepers were in Somalia, will satisfy their will to wholeness through the degradation and containment of Others and will seek ways to defend themselves against 'the overwhelming castration anxiety brought about by war.'[112]

Given the racist and violent features of the masculinity exhibited by the Airborne Regiment, and given the colonial context of Operation Deliverance, it is not surprising that violence was enacted on the bodies of Somalis. The soldiers appeared never to have lost their sense of being in alien, hostile territory, a space filled with night terrors and the possibility of engulfment by the degenerate Other. One soldier described patrolling at night 'like walking into a twilight zone.'[113] Others felt that they were in 'Nam' and took to calling Somalia 'Som,' an interesting appropriation of an experience that most Canadian soldiers of this age group could only have known of indirectly through popular culture.[114] Some saw Somalis as polluted people whom one should not touch unless wearing gloves.[115] When the soldiers noticed that Somali men often held hands, many assumed they were mostly homosexuals.[116] Somali men were criticized as irredeemably sexist and as not valuing human life as the Canadians did.[117] The alien race, the homosexual Other, the unmanly man, these all became the mass. Somalis were thought to all look alike, thereby increasing the soldiers' sense of frustration that they were unable to tell who was friend or enemy.[118] A profound sense of threat infused everyday activities. As one soldier put it: 'The guy who passes by in the morning with his cart could just as well turn up the next night with a grenade. We never knew what to expect.'[119] Even children (and contact appeared to be mostly with children, teenagers, and young men) were not exempt from the mass: 'The kid between 7 and 23 years old was your enemy.'[120] As the enemy, and therefore undeserving of Canadian generosity, Somalis quickly become subjects requiring violence.

Reproved early on for the aggressive practices of his troops towards the Somali population, Major Anthony Seward privately noted in his diary that the humanitarian cast of the mission, officially known as 'hearts and minds,' was 'bullshit.'[121] Ungrateful, thieving Somalis, who were thought to be laughing at Canadian soldiers,[122] and for whom the soldiers had an arsenal of racist epithets, culturally understood nothing but violence: as more than one soldier commented, '[E]veryone was beating Somalis.'[123] Theweleit's mass from whom the soldier had to protect himself would not be inaccurate in this context, especially given that the actual threat appeared to be minimal. *African Rights* reported that Belet Huen remained peaceful throughout 1993.[124] As the inquiry found, the Somali militia had long ago left the area of Belet Huen, and the area was largely made up of starving refugees. There were few hostile encounters and little evidence of danger of the kind that would require preparations to prevent armed incursions or even sabotage. No Canadian personnel were killed or wounded by Somalis.[125] The sense of threat seemed to grow in inverse proportion to reality; as the threat diminished, the more extreme incidents of peacekeeper violence occurred.[126]

The 'King of Belet Huen'

On 28 January 1993, after just over one month of being in Somalia, Lieutenant Colonel Carol Mathieu announced at his regular briefing to squadron leaders that owing to the thefts occurring in the camp, the troops were authorized to shoot anyone seen fleeing the camp. The men were advised to 'shoot between the skirt and the flip-flops,' language that both feminizes (in a typical orientalist gesture towards Muslim men) and degrades, even while it implies shooting to wound rather than to kill.[127] When two Somalis were shot on 4 March the Lieutenant Colonel's orders given in January came under scrutiny.

Charged with changing the rules of engagement to permit the use of deadly force against intruders, whether or not they were armed, Lieutenant Colonel Mathieu defended his actions first by describing the perilous conditions in Belet Huen that justified the use of stern measures and then by arguing that he had not changed the rules of engagement and that he had never counselled his men to abandon the usual steps to be taken before firing – namely, to warn intruders and to ascertain whether the intruder had a weapon.

In Mathieu's interview with military police in May and July 1993, and in his testimony to the Commission of Inquiry in the winter of 1997, a story emerges of a Somalia in which powerful Northern men encounter strange, warring peoples – in Mathieu's eyes the eighteen tribes of Belet Huen, who were not content and who resented the presence of peacekeepers.[128] On New Year's Day, an intoxicated Mathieu and another senior officer drove through a Canadian checkpoint. Mathieu reportedly announced to the soldier who asked for the password, 'Don't you know who I am? I am the king of Belet Huen.'[129] Mathieu would later suggest that the soldiers' testimonies of this incident amounted to mere 'histoires de pêche' ('fishing stories'), tall tales that soldiers tell to enhance their own reputation.[130] Far from viewing peacekeeping in Somalia as something to be joked about in this manner, Mathieu described instead his sense of being in the middle of 'killing zones,' a place where extreme vigilance was called for and where you could not even take the chance to go out at night alone.[131]

Insisting that Somalis were consummate looters who had even managed to break into the heavily guarded American compound in Mogadishu, Mathieu maintained that although conditions in Belet Huen were vastly different from those in Mogadishu (a point raised by Peter Desbarats, one of the commissioners), they are nonetheless 'the same Somali[s] and they travel.'[132] Duplicitous and dangerous, Somalis were also desperate. They were desperate enough to steal empty cardboard boxes. Wishing to respect local hierarchies, Mathieu had instructed his troops never to give a Somali anything, not even empty boxes, since gifts had to always go through the local chiefs and elders.[133] It paid to exercise caution and to respect custom, not only to avoid embarrassing moments (such as when Americans hired a Somali woman to wash their clothes, without realizing that she was culturally prohibited from washing the clothes of strange men) but also to manage a people who would be likely to grab as many boxes as possible in order to sell them.[134] In an atmosphere of theft, duplicitous natives, and strange customs, it made sense, Mathieu told the Inquiry, to step up cautionary measures, especially with increased thefts. Vigilance was particularly necessary because a Somali national had been killed in an encounter with Canadian troops in February 1993. Somalis believed in an eye for an eye, explained Mathieu, and he didn't want to make himself vulnerable to reprisals.[135]

The vulnerability of Canadian troops to wily Somalis remained at the core of Lieutenant Colonel Mathieu's defence of his actions. If a looter failed to stop on command, the troops could shoot to wound: 'anyone seen running away from lines with kit will be fired at,' whether or not they were armed.[136] Repeating his explanation to the Inquiry a few years later, Mathieu stuck resolutely to his position that he had respected the rules of engagement, merely advising his troops that after dutifully following the warning steps, they could shoot if the suspect appeared to have hostile intent – for example, if he was stealing critical equipment. When questioned by an incredulous commissioner as to what constituted critical equipment, Mathieu responded:

COMMISSIONER DESBARATS: But I mean that if you stole a radio that was a critical piece of equipment?

LIEUTENANT COLONEL MATHIEW: Then you do ... like you follow my graduated response because you need to capture that radio back. Because with that radio, they can spy on you and they can use it against you.[137]

Pressed repeatedly to explain how a radio could constitute a threat of imminent use of force, the condition under which Canadian troops could fire their weapons, Mathieu maintained that even the loss of a radio could threaten a mission and that to protect oneself from such thefts by shooting at looters was really only self defence. Indeed, the very problem with Somalis was that 'ils voulaient tout avoir' ('they wanted to have everything') and presumably would not know when to stop.[138] In the rules of engagement, Mathieu asserted, there is also 'a place where you're entitled to use deadly force to protect your equipment.'[139] Anyone penetrating the wire in the area of the valuable American Black Hawk helicopters, for instance, committed if not a hostile act then an act that had hostile intent. The helicopters were so necessary to evacuate the wounded, Mathieu testified, that no chance could be taken that they would be damaged.[140]

Lieutenant Colonel Mathieu's perception of the conditions under which peacekeepers could shoot startled a few of those present at the briefing on 28 January. Despite claims that he did not order his troops to shoot intruders, and that he implied that the regular steps of warning and ascertaining hostile intent should be followed, one witness after another testified at his court martial that what was mainly understood was that anyone running away should be shot. Captain P.W. Hope, for example, who appeared to share Mathieu's perception that Somalia was 'a wild west show' where there was an organized attempt to 'sabotage our operation,' wrote in his notebook that day that anyone running away or carrying Canadian property could be shot at.[141] When pressed about the incidents of theft that might have justified this response, Captain Hope could recall only that a few bullets and gas cans had been stolen and that Somalis often carried knives.[142] Major R.D. Mackay noted the phrase about looters running away in his notebook[143] and recalled the word 'flip-flop' being used. Major C. Magee, the commander of 3 Commando, testified that in his experience the looters were usually unarmed young kids and that only some teenagers had knives. Few items of value were stolen. He interpreted the Lieutenant Colonel's words to mean that the use of force was permitted unless a soldier was absolutely sure that the suspect was not carrying a weapon.[144] He recalled his reaction to the order: 'My concern with it ... though was one of the soldiers shooting somebody, coming up to a person he had shot and realising that he had killed a kid or a young teenager for something that wasn't all that important.'[145]

Other soldiers posted at a nearby camp in Matabaan explained their surprise at the 28 January briefing. Children stealing small items from the camp was a completely normal problem, posing no real threat, and many soldiers felt it could be dealt with without resorting to the strategy outlined that day to shoot anyone seen leaving 'with something in his hands.'[146] On the first of February, Major Seward who himself would later approve of aggressive actions against Somalis, nevertheless wrote to his wife of his own worries after the briefing:

> I'm bewildered; he had issued direction to act in this fashion a week earlier. Further, he had amended (unlawfully) the rules of engagement ordering us to open fire on individuals pilfering the camp. These individuals are teenage Somalia! [*sic*] (Please keep this to yourself as I know you will.) His direction is a constant change from 'heart and mind' to killing children that is perplexing and disturbing. I can't help remember that we jailed Kurt Myer for fifteen years in the Dalhousie prison for killing Canadian soldiers and here we are with orders from a battalion commander to shoot at boys![147]

Dismissing Seward as keeping 'une drôle de journal' ('a funny diary'), Mathieu's response to commissioners who asked about his views on Seward's letter was to remind them that men were very often stressed in the military under conditions like Somalia. He also intimated that Seward had personal problems.[148]

For all those who later testified that they felt discomfort with Lieutenant Colonel Mathieu's directive to shoot Somalis caught fleeing the Canadian camp, there were others who took the directive as a green light to engage in violence against Somalis. Chief among these was Captain Michel Rainville, a soldier who had a record of taking inappropriate and overly aggressive actions and whom Brigadier General Ernest Beno, in suggesting that Mathieu consider not taking him to Somalia, characterized as a 'Rambo type.'[149] (Three months after he returned from Somalia, Rainville was arrested and charged with possession of weapons belonging to the Canadian military. He was convicted and fined $3,000.)[150] Before going to Somalia, Rainville engaged in several disciplinary incidents, including leading his platoon on an assault of the residence of the lieutenant-governor in Quebec City, in which they tied up guards and handled them aggressively in order to test the compound's security.[151] He also posed for a newspaper photo wearing battle fatigues and brandishing knives.[152]

Mathieu's response to the suggestion that three men (including Rainville and Seward) might have discipline problems if posted to Somalia was to consider that the men who make trouble were 'des hyperactifs' ('hyperactive men') and often the men with initiative.[153] Regarding Rainville as perhaps 'un peu trop exhubérant' ('a little too energetic'), Mathieu nonetheless had confidence that he was an ideal platoon leader.[154] After a pump went missing at the Somalia base camp and claiming that he feared that a sabotage of the helicopter area was imminent, Mathieu charged Rainville with the task of patrolling the helicopter area and augmenting security in the engineers' compound. While increased lighting (through the installation of a tower) was an obvious way to augment security, Rainville and his platoon chose instead to patrol the area with night- vision goggles, relying on strategically placed food and water as bait to entice Somalis walking nearby. Their objective, as Rainville consistently maintained at his court martial and at the Inquiry, was to capture Somalis.

The 4 March Incident: Rambo in Action

Of the multiple violent encounters between Canadian troops and Somalis[155] – incidents involving firing into a small crowd demonstrating at a bailey bridge, killing one of the demonstrators and disabling at least two others (a crowd likely to have been one of fifty people but which the military reported as 300),[156] the administering of severe beatings to prisoners, and clandestine searches involving a Canadian captain dressing in Somali clothes while on patrol – the 4 March incident has come to symbolize (along with the killing of Shidane Arone) the essence of what went wrong with the peacekeeping encounter in Somalia. On the night of the fourth, two Somalis – Abdi Hamdare and Ahmad Aruush – were walking near the perimeter of the camp.[157]

While there are conflicting accounts of what transpired that night, it is agreed that the Recce Platoon were laying in wait for intruders – equipped with their night-vision goggles – and may even have gone so far as to bait the Somalis. It is also indisputable that the Somalis were shot in the back, as they fled away from the camp, and therefore, could hardly have constituted a threat.

According to the Recce Platoon members, the Somalis were behaving as if they were planning to penetrate the perimeter of the camp. When (possibly) startled by the sound of radio communication between Rainville and his men, Hamdare and Aruush took flight, running away from the camp. Rainville shouted 'get them' or perhaps 'don't let them get away,' and a heated pursuit ensued. Corporal Smetaniuk dropped his weapon, kit, and helmet in order to pursue the Somalis on foot. (Shedding of the weapon and helmet was interpreted by the Commission as an indication that the platoon members were clear that the Somalis did not represent a threat.) At the same time Master Corporals LeClerc and Countway each fired one round of bullets, wounding both Aruush and Hamdare in the back and legs. Hamdare remained lying where he fell and was soon captured by platoon members, but Aruush attempted to get up and continue his flight. As Aruush rose to a 'push up position,' Countway fired a second round of bullets 'at close range,'[158] mortally wounding Aruush.[159]

Survivor Abdi Hamdare's account is somewhat different. According to Hamdare,[160] he and Aruush had no intention of burglarizing the camp. They had been walking a long time, were thirsty and, on the assumption that the camp was there to offer humanitarian aid, approached the camp in order to ask for water. As they approached the fence they were fired upon. Hamdare and Aruush 'ran away in panic and disbelief.' In Hamdare's words:

> Instantly my companion was shot and he fell to the ground on the spot and as I looked at him I was shot too. My companion managed to move before me. At that time an armed man, you know, from the Canadian forces came out of the camp. Luckily, I fell under a shallow cliff and he could not see me. What he did was that, he followed the other man and shot him on that spot, the face. Over there on his front body part. And I saw the shot clearly. Some other Forces ran out of the camp after him, and when he started to come running after me, the other Forces held him by the hand and stopped him.[161]

Both Aruush and Hamdare were transported to the hospital. The medical officer, Major Barry Armstrong, and the junior medics who examined the dead body of Aruush recalled their shock at seeing the level of violence inflicted. Sergeant Thomas Riley Ashman submitted in his voluntary statement, 'We [himself, and other medical personnel in attendance] had been told earlier that he had two chest wounds so it was with some shock we first saw the massive neck wounds as we were not told about these.'[162] Major Russell Brown recalled: 'The body was covered with a cloth, when we exposed the patient, I was initially shocked to see the extent of injuries to the neck and head. So much so, that I decided against intubating the patient because I felt the anatomy was sufficiently destroyed to make the exercise not useful.'[163] For Master Corporal Butler, the 'horror of the body [was] unbelievable.'[164] Aruush, identified as the man who had been shot that night, was Butler's age.

Butler also assisted in removing buckshot from Hamdare's body. Referring to the death of an American soldier blown up when his jeep drove over a land-mine, Butler's diary entry reads as follows:

> I spent 3 hours in the OR picking buckshot off a Somalian back, ass and feet. Tell me he was attacking, more like running away. This should be interesting. I don't know whose [sic] worse the Canadian or Somalian, we kill people for stealing water and gas. Shoot them in the back. They mine the woods to kill us.[165]

Private Kyle Brown (one of the Cree soldiers later charged in the torture and murder of Shidane Arone) recalled that as he listened to the activities of the Recce Platoon that night, and to the shouts of his comrades, it brought to mind the 1988 movie *Mississippi Burning*, which depicts white men hunting down and killing Black men.[166] In military courts, other soldiers would recall only the pedagogic purpose of the night's activities. Using language that suggested his understanding of the encounter as simply one of teaching children a lesson, Master Corporal Leclerc explained what had to be done with anyone found breaching the wire of the camp: 'Si tu vois quelqu'un qui essai d'entrer dans le périmetre, de le prendre and de le capturer de façon à faire un exemple, tu le captures et tu lui montres, OK on niaise plus la, il y a plus personne qui rentre ici.' ('If you see someone trying to breach the perimeter, take him and subdue him in a way that will set an example, you capture him and you show him "OK, we are not fooling around anymore, nobody comes in here again."')[167]

The sense that the men of Recce Platoon may have seen themselves as Rambo executing a well thought out plan to entrap saboteurs is nowhere more evident than in the testimony of Captain Rainville who coordinated their activities that night. At his court martial, Rainville's defence lawyer was careful to set the scene on the night of 4 March, questioning his client about the extreme heat of Belet Huen, the utter darkness of the desert at night, and the presence of sand everywhere. Confirming the extreme climate, Rainville further attested to his sense of the warring tribes, the utter anarchy that prevailed in Somalia, the increasingly hostile responses of Somalis who had guns and who used drugs and the increasing tension among his men.[168] For example, by late February, following a demonstration in which Somalis threw rocks at Canadian troops and in which a Somali was killed, Rainville testified that the sense of vulnerability among his men was rising. Then on 2 March, an American was killed by a land-mine and on 4 March, it appeared that a fuel pump had gone missing (it was later found). These were significant events for Rainville and others, although the American soldier was killed at a place that was 80 kilometres from the Canadian camp at Belet Huen.[169] As Theweleit reminds us, fascist violence was 'often produced in acts of violence following directly from the sight of the bleeding bodies of the soldier males, fallen comrades or "news" of the effects of the "red terror" on their own people.'[170] At that point, Rainville was ordered to beef up security around the engineers' compound and particularly where the American Black Hawk helicopters were kept. His moment had clearly arrived.

Captain Rainville embarked on his mission with considerable enthusiasm. It is interesting to take a closer look at his own perceptions of what he was doing that night. As he explained to the commissioners of the Inquiry, he immediately rejected the idea of increased lighting for the area in order to deter infiltrators. Somalis were difficult to catch, he suggested, because they easily outran Canadian troops once outside the wire. Intruders who fled were only going to keep coming back, anyway.[171] The objective was to capture saboteurs, not to deter them. The installation of additional lights would only impair the night-vision provided by the goggles. Rainville decided to use food and water as bait and to deploy soldiers in teams to lie in hiding, waiting for the night's first intruders. As he candidly explained, '[J]e voulais appréhender le monde' ('I wanted to catch everyone").[172] For Rainville, the mere penetration of the wire of the camp was either 'un acte de sabotage ou un acte de terroriste ... Ça était clair dans notre tête' ('an act of sabotage or an act of terrorism ... That was clear in our minds').[173]

As night fell, an excited Rainville, as one of his men testified, began to enact the script he had carefully prepared.[174] The soldiers did not have long to wait. Two Somalis soon came into view and appeared to be pointing to the bait. In Captain Rainville's account, he yelled, 'I've got one.'[175] The wounded man's wrists were bound and Rainville radioed his team that the second man was running their way. He did not mention that the man was unarmed and, later, there was a dispute at the court martial as to whether Rainville had already discovered a knife on the first man or whether this discovery came later. His men testified that it was one of them who later found the knife and kept it since no one asked for it.[176] For Rainville, the assumption was that all

Somalis were armed and dangerous, and if they fled, it was not in order to save their lives by avoiding Canadian bullets but because they did not want to be caught in the act of sabotage.[177] Moreover, as he declared to the commissioners, '[L]a vie de mes hommes compte beaucoup plus que n'importe quelle autre view qui s'était là-bas en Somalie.' ('The lives of my men are much more valuable than any other life in Somalia').[178] When the second Somali, Aruush, was shot a second time as he tried to flee, Rainville called for an ambulance (the sequence of this is in dispute) and then ordered that a picture be taken of the dead man. In his account, the request for a photo was made because he knew that there would be an investigation. It was not, as the Commission's lawyer suggested, because Rainville wanted a trophy photo.[179] It only remained to congratulate his men for a job well done and later to consider one of them for a citation.[180]

The accounts of Rainville and his platoon that night confirm that the men either believed or wanted to tell a story of professional soldiers entrapping and killing well-trained, armed Somali militia who were out to sabotage, or at least to steal. Few could pin down any major thefts that had occurred in the camp and, when scrutinized, the story did not hold up that a sabotage of the fuel pump was imminent. As Commissioner Desbarats pointed out, a fuel pump was half the size of a refrigerator and weighed more than 90 kilograms (200 pounds). It was unlikely that one could just walk away with it, as Rainville claimed. There were surely sophisticated ways to disable such a pump.[181] As well, it seemed unlikely that saboteurs would wear white shirts, as one of the Somali men had done that night.[182] Yet these details did not trouble the soldiers or any of their leaders. Indeed, Lieutenant Colonel Mathieu congratulated Captain Rainville on a job well done and maintained throughout all the legal proceedings that Rainville's plan had been a sound one.[183] Although the platoon took care not to mention in their reports the use of the bait and the deliberate entrapment of Somalis, each soldier would maintain that he had a job to do that night, a job that was officially sanctioned: to capture Somalis. This task, Rainville's defence lawyer reminded the military court, must be contextualized as part of 'une mission plus globale' ('a more global mission').[184] The activities of Captain Rainville's recognizance platoon were indeed a regular part of the peacekeeping mission. Chief medical officer Barry Armstrong described the capture of Somalis as occurring at least once a week,[185] while Captain Rainville maintained that there were apprehensions of Somalis every day.[186]

The death of Ahmed Aruush on 4 March did not prevent Lieutenant Colonel Mathieu from congratulating Captain Rainville on his successful mission that night and from confirming that he was to carry on performing the same tasks.[187] The death of Ahmad Aruush and the wounding of Abdi

Hamdare did, however, disturb Major Barry Armstrong who examined the bodies. His statement, prepared two days after, tersely described his concern about Aruush's death: 'A plausible hypothesis is that he was shot in the back by a high velocity rifle, remained alive, and was dispatched a few minutes later by two or more high velocity rounds to the head and neck.'[188] In a statement to military police six weeks later, Major Armstrong described more fully his growing conviction that there had in fact been a homicide.

Major Armstrong noted that Somalis had previously breached the compound on 21 February, at which time multiple shots were fired with lethal intent but with no effect. In chasing the intruders, Canadian soldiers drove through the tent of a Somali family in the village and injured a small boy. Major Armstrong asked his superior Major Jewer to raise the issue of excessive force that day, believing that Canadians were escalating their acts of violence against Somalis. On 4 March, he was called to attend to the injuries of Abdi Hamdare and to examine the body of Ahmad Aruush. Aruush, he concluded, had been shot in the neck while lying on the ground. No razor cuts were visible on either man which would have been compatible with the story of their having breached the wire. After completing the examinations, Major Armstrong went to bed and was awakened by the duty officer with an order to provide a report to Mogadishu about the dead man's injuries. He did so indicating his view that a homicide had taken place.

The following day at the regular briefing, the Orders group was informed that the two men were shot trying to get through the wire near the helicopters, critical coalition equipment for medical evacuation. Remembering that helicopter service was refused for the transport of severely injured Somalis, Armstrong rejected the idea that the two Somalis had threatened the equipment. He wrote his first memo of his allegations to his immediate superior and copied to it to Lieutenant Colonel Mathieu. Mathieu, Armstrong recalled, disagreed with him saying that if a police officer in Canada told a criminal to stop and he didn't, the policeman would be justified shooting him in the back. In a letter to his wife on 13 March, Armstrong conveyed his sense that there 'is a very big racist thing going on here' and that a cover up was in process. This letter was leaked to the Canadian press in April and a military police investigation soon followed.[189] Interviewed by military police on 23 April 1993, Armstrong suggested that as a result of his allegations, he was under increasing pressure to leave Somalia.

From the first moment he responded to Armstrong's allegations, through two court martial proceedings and when fielding questions from the commissioners of the Inquiry, Mathieu steadfastly maintained that Captain Rainville's plan and its execution of it on the night of 4 March, 'faisait du sens' ('made sense').[190] Interrogated by military police in April about his response to

Armstrong, he began by making clear that he had investigated the platoon's activities and had assessed the terrain with Captain Rainville, carefully considering the dark, windy conditions and what it was possible to see through the night-vision goggles. Mathieu concluded that there had not been a murder that night and he submitted his conclusions to Colonel Labbé in a short report on 6 March. Colonel Labbé returned the six-page report requesting more information, a request Mathieu complied with over the next week, adding several more pages of information. Claiming that he was preoccupied with all the 'taponnage' ('odds and ends'), he was only able to submit the revised report sometime later, bearing the same 6 March date and incorporating additional information but making no mention of Major Armstrong's allegations.

In his report, Mathieu rejected the suggestion that he had attempted to cover up the allegations, and joked that it would have been very easy to cover up but that he was 'très honnête, plus catholique que le pape dans notre façon de rapporter les faits' ('really honest and more Catholic than the Pope in the reporting of these facts').[191] As he elaborated, when Armstrong made the claim that a Somali had been 'dispatched' that night, he did not consider the hypothesis credible and in any event, he had little time to waste on something that appeared 'un peu farfelu sur les bords' ('a little outrageous and far fetched').[192] (As French-language speakers, both Mathieu and the military police speculated on the different meaning of English figures of speech such as the word dispatch.)[193] Armstrong, Mathieu observed, was a doctor who did not fully understand military operations.[194] As Mathieu put it plainly, '[L]ui c'est un docteur. Moi je ne vais pas lui dire comment faire ses opérations' ('He is a doctor. I don't tell him how to perform operations').[195] If Armstrong's allegations appeared 'farfelu' and 'sans fondement' ('far-fetched' and 'without foundation'),[196] Armstrong himself was considered confused. He assumed one could see clearly with night-vision goggles, for example. For these and other reasons, Mathieu did not pursue the matter with his superior Colonel Labbé, who felt that excessive force might have been used that night. However, neither man considered the event on 4 March a serious enough one to launch a police inquiry, nor even to probe why the duty officer that night had woken a sleeping Armstrong asking that he call Mogadishu with his medical report. Mathieu claimed not to be interested in whatever Armstrong had to say to Mogadishu. Finding this assessment of the situation 'un peu stretché' ('a little stretched'), military investigators continued to press Mathieu for an explanation of his dismissal of a senior officer's concerns that a homicide had been committed, an approach Mathieu described as making him feel as though 'on a commencé à me traiter en bandit' ('they began treating me like a criminal').[197] He contented himself with repeating that he was completely satisfied that his men had acted properly.

The shootings of 4 March might have remained an internal and non-police matter, particularly after the Canadian media were given the story of 'highly trained saboteurs' infiltrating the camp.[198] Colonel Labbé proposed that there be an internal investigation and then one by American military personnel, an idea that never came to fruition but one that the Inquiry felt was proposed because Labbé knew he could control the outcome.[199] It was only after Armstrong placed a note alleging murder under the hotel-room door of Lieutenant Colonel Tinsley in Nairobi, that there was some reaction from military headquarters in Ottawa. By then, there was an irretrievable loss of evidence. As Major Buonamici testified, military police had concluded in a memo written 24 April that Mathieu's investigation was poorly conducted and that there was a distinct possibility the 'environment may have encouraged unstable members of the unit to believe that they were immune to censure for brutal acts.'[200] By November 1994, however, it was still the military's public position that Major Armstrong was 'a very idealistic medical officer whose military judgement has sometimes been questioned.'[201]

Lieutenant Colonel Mathieu was eventually court-martialled for giving an order that infiltrators could be shot at. Captain Rainville was also charged with contravening the rules of engagement regarding the use of force. Neither Mathieu nor Rainville was found guilty in military courts, the latter on the basis that he had simply been following orders. In the end, duplicitous natives and hazardous conditions, succinctly summed up by his defence lawyer, would make of Mathieu's actions and responses those of a reasonable man:

> J'aimerais vous rappelez ce que mon confrère n'a pas fait, les conditions extrêmes qui existaient là-bas: les températures dans les 40, 50 degrés; le désert; le vent; le sable; l'anarchie totale; l'absence de toute forme de gouvernment local ou autrement; aucune force d'ordre qui n'existait (I want to remind you what my colleague did not mention, the extreme conditions that existed over there: temperatures of 40, 50 degrees; the desert; the wind; the sand; complete anarchy; the absence of all forms of government; local or other; no form of order existed).[202]

In Africa, who can be a saint?

There is much that can be written about the shootings (and the torture and murder of Arone discussed in chapter 3). Here, I limit myself to comments on what these events tell us about the colonial nature of the encounter. Ridley's two forms of violence come to mind: 'teaching-the-natives-a-lesson' violence and self-justifying violence, where the colonizer reassures himself that he is intact and in control. One of the soldiers interviewed by Donna Winslow comments on the men who engaged in torture and killing: 'Yes they were wrong but they were frustrated inside, they were scared. If scared, drunk or frustrated civilians beat someone up, it will probably go by relatively unnoticed in the press. But it becomes a big thing because it's the army.'[203] (The home front never understands what life is like in the colonies.) Theweleit speaks to this fear in fascist men as a fear of decomposition, one that requires no armed external enemy but 'is predicated instead on the existence of threats within his own interior.'[204] Intending to render the surreal quality of the violence that springs from an internal sense of disintegration, Theweleit dramatically describes the feelings of the torturer and, specifically, his sense that he is the victim. The man

> seeks out what is threatening and horrifying. Having been aroused to the point where he can no longer stand up, by the eyes of the murderers (stabbing him *in the back*), by executions, embryos, the smell of sweat, razor blades streaming with blood, he simply has to see the syphilis. It represents something oh-so-tantalizing – but he finds it unendurable. It now begins to pursue him; later, he kills it. Only the act of killing allows him to escape the unreality of his feelings, the unfulfillment whose burning flame consumes him. The act of killing becomes a direct affirmation of his own reality: it is not I who am the ghost, but others – see how they disappear ... (when shots are fired).[205]

The rapist or the torturer imposes his own meaning on the victim's body, and in so doing gives himself definition and substance.[206] The Black man's body, Frantz Fanon comments, is overdetermined from without. It is the space on which is projected the colonizer's traumas, as is the woman's or the child's body[207] the space on which men can become men. Theweleit's men are prone to fragmentation because armour against such an overwhelming mass necessarily has chinks. They are embittered.[208] Canadian soldiers reported that *they* felt 'violated' by the Somali infiltrators.[209] As one soldier candidly explained to a military court, '[I]t felt as if we were being mistreated. We do so much and have it thrown back in our face by the infiltrations.'[210] Others would go so far as to claim that 'they wanted us to shoot them.'[211] For such men, beatings and killings inflicted on the Somalis would have been fortifying. Ritual flogging 'forces victims to participate in a negative coitus.'[212] In this world of men (no women are mentioned in the Somalia Affair), the enactment of violence on the bodies of Somalis kept the terrors at bay.

Conclusion

Societies 'afflicted by racism and caught in the siege mentality of war or threat of war' teach people to respect and defer to authority and 'attenuate the sense of personal responsibility,' concludes Christopher Browning in his exploration of the ordinary men conscripted as soldiers by the Nazis – men who so casually committed the murder of Jews.[213] Peacekeeping today is a kind of war, a race war waged by those who constitute themselves as civilized, modern and democratic against those who are constituted as savage, tribal, and immoral. Already organized to produce men who do not think on their own, militaries operating on the basis of these racial premises invite brutality. It is not the exceptional man who commits, condones, or simply watches brutal acts, Browning suggests; it is the exceptional man who does not.

What is to be gained by characterizing peacekeeper violence as colonial or racial violence rather than simply violence typical of the hypermasculine world of militaries? The racial nature of the encounter, the overriding sense that white armies were in Africa to keep the natives in line, provides one critical reason. Another equally important reason is that colonial violence implicates us all. It is violence done in our name. In his preface to Frantz Fanon's *The Wretched of the Earth*, Jean-Paul Sartre addresses those Europeans who will be tempted to distance themselves from the colonial violence Fanon describes in Algeria:

> But, you will say, we live in the mother country, and we disapprove of her excesses. It is true, you are not settlers, but you are no better. For the pioneers belonged to you; you sent them overseas, and it was you they enriched. You warned them that if they shed too much blood you would disown them, or say you did, in something of the same way that any state maintains abroad a mob of agitators, *agents provocateurs*, and spies whom it disowns when they are caught.[214]

We might keep Sartre in mind when we consider what happened to the violence of peacekeepers, so carefully recorded in diaries, photos, and videos. Where did the violence go when it came back to North? In later chapters, I discuss its alchemical transformation in the law when the bruises and blows on Black bodies became the wounded psyche of the nation and its soldiers.

CHAPTER 3

'Outwhiting the White Guys?'
Men of Colour and the Murder
of Shidane Abukar Arone

To join the nation you must forget the violence done unto you, much as joining
the family requires forgetting the possible violence of abuse, incest, and neglect.
Abouall Farmanfarmahan, 'Did You Measure Up?'[1]

The photo shows a handsome, well-muscled, shirtless young soldier in a
bunker, wearing sunglasses and apparently posing for the camera under the
hot sun. Taken only hours before he allegedly tried to hang himself with his
bootlaces, the photo freezes forever a seemingly relaxed young man at the
height of his physical powers. A second photo, taken two days earlier, shows
the same young man posing this time with the battered and bloodied body of
a handcuffed and blindfolded Somali teenager. In a third photo, another
young soldier appears beside the teenager's battered body. Like the first, this
second man appears to be of Aboriginal ancestry. From newspaper reports we
learn that the man who apparently tried to hang himself by his bootlaces is a
Cree soldier, Master Corporal Clayton Matchee, originally from a small
reserve in Saskatchewan. The second man is Private Kyle Brown, also part
Cree and from a city on the Canadian Prairies. The Somali teenager was
Shidane Arone.

These pictures disturb us, and not only for the obvious reason that a teenager is shown to have been so brutalized. Matchee's expression haunts us. He
is described as 'smirking,'[2] an inadequate word for the mood of the man who
smiles tightly for the camera and points to Arone's battered head, directing
our attention to the results of his handiwork. It is as if to say, 'See what we do
for you?' And we feel the strong impulse to distance ourselves from the
graphic brutality, from Arone curled in a fetal position.

To achieve any kind of distance we must exorcise Matchee first and foremost, and to a lesser extent Brown, whose unease is especially evident in comparison to Matchee's confidence. They are monsters, we say, but we are not altogether convinced. For one thing, race bothers us. Why are two Aboriginal men beating a Black man so mercilessly, we want to ask, remembering somewhere on the edges of memory that in Canada, the bodies curled in a fetal position are Aboriginal ones as often as they are Black. Most of the time, we stifle the question but it surfaces during the military trials and the public inquiry and refuses to go away. How does race operate here?

The three photos were among sixteen taken by Private Brown on the night of 16 March 1993. It was Brown's reporting of what occurred that night, and the handing over of his film that resulted in the arrest of Clayton Matchee for the torture and murder of Shidane Arone. Admitting that he himself hit the prisoner, Brown, one of the lowest ranking soldiers in the regiment, was also charged with torture and murder. Private David Brocklebank, a white soldier from a small farming community in Prince Edward Island, was arrested for aiding and abetting the torture as was another white soldier, Sergeant Mark Boland. Boland as the section commander, Sergeant Perry Douglas Gresty, and their superiors in the chain of command, Captain Sox, Major Anthony Seward, and Lieutenant Colonel Carol Mathieu, all white men, were also charged with negligent performance of duty for giving or passing on orders to abuse prisoners detained by Canadian peacekeepers in Somalia.

The involvement of white soldiers notwithstanding, the role of men of colour in peacekeeping violence became a central issue for many who tried to understand what would have motivated Aboriginal Canadian soldiers to torture to death Shidane Arone. Although Matchee was declared unfit to stand trial owing to severe brain damage, resulting from the attempted hanging (some question remains as to whether he tried to commit suicide), he and Private Brown remained the two figures at the centre of the crime, making it easy to connect what had occurred with racial minority men. All others who were charged remained in the category of onlookers or accomplices and of these men, those bearing the greatest responsibility were all working class, of lower rank, and with less education than their leaders. At first glance, this raced and classed ranking of who was most culpable appears justified. Matchee and Brown appear to have led the torture of Arone. Similarly, of the many men who dropped into the bunker that night, it was Private Brocklebank and Sergeant Boland who next come into view as most implicated. The context surrounding the event, however, complicates this picture immeasurably, as I discussed in chapter 2. Practices were in place to humiliate and degrade prisoners and orders were given to abuse them. When most of this broader context remained unconnected to the actions of the soldiers, and when race and class facilitated a convenient marking of some men as innately less civilized, it was men from subordinate groups who ended up bearing almost exclusive responsibility for the crimes committed in Somalia.

In the military trials, the men of colour were marked as the few bad apples in an otherwise good barrel (it seems unlikely that the reference was to the men's Aboriginality – red on the outside, white on the inside – but the expression was repeated time and time again by those seeking to explain the violence). For the most part, the role that their racially subordinate status might have played in their activities in Somalia was only superficially explored, avoided perhaps because such a discussion takes us too close to a consideration of race and dislodges the determined racelessness of the law. Race nonetheless remained the hidden logic shaping how we understood the arguments advanced by the lawyers. Both prosecution and defence lawyers agreed that Somalia was a lawless land in which well-intentioned peacekeepers were besieged by ungrateful Somalis, an encounter that required 'rough justice.'[3] Race – their savagery and our civility – was invoked to help us understand the aggressive actions of white soldiers and leaders.

The men of colour enjoyed no such indemnity. Because of the severing of the murder of Arone from other acts of peacekeeping violence, it became possible to regard Matchee and Brown as exceptions, as men who took rough justice too far. Although the reasons for their excesses were never exhaustively probed, the question of *their* race hung in the air. Whether described as monsters, as bullies, as exceptionally weak soldiers, or even as men victimized by racism, they absorbed in their bodies the violence of the Canadian peacekeeping encounter in Somalia. In contrast, white soldiers and leaders remained ordinary and unmarked, except in some instances by their class. Comparatively innocent of wrongdoing, white men were cast as lesser players, guilty of negligence and poor leadership, if anything but not guilty of torture and murder. In part one of this chapter I explore this theme of how white innocence depended on Black culpability, an old colonial dynamic reconfigured in the arguments presented in the military courts.

For all the marking of men of colour as bearing primary responsibility for the violence, it is equally important to note that Brown and Matchee *did* engage in acts of violence. While singling them out has the impact of hiding the complicity of others, their own actions must be examined. In part two, I explore what we can know about racial masculinities in such a context, one I have been describing as overdetermined by race. Principally I consider whether we might understand their actions as compensating for their diminished status as men through engaging in acts of subordination against lower status groups, a process popularly described as 'outwhiting the white guys.' Such compensatory theories have two important pitfalls. First, they suggest that men of colour and other subordinate masculinities have the most incentive to engage in acts of violence because it is they who have the most to prove about their manhood. Second, a compensatory framework, through an analytical focus on men of colour, can leave unexamined hierarchical relations among men – how, in different ways, each group of men is drawn into producing and sustaining a racially ordered and gendered society. I negotiate these pitfalls searching for a way to understand the violence of men of colour in the Somalia Affair without excusing, pathologizing, or exceptionalizing their behaviour and, importantly, without obscuring the highly racial terms of the encounter between Canadian peacekeepers and the Somali population.

Instead of a compensatory framework, I propose an anticolonial one for considering the role of men of colour in peacekeeping violence. The terms and conditions of membership in a white nation include that men of colour must forget the racial violence that is done to them, as Abouali Farmanfarmalian observes. But passing as ordinary men requires more than an act of forgetting. Joining the nation, as chapter 2 showed, also requires that men actively perform a hegemonic masculinity in the service of the nation. This masculine ideal includes engaging in acts of racial domination. The ideal man is one who is superior to both women and racial minorities. For racial minority men, joining the nation requires, then, both forgetting racial violence and engaging in racial violence. While there can certainly be a compensatory element in the participation of men of colour in racial violence (the violence provides a prestige that would not otherwise be available), it is important to see that racial minority men's participation need not spring primarily from an impulse of compensation. If an ideal man is one who engages in practices of dominance, then all men have incentive to do so. The exceptional man would be the man who rejects these terms and conditions unequivocally.

Although men of colour have as much to gain from engaging in racist acts of violence as anyone else – no more and no less – their investment in such hegemonic practices can also be undermined by their own experiences of subordination. If we think of Gramsci's notion of hegemony as Anthony Chen reminds us to do, that is as involving 'not only pure coercion but also struggle over prevailing conceptions of the world' then we should remain alert to the complex negotiations that attend how subaltern men both resist and contribute to their own oppression.[4] A compensatory framework pays attention to how subaltern men contribute to their own oppression, and ignores how they resist. An anticolonial approach incorporates both dynamics and it has the added virtue of reminding us what the hegemonic ideal is that all men must negotiate, an ideal captured in Erving Goffman's description:

In an important sense there is only one unblushing male in America: a young, married, white, urban, northern, heterosexual, protestant father of college education, fully employed, of good complexion, weight, and height, and a recent record in sports. Every American male tends to look out upon the world from this perspective ... Any man who fails to qualify in any one of these ways is likely to view himself – during moments at least – as unworthy, incomplete, and inferior.[5]

Men negotiating this hegemonic ideal while peacekeeping in Somalia would have been even more drawn into the racial dominance at the core of the ideal since peacekeeping was principally enacted as an encounter between a modern, civilized, Northern nation and a backward, African one.

I. 'A Significant Opposition of Values'

Native society is not simply described as a society lacking in values. It is not enough for the colonist to affirm that those values have disappeared from, or still better never existed in, the colonial world. The native is declared insensible to ethics; he represents not only the absence of values, but also the negation of values. He is, let us dare to admit, the enemy of values, and in this sense he is absolute evil.

Frantz Fanon, *The Wretched of the Earth.*[6]

The Order to Abuse Detainees

As I discussed in chapter 2, men who understand their role as bringing order and civilization to Africans, and who view themselves as confronted with ungrateful and thieving natives (albeit children and youth), will resort to violence to conquer their own fears and to convince themselves that they are indeed men in control, successfully defending the values of their nation. Nowhere is this more evident than in Major Seward's account at his own court martial of why, on the eve of Shidane Arone's death, he gave an order to abuse detainees and to make an example of anyone caught breaching the perimeter of the camp. Known for his aggressive training methods (and, as pointed out earlier, identified by Brigadier General Beno as someone who should not go to Somalia, a recommendation ignored by Lieutenant Colonel Mathieu), Major Seward knew of discipline problems within the ranks but failed to do anything about it.[7] In court, Major Seward outlined the context for his order by explaining that his intent was to avoid a recurrence of the 4 March events. A soldier 'dealing with mixed emotions,' and torn between his desire to accomplish something and his discontent with ungrateful Somalis, could not easily draw a distinction between a petty thief and someone bent on stealing weapons, ammunition, or vital material.[8] Seward elaborated on the tensions he felt obliged to mediate:

> It was hard for anybody from that battle group, from lieutenant-colonel down to trooper, to accept the fact that we were here ... we were there in that country on a voluntary basis to do a difficult mission and then be treated in that way. But I think that the individual soldier, he was dealing with what for him was a significant opposition of values.[9]

Beleaguered by rock-throwing and thieving natives, soldiers were likely to shoot to kill. To avoid this outcome, Seward ordered three actions: clean the camp of any items likely to attract thieves; improve the defence provided by the wire around the camp; and capture infiltrators. Seward testified that he emphasized this third order (given to Captain Sox) by saying, 'I don't care if you abuse them but I want those infiltrators captured. I do not want them running around my bivouac.'[10] When asked for clarification by Captain Sox on how he wanted infiltrators abused, Seward replied: 'No. Abuse them if you have to. I do not want weapons used. I do not want gunfire. I do not want another Recce Platoon killing.'[11] Guns, Seward further explained to the court, were of little help in apprehending an infiltrator since Somalis did not respond to warning shots. Short of shooting them, a physical battle was the only way to stop infiltrators, and it was presumably at this point of apprehension that abuse was approved. Since Shidane Arone offered no resistance whatsoever when he was caught breaching the perimeter of the camp, it would become a central point in the various military courts whether Seward's words meant that 'abuse' was also approved for prisoners held in detention.

Major Seward presented himself to the court as someone who repeatedly had to restrain his men from engaging in activities that crossed the line from peacekeeping to violence. For instance, he described stopping his men from painting white the hands of Somali children caught stealing.[12] In another incident, he checked that children who were being threatened by a soldier with a machete were only being taught a lesson in a humorous manner.[13] Seward testified of his own remorse, wondering whether the need to capture infiltrators and teach them a lesson could have been communicated without the use of the word 'abuse.'[14] The prosecution pointed out that there had, in fact, been only one successful infiltration of the camp,[15] and that the soldiers' frustration had more to do with their experiences in the town where they were being spat at and where rocks were thrown at them. Seen in this light, Major Seward's response to infiltrators seemed unnecessary and dangerous. For the most part, the court did not agree. Although Major Seward was found guilty

of negligent performance of duties for giving instructions to abuse, he was
sentenced only to a severe reprimand. Upon appeal, the court imposed a sentence of three months and dismissal from the Canadian Armed Forces.

Regardless of how we assess his complicity, what Seward's testimony so
clearly confirms is the shared understanding of many of the leaders of Canadian
peacekeepers in Somalia: the natives had to be kept in line, often through violence. Indeed, as Frantz Fanon reminds us in the quote above, the native is considered insensible to ethics, 'absolute evil' that only violence will contain. The
majority of men seemed to share this understanding of their duties in Somalia.
The occasional moment when the basis for this view was questioned, such as
when the prosecution pointed out that infiltrations of the camp were relatively
rare, seemed not to have a bearing on how Major Seward's explanation for his
order should be assessed. At a briefing of his platoon commanders, Captain Sox
passed on Major Seward's abuse order to J.K. Sergeant Hillier when he
instructed him to conduct a standing patrol outside the perimeter of the camp.
At the court martial of Captain Sox, his counsel argued that Sergeant Hillier
was initially concerned about the use of the word 'abuse' but clarified with his
superior that, in fact, the rules of engagement had not changed. The word
merely indicated that soldiers were 'to use the amount of force necessary.'[16]

Sergeant Boland, also present at the Sox briefing, testified that he did not
understand the words to mean a carte blanche for violence. Contradicting
himself later, he declared that he had not passed on the order to his section
fearing that they were not 'mature' enough to interpret it.[17] Whatever apprehensions Sergeant Boland acknowledged having did not prevent him from
discussing the abuse order with Clayton Matchee moments before the latter
began his most savage beating of Shidane Arone. Boland defended his discussion of abuse with Matchee as amounting to 'gossip' and not to the conveying
of an order.[18] Only one sergeant asserted that he felt discomfort at the Sox
briefing and, although he did not seek clarification, Sergeant Lloyd did com-
municate to his section that he would personally jail anyone who roughed up a
prisoner.[19] It would have been enormously difficult for the court to sort out
the meaning of the abuse order, given such varying responses. Most significant of all, as Captain Sox's counsel argued, procedures adopted in Somalia
may not have been like procedures adopted in other peacekeeping situations.[20]
Although he did not elaborate, the implication, as others such as Major
Seward made clear, was that Somalia required an unusual level of military
aggression having, as it did more than a fair share of unruly natives.

On the night of 16 March, Hillier's patrol set out to capture infiltrators 'as a
demonstration of Commando vigilance and intolerance of infiltrators.'[21] When
Hillier's patrol captured Shidane Arone, he was brought to Captain Sox.

Through an interpreter, Sox questioned Arone about what he was doing there and he replied that he had been looking for a lost child. Private Brown recalled that Captain Sox then berated and taunted the prisoner, showing him different items of value and asking him if he wanted to steal them, a statement that was not corroborated by others who were present but consistent with the incidents described in chapter 2 where soldiers felt that Somalis had to be repeatedly instructed, disciplined, and taught a lesson.[22] Brown also testified that Sox threw the prisoner to the ground and put his knee on his back.[23] That it had been a regular practice to capture and humiliate Somali detainees was not introduced during these military trials, although trophy photos (the few that survived the order to have them destroyed) provide clear evidence that this was the case. In several of these photos, soldiers hold detainees in exactly the same position as in the photos Brown took of Matchee and Arone. Captives are tied up, blindfolded, and restrained with a baton, and sometimes made to wear a sign around their necks with the word 'thief' written on it, while grinning soldiers stand proudly beside them.[24]

As the military trials progressed through the ranks from Major Seward to Captain Sox and ultimately to Sergeant Boland, a picture emerges of a peacekeeping force who understood its duties in Somalia as duties requiring the aggressive treatment of Somalis. In his suggestion that the incidents of 4 and 16 March formed 'a commonality of location, timing, and subject matter,' the judge advocate at Sergeant Boland's court martial alluded to this feature of peacekeeping in Somalia.[25] In evidence given at Boland's trial, peacekeeping-training expert Colonel Kenward candidly explained that as peacekeepers, the Airborne Regiment had to be prepared for war. Although he acknowledged that he did not know the details of the Somalia mission, he suggested that it was a situation that often required 'offensive action.' As he testified, 'the forces deployed (in Somalia) had to deal with some very difficult situations where they had a local population that was not always understanding of what was trying to be accomplished, were very demanding of the people on the ground and sometimes displayed hostility.'[26] This, Colonel Kenward felt, along with 'the harshest physical environment that we have put Canadians into in UN operations' helps to assess the context of the abuse order and the practices devoted to apprehending infiltrators.[27] These two assertions, that Somalia required aggressive military action and that the social and climactic environments were extraordinarily difficult ones, enter the stories told in military courts as mitigating circumstances that ought to help us understand the violence of peacekeepers, circumstances also named as contributing to trauma. As premises, they are very seldom interrogated. Whenever these two factors prove insufficient to excuse the men's behaviour, an alternative argument takes its place, one about men who are inherently unable to remain disciplined – men, that is, who are handicapped by their class or racial backgrounds.

His identification of the special factors prevailing in Somalia notwithstanding, Colonel Kenward served as a witness for the prosecution of Sergeant Boland who was charged with negligently performing a military duty through (among other things) passing on the abuse order to Master Corporal Matchee and discussing with him various ways to torture Shidane Arone. Questioned about the responsibilities of a platoon commander such as Sergeant Boland under these circumstances, Kenward outlined the general duty of the platoon commander to ensure that his subordinates used proper judgment and obeyed the law while carrying out their duties. Without mentioning Sergeant Boland as an example, Colonel Kenward suggested that where 'you have somebody who is not going to take full responsibility for the position they occupy and have an understanding of what their accountability is,' there would be 'a breakdown of order.'[28]

At his court martial, Sergeant Boland became the man in Kenward's hypothetical example, somebody who did not take responsibility for the position he occupied. Both the prosecution and the defence explained Sergeant Boland's irresponsibility and lack of accountability by pointing to his grade eight education and his talents as a field soldier rather than an 'academic.' Witnesses described Sergeant Boland as hard working, reliable, loyal, and diligent, and the prosecution used this testimony to argue that Boland was simply an average soldier. Only Major Seward used superlatives in his testimony of Sergeant Boland's character, but Seward's words described a soldier who was 'a natural' in operations, one who conducted 'one of the ballsiest actions of Operation Deliverance' in leading a seizure of weapons from 'bandits' in Elgal village.[29] Defence counsel, anxious to contest the prosecution's picture of a man who showed no remorse and whose actions were on the high end of the negligence scale, argued that his client was intimidated by the array of senior military officers in the court. His client would have answered 'in a more relaxed tone of voice' if he hadn't felt that he was on the parade square.[30] That Boland was a simple infantry soldier with a grade eight education is mentioned no less than three times in the defence counsel's closing address. The court is told that Boland, 'given his abilities, his intellect, what he has to offer life,' has simply done his best in the Canadian Armed Forces, one of the few places left where a man with a grade-eight education can go.[31] Boland was a man who shone 'where academic skills were not as important,' a man whose finest hour was in Somalia.[32] His platoon was one of the most successful in seizing weapons from the civilian population, a job that required diplomacy as well as courage, and skills that were a 'lot to ask for a fellow with grade 8.'[33]

His marking as a poorly educated man aside, Sergeant Boland's own testimony was riddled with inconsistencies. He appeared to understand the abuse of prisoners as a regular part of peacekeeping operations. The prosecution argued convincingly that his negligence that night far exceeded a failure to act. Instead, his actions positively contributed to the torture. For example, he indicated to Private Brown, whom he considered to be a soldier who needed direction, that he didn't care what Brown did to Shidane Arone as long as he didn't kill him. The same words were uttered to Master Corporal Matchee with whom Boland discussed the abuse order. Boland also suggesting the use of a phone book or a ration pack when beating the prisoner (so as to prevent marks) instead of burning the soles of the prisoner's feet with a cigarette. Claiming that he did not know of Matchee's reputation (something that many testimonies contested) and so did not take him seriously that night, Boland defended his negligence as owing to not feeling well. When he suggested that Matchee use the phone book, a technique used by anyone wanting to hide the marks of a brutal beating but also specifically used on the Canadian Prairies by white policemen who beat Aboriginal men held in their custody, Boland claimed that his comments here were intended as a joke and that Matchee did not seem to understand them. It seems unlikely that Matchee would not have understood the allusion to phone books since he himself was an Aboriginal man from the Prairies, and specifically from Saskatchewan, the province where investigations into allegations of police brutality against Aboriginal men confirm that the phone book technique is a well-known one.[34] Boland's counsel argued that it was merely Boland's bad luck to have Matchee in his section and that Boland had a tough job to do given the hostility of the local population.[35] Pleading guilty to the charge of negligent performance of duty and not guilty to the charge of torture (the guilty plea automatically cancelled out the second charge), Boland was initially sentenced to three months detention and to an automatic reduction in rank from Sergeant to private. Upon appeal, his sentence was increased to one year.

Amidst all the talk of the abuse of prisoners, how then did the rank and file behave on the night of 16 March? Some time before nine o'clock that night, when Private Brown helped bring Arone to the bunker, he was asked by Captain Sox to tell Master Corporal Matchee to report to the bunker for the commencement of his shift to guard the prisoner. At 9 p.m., Sergeant Boland relieved Matchee at the bunker and in the presence of Warrant Officer Murphy, and Captain Sox asked Matchee to remove the bindings from Arone's feet because they were too tight. His wrist bindings were replaced with loosely secured metal handcuffs. Another soldier secured the riot baton under Arone's arms. A rope was tied to one end of the baton, looped around the bunker roof beam, and then tied to the other end of the baton, securing the prisoner to the bunker. Matchee pulled off a cloth Arone was wearing around his waist and tied it around Arone's head, and then proceeded to pour water on the cloth as Arone choked. Sergeant Boland objected and Matchee removed the cloth only to replace it later. Matchee left shortly after.

At 10 p.m., Private Brown arrived to relieve Sergeant Boland. He was accompanied by Matchee. Brown punched Arone in the jaw. As Boland left the bunker, he told Brown and Matchee, 'I don't care what you do, just don't kill the guy.'[36] Both Brown and Matchee started to kick and hit Arone. After allegedly saying, 'I want to kill this fucker, I want to kill this guy,' Matchee left the bunker to have a beer with his friend Corporal Matt McKay who was on bed rest.[37] Boland joined the two. Matchee began to discuss what he and Brown had done and to consider burning the soles of Arone's feet with a ciga-rette. It was at this point that the conversation ensued about using a phone book or a ration pack to ensure that there would be no marks left on the pris-oner. Matchee returned to the bunker with a ration pack and started to beat the prisoner in earnest for the next three hours. We do not know conclusively what Matchee's role was. For his part, Brown testified that he himself punched the prisoner a few times while Matchee severely beat him and burned his skin with a lit cigar. Brown took photographs of Matchee and the prisoner, and also posed for a photo himself. Matchee then beat Arone with a stick (and in two accounts sodomized him with the stick). Brown claimed that he tried three times to get Matchee to stop and the only way he could do so was to take pho-tos, because Matchee did not torture Arone while the photos were being taken. Brown came forward two days later to tell his story, resulting in his own arrest as well as Matchee's.[38]

Throughout these events, a great number of soldiers heard Arone's screams – eighty, according to one estimate.[39] Brown and Boland both allege that War-rant Officer Murphy savagely kicked the prisoner, conveying to Matchee what had already been generally affirmed in orders given by Major Seward earlier that day – that it was okay to abuse the prisoner.[40] Private David Brocklebank lent his pistol for a camera shot of Matchee holding the gun to Arone's head. Another soldier lent Brown some film and others allegedly also kicked Arone or witnessed the acts of torture. The details of the night of 16 March that emerge from the numerous military court proceedings only confirm the abso-lute normalcy of the event for all the soldiers. Master Corporal J. Giasson 'peeked in' to see Arone in the bunker that night out of 'normal human curios-ity,' an attitude that might indicate how normal the abuse was in that setting.[41] A visiting squadron dropped in to see the prisoner in the bunker.[42] Men seemed to come and go quite casually, thinking little of it. The testimony of Corporal Brady John MacDonald is instructive in this respect.

As the duty signaller in 2 Commando that night, Corporal MacDonald saw the prisoner being brought in and noted that Captain Sox recorded in the log book that the prisoner was a sixteen-year-old man who claimed he was looking for a lost child. Sergeant Major Mills, Major Seward, and Captain Sox also observed the prisoner being taken to the bunker. Some time after, all three heard a yelp or, as MacDonald put it, 'a long dragged out howl.'[43] Mills asked: 'What are they doing to him out there?' but no one answered.[44] It is telling that when he heard the yelp, MacDonald was not concerned to enough interrupt his playing of *Game Boy* (a video game). When there was a second yelp sometime later, only MacDonald and the Somali interpreter Mohammed heard it from the signaller's station; the others had departed and Sergeant Gresty was sleeping on duty.

At Private Brown's court martial, MacDonald also testified that later that night Matchee came in to the signaller's station to bum a cigarette and made the comment that now the Black man would fear the Indian as he did the white man, a statement that may have alluded to a scoring game within the unit with respect to Somalis. When he was about to go off duty, MacDonald went to check out the bunker for himself. He found Brown on the stairs,[45] and Matchee was hitting the prisoner in the face with a riot baton as well as kicking him. Matchee asked Brown to hold up the prisoner's face for MacDonald to see. Macdonald noted that the prisoner's face was badly swollen. He also noted that Matchee was in a chipper mood. MacDonald then returned to Sergeant Gresty and reported that the prisoner was 'getting a good shit-kicking,'[46] before returning to his tent and going to bed. Brown came in shortly after to ask if anyone had heard the screams. He received no reply.[47] In this account, even though MacDonald presents himself as having reported the event, it seems clear that he was not overly troubled by it. No one thought it significant enough to find out from Brown what had happened or to discuss the screams.

On duty in the watch-tower that night, Master Corporal R.E. Campbell testified that around 9:30 p.m. he heard screams and saw flashes of light coming from the bunker. He described the sounds he heard: 'The only way I could describe it was from my childhood on the farm. We used to slaughter our own animals. If an animal was not put down properly then as they were finished off they would still be alive and conscious and that sound was very close to what I heard.'[48] His graphic and disturbing description notwithstanding, Campbell did not investigate or intervene further. As he explained in his statement to military police shortly after the event, he had heard howls on previous occasions and he felt that the practices that gave rise to them 'seem to be accepted.'[49] Campbell testified at Brown's court martial that at least three bodies were present in the bunker most of the time and that he assumed that what went on there was the business of 2 Commando. Other soldiers also did not report what they heard, testifying that screams in the night were a common occurrence. As the notes of Master Corporal Joseph Montreuil revealed to military police, several Somali youth were beaten in custody. Somalis, Montreuil wrote, seemed to be 'fair game.'[50]

Visitors to the bunker commented to Matchee and Brown that they had 'a nice trophy.'[51] Others thought little of the picture taking; in Somalia, pictures were routinely taken of 'the good, the bad and the ugly.'[52] When Master Corporal Giasson visited the bunker that night around 11:20 p.m., Matchee invited him to see the prisoner who was sitting in the bunker with his ankles tied up with plastic straps and his arms tied to a riot baton secured to the beam of the bunker. He had a cloth over half his face, his bottom lip was cut and bleeding, and he was semi-conscious. Matchee is alleged to have said to Giasson, '[I]n Canada we cannot do that and here they let us do it. The NCO is aware of it, the officer is aware of it and even the NCO gave him the boot and there is six or eight people in line for the same treatment.'[53] Matchee then took a metal pipe that Giasson had. The latter left, testifying that he was scared. He discussed this incident with a fellow worker and then reported it to his commanding officer the next morning.[54]

Something about the night's ordinariness is also evident in Private Brocklebank's testimony at his own court martial. Brocklebank, then twenty-six years old and a grade-twelve graduate who had recently discovered that he had Tourette's syndrome, testified that he had absolutely no knowledge of how prisoners ought to be treated.[55] When he dropped by the bunker, Matchee asked him for his gun, ostensibly in order to pose with it in photographs. Two photos were taken of Matchee and the bleeding prisoner, and Brown (at Matchee's invitation) posed for a third. During his time in the bunker, Brocklebank saw Matchee hitting the prisoner, and several other soldiers dropped in during this time. Brocklebank asked Matchee if anyone had seen this, to which Matchee replied that Warrant Officer Murphy had also kicked the prisoner and that Captain Sox had ordered him to beat the prisoner.[56] According to Brocklebank, when Matchee left temporarily, he tried to arrange the prisoner's feet so that Matchee would think he hadn't moved. Brocklebank surmised that Matchee hit the prisoner whenever he moved. He testified that he also tried to give the prisoner water. Later that night, Matchee (although now off duty) returned with Brown (who was on duty) in order to further beat Arone. Matchee and Brown stayed on even after Brown went off duty and was replaced by Brocklebank. Arone is said to have died at 0014 hours on 17 March.

The following day, Brocklebank asked Warrant Officer Murphy if he had hit the prisoner. When the answer was no, he reported Matchee to Captain Sox, although he maintained at his court martial that he thought Matchee was only following orders. There were some inconsistencies in Brocklebank's account. For example, he maintained that he was in shock that night but he also declared that he did not believe that the prisoner was in any danger of his life. Again in this testimony, one has a sense that the event did not profoundly shock anyone. Although it worried Macdonald and Brocklebank a little, neither knew how to explain the event in hind sight. Although it was not introduced at his court martial, Private Brocklebank was also the soldier uttering racist and violent epithets on a video taken by Canadian Airborne Soldiers while serving in Somalia.[57]

Ironically, it is the very ordinariness of the violence and everyone's participation in it, *as well as its necessity in Somalia* that became the basis of Brocklebank's successful legal defence by a high profile criminal lawyer. In presenting Brocklebank as simply an ordinary man doing what everyone else was doing, his counsel, Edward Greenspan, was careful to remind the court that it was Matchee and Brown who are the monsters. Brocklebank was charged with failing to protect Shidane Arone, a civilian, from acts of violence which he knew were occurring. A reasonable person, the Prosecution argued, would have intervened to stop the violence. A reasonable soldier would not have watched the beating for over forty minutes and then walked away to make a phone call home, commenting along the way to a fellow soldier that he hoped the prisoner doesn't die.[58] To defend him, Brocklebank's counsel sought to demonstrate that Brocklebank's responses did not represent a 'marked departure from the norm.'[59] Rather, Brocklebank was simply 'a young kid from Charlottetown, Prince Edward Island, [from a] nice family,'[60] who simply obeyed an order from his superior officers (Seward, Sox, and ultimately Matchee). These officers (with the exception of Matchee) were not evil men or 'Nazis,' their orders notwithstanding.[61] Instead, 'there existed a state of facts which caused reasonable men, decent people to believe in those circumstances that that abuse order was justified in the circumstances in which they found themselves.'[62]

Like all the other soldiers, Private Brocklebank was a man 'in a hostile country,' doing a 'dangerous job' in 'a harsh and hostile climate.'[63] He was merely 'acting on orders as he has done thousands and thousands of times before.'[64] Most important of all, many men witnessed the beating and did nothing to stop or discourage it. In his address to the court, Greenspan carefully itemized the actions of twenty men who either participated , witnessed the torture or heard about it, and who did nothing. He concluded: 'The order was out, beat the prisoner, and nobody saw it as manifestly unlawful.'[65] Should he have chosen to complain, Greenspan concluded, Brocklebank would have had no one to tell. He would, in fact, have had no basis for a complaint since the order to abuse the prisoners was clearly not unreasonable given the circumstances of Somalia.[66] Somalia, Greenspan made clear, was not a police station in Metropolitan Montreal or Toronto, presumably where such activities would be illegal.[67] Private Brocklebank was acquitted of all charges.

II. The Bully and the Weak Soldier

In military trials, the evidence that there was a widely shared understanding among Canadian troops and their leaders that the abuse of Somalis was both normal and necessary did not operate to exonerate either Brown or Matchee. Private Brown was sentenced to five years imprisonment and dismissal with disgrace from her Majesty's service. Unlike Private Brocklebank, who was considered to be acting reasonably and who was merely doing what everyone else was doing, Matchee and Brown were pathologized and shown to be exceptions to the rule. Brocklebank's counsel, Edward Greenspan, presented Brown as 'a very different kettle of fish,' a man who knew all the facts and, of his own volition, deliberately removed his kit and proceeded to beat the prisoner because he despised thieves.[68]

In Greenspan's defence of Brocklebank, Brown was painted as deliberately cruel. The prosecution in Brown's trial took the same approach. A similar strategy was followed with respect to Matchee who was variously described as a 'braggart and a liar,'[69] 'disruptive, dishonest, an aggressive bully,'[70] as someone who, on the night of 16 March, had 'already drawn blood'[71] and who went looking for more, 'an overbearing person who tried to get the upper hand' and 'control people,'[72] and 'a cowboy who wouldn't follow the book.'[73] What then of the bully and the weak soldier on the night of 16 March? Can we understand their actions, as I have proposed above, as part of a general encounter between Somalis and men who thought of themselves as colonizers, or were they exceptions, men who were simply compensating for their own diminished status as men marked by their racial origins? What did being Cree or part Cree have to do with their actions that night? In a military made up of just 2.1 per cent Aboriginal soldiers and 3.1 per cent soldiers of colour, and in a regiment that boasted several white supremacists, what role did racism play?[74]

Torture and murder are not unusual events in times of war. Scholars often explain the breakdown of morals as arising from the necessary dehumanization of the enemy that occurs in war. It is argued that military discipline restricts a soldier's capacity to think for himself. Jonathan Glover, for example, explains the massacre of Vietnamese civilians by American troops at My Lai as due to two contradictory features of military discipline. Where military discipline is absent, soldiers can become like a pack of wild men; where it is present, the pressure to conform can mean blind obedience.[75] Soldiers' isolation and solidarity, Glover suggests, can create 'a private moral world with its own social pressures.'[76] In Vietnam, these factors, along with the dehumanization of the enemy resulted in 'a cult of hardness which stigmatized moral doubts as sentimental weakness.'[77] Lieutenant Calley, who led the massacre, was said to be a man who was not widely respected and who desired above all to show that he was indeed a tough man. Such explanations are premised on the exceptional circumstances of war, and on the exceptional conditions of military life. In Calley's case, they are also premised on the notion of an exceptionally dysfunctional man. The thesis of Calley's exceptionality precludes a more systemic explanation as it directs us (and the court) to look for the unusual in individual biographies to explain the violence. We are diverted by this, and we do not look at the everyday context to understand what some men chose to do, while others did not.

The everyday context of peacekeeping, I have been arguing, is a colonial one, where Europeans think of themselves as bringing order and civilization to a darker race. What of the violence of colonized or subordinate men in such colonial situations? Are such men those of whom Fanon writes when he describes the native deprived of an outlet for his anger against the colonizers, the man who dreams of aggression and who will first 'manifest this aggressiveness which has been deposited in his bone against his own people?'[78] Matchee's and Brown's Aboriginal ancestry cannot of course be said to hold the same kind of subordinate status as the Somalis towards whom they were violent. As members of a Northern nation that claimed its own moral superiority over Africans, Matchee and Brown occupied the role of colonizer even while their own status within the military was a racially subordinate one. Interest in their unique racial positioning emerged as an issue in legal processes as it did in the media when the story of peacekeeping violence became headlines. This interest in the violence of men of colour was not simply a prurient one, although there have been those anxious to show that racial minorities are racist towards one another, and others for whom race always means the race of the subordinate group and not the race of the dominant one. The question of Matchee's and Brown's race remained on the table, I suggest, because both men indicated that they themselves were often compelled to negotiate race in Somalia and in the military. Their actions and accounts leave us with the nagging suspicion that racial minority men's experiences of racism in the military and in Canadian society does offer a clue about Matchee's and Brown's activities on the night of Arone's murder.

That racism had something to do with what happened on 16 March has engaged many commentators. The murder had the characteristics of a 'lynching,' concluded an expert in cases of police brutality who was commissioned by the Inquiry into events in Somalia: 'The mob – in this case the CAR [Canadian Airborne Regiment] members within earshot – was not standing around ready to 'string up the rope,' but they could not have helped hearing Arone's cries; they had to know what was happening to him and they did nothing to stop it.'[79] Suggesting an altogether different operation of racism, one that has to do with the idea of compensation, a contemporary of Matchee's from the same small town commented that the murder of Shidane Arone seemed 'an almost ritualistic act of racism.'[80] For Warren Cariou, a childhood acquaintance of Clayton Matchee, to look for an explanation of these terrible actions means to start with what the troops brought with them to Somalia. Clayton Matchee, Cariou writes, grew up in an environment of extreme racism towards Aboriginal peoples. Some of this was evident in the hate mail, phone calls, and bomb threats his family received when the events of 16 March became known to the Canadian public. Callers were clear: 'Indian, welfare bum. You deserve to die. You should be dead.'[81] In his childhood, Cariou recalls, the Native kids he grew up with quickly learned two things in their search for approval: 'whiteness is power and [that] the way to become white is to be a racist.'[82] Matchee, in Cariou's memory, was a kid who wanted desperately to fit in. With a white mother and an Aboriginal father, Matchee's dark skin nevertheless ensured that he was always regarded as Native. Few knew or cared about his mixed heritage. Matchee would have been familiar with racist hazing rituals from sports teams, and he would have learned early on that belonging required that one gave as good as one got. Perhaps the most telling sign for Cariou that Matchee sought to transcend his own colour through racism against Somalis were the pictures Matchee demanded that Kyle Brown take of himself, barechested, powerful and muscled, holding up the head of a semi-conscious Shidane Arone. The schoolboy, whom Cariou remembered as taking pains to cover up his physique and his skin, had finally found someone who came off worse in comparison.

Cariou's explanation for Matchee's behaviour was proposed by others. Journalist Tony Hall described Matchee's actions as actions meant to 'outwhite the white guys.'[83] That is, they were an attempt to outperform white soldiers in a context in which violence against Somalis was the measure of masculinity. Posing questions about Matchee's alleged suicide attempt, Hall wondered if Matchee's behaviour (specifically in boasting that now both Black and white men should fear the Indian) was not, in fact, calling unwelcome attention to 'the interlocking cycles of racism' against men of colour in 2 Commando unit of the Canadian Airborne Regiment and against Somalis. He proposed that Matchee be seen 'as a victim as well as a perpetrator of a pervasive Canadian racism, which the Airborne [R]egiment only reflected rather than epitomized.'[84] The Inquiry itself pursued the victim/perpetrator line of argument. It asked interveners to help commissioners to understand whether Matchee and Brown might have felt that they had a lot to prove to a unit of soldiers, some of whom were card-carrying members of white supremacist groups.[85] While this line of thinking has the virtue of reminding us that white soldiers were also violent and racist, it can lead to the position that men of colour were more violent because they had the most to prove.

The idea of compensatory practices begins with the contention that privileged status along one axis – in Matchee's and Brown's case this would be membership in the Armed Forces of a white, Northern nation on duty in Africa – enables such men to engage in acts of subordination (in this case, violence against Somalis) to compensate for the devaluation they experience along another axis' (in this instance, Aboriginality). Sociologist Karen Pyke, writing on class-based masculinities, has argued that there are higher levels of domestic violence in the marriages of lower-status men. Disempowered on their jobs and in society, lower-class men bolster their sense of self through violence against their wives. As Pyke puts it, '[I]n the absence of legitimated hierarchical advantages, lower-class husbands are more likely to produce hyper masculinity by relying on blatant, brutal and relentless power strategies in their marriages, including spousal abuse.'[86] In so doing, the men 'compensate for their demeaned status, pump up their sense of self-worth and control, and simulate the uncontested privileges of higher-class men.'[87] Although Pyke makes the claim that lower-status men rely more on overt violence than do middle-class men, she reminds us that their hypermasculine behaviour benefits middle-class men in two ways: middle-class men benefit from the 'mystique of men's superior prowess' and, at the same time, they emphasize their own greater rationality as evidence of their superiority over working-class men.[88]

Even if one were not to take the compensatory argument fully in the troubling direction suggested by Pyke and others,[89] which leaves lower-status men with more potential and reason to be overtly violent than elite men, it seems obvious that men of colour make 'hegemonic bargains' when up against the demands of hegemonic masculinity.[90] As Anthony Chen's research with Chinese-American men reveals, both dominant and subordinate men succumb, in different ways and trading with different assets, to the powerful pull of hegemonic ideals of masculinity. To negotiate a dominant masculinity that is deeply racist, men of colour sometimes agree to engage in behaviour that makes them complicit with white supremacy.[91] The men in Chen's sample adopt one or more of at least four possible strategies, only three of which are hegemonic bargains. Some choose a strategy of compensation in which they trade their assets (for example athletic ability) for belonging to the dominant group of men, men who most conform to the hegemonic ideal. Others attempt to secure belonging through deflecting attention away from their own short-comings (as ideal men) by doing things that will buy them some respectability. For example, a man who is unable to conform to the hegemonic ideal of a man who excels at sports may buy belonging through becoming adept at using com-puters. A third strategy that keeps the hegemonic ideal in place is denial: sim-ply affirming that the prevailing stereotypes do not apply. A fourth strategy, however, and one which does not result in a hegemonic bargain, is the strategy of repudiation: rejecting the hegemonic ideal and taking pride in being Asian. In Chen's work we are forcefully reminded that men of colour negotiate hege-monic masculinity under a set of conditions that determine which options are available. Chen urges us, as does James Messerschmidt, to consider the struc-tural conditions, that is to say, the wider hegemony under which hegemonic masculinity is negotiated.[92] In the context of peacekeeping, we might consider these conditions to be the colonial nature of the encounter between Western peacekeepers and the local population. All the men negotiate masculinity under this overarching constraint.

Violence is a readily available option for the making of self in militaries and in police forces, and the conditions of peacekeeping are no different. Subordi-nate men, especially working-class men, are often in situations where oppor-tunities for certain kinds of violence present themselves. Angela Harris describes this dynamic as it operates in police forces:

> Police officers in poor urban minority neighbourhoods may come to see them-selves as 'law enforcers in a community of savages, as outposts of the law in the jungle.' 'Us' versus 'them' collapses into 'us' versus the nonwhites' (White suprem-acist activity is as present in the police as it is in the military) and rogue police officers, like private perpetrators of hate violence, are provided with ample oppor-tunity to prove not only their patriotism but their masculinity.[93]

In the peacekeeping context of Somalia, Canadian soldiers had a great deal to persuade them that they were in an intensely racial, indeed colonial setting and their opportunities for violence would have inescapably followed the racial route Harris describes. In such a context, a racial-minority man has an oppor-tunity to engage in violence against other racial minorities without feeling, in Harris's words, 'that he has betrayed his race.'[94] Violence after all, as I have argued with respect to peacekeeping and Harris has argued for the police, is deemed necessary to control savages. Violence against Somalis easily became patriotic duty and it provided an opportunity for men to prove their manhood. All the same, when we think of ultra-violent Black men, savage Aboriginal men, and 'super macho' working-class men, we come dangerously close to reproducing race and class stereotypes, and it is not easy to steer clear of them when considering the violent acts of lower-status men. With respect to Matchee and Brown, if we acknowledge the investment racial-minority men have in being seen as real men, we walk a fine line between pathologizing them as savages and maintaining that they are simply engaging in practices produced by the colonial situation (whites and minorities in North America, Somalis and Northern peacekeepers in Somalia) in which they find themselves.

Importantly, the facts do not always bear out the finding that racial-minority men are more violent than other men in either the policing or military context. Jean-Paul Brodeur, rejecting a compensatory line of argument, suggests that minority police have not in fact been shown to overidentify with the norms of the majority group. He speculates that much of what we hypothesize about the behaviour of racial minorities in the police or the military comes from work done on prisons and concentration camps where, in the case of the latter, those selected to police their own were only able to escape their own subordinate status through violence. It is critical to remember, Brodeur writes, that any violence among subordinate groups pales in comparison to the violence of the dominant group towards the subordinate group.[95]

Brodeur's reservations about compensatory masculinity theories as they might be applied to the police are sustained in the study by Laura Miller and Charles Moskos. Peacekeeping missions have their share of 'warriors,' who are apt to be violent, and 'humanitarians,' write Miller and Moskos in their analysis of American peace keeping troops' attitudinal patterns in Somalia. As with Canadian troops, American troops went to Somalia with high expectations, anticipating that they would be engaging in humanitarian activities and that they would be appreciated by a grateful and hungry local population. Soon thereafter, disillusioned American troops began to feel that Somalis were neither grateful nor starving and were, in any event, their own worst enemies. Miller and Moskos identified two responses to this situation:

> One pattern reflected a 'warrior strategy,' in which soldiers generalized the behavior of gunmen and rioters to all Somalis and treated the entire population as potential enemies. The other pattern was based on a 'humanitarian strategy': soldiers following this pattern were offended by negative stereotypes of Somalis, eschewed the use of force, and sought to contextualize Somali behavior by seeking cultural and political explanations.[96]

Significantly, while the 'warrior strategy' was adopted mostly by white men, the 'humanitarian strategy' was adopted mostly by women and Black soldiers.

Miller and Moskos also show how quickly 'warrior strategies' entailed violence. American troops exhibiting this pattern frequently expressed a profound sense of threat: 'We can't tell the good guys from the bad guys'; 'A boy who smiled and waved one day could become a fervent rock thrower on another.'[97] Somalis in this view only understood force. As one soldier told Miller and Moskos, '[W]e should beat them and scare them some, or shoot one and make an example.'[98] In contrast, 'humanitarians' often observed that Somalis were treated as less than human, that their situation was a desperate one which drove them to desperate measures, and that they were culturally different from Americans and so did not always understand what was done for their benefit. For some of the Black soldiers, their own experiences of racism were mirrored in the white soldiers' treatment of Somalis. As one Black soldier explained, he was offended by 'the constant anti-Somali remarks from whites, including jokes about wanting to intentionally run down Somalis on the road.'[99]

It seems obvious that without the benefit of personal experience of racism and sexism, and without an opportunity to engage in critical thinking about the terms and conditions of the encounter, soldiers more easily become warriors. Yet the terms and conditions of the peacekeeping encounter *are* colonial. Northern armies do officially set out to save and civilize Southern nations and the peacekeeping encounter discourages individuals from exploring their countries' complicity in the conditions they have come to fix. It is not surprising, then, that warriors of all races are a consistent feature of peacekeeping, but it is also not surprising that women and racial minorities, reminded so forcefully of their own subordination, would reject warrior modes of operation. It is this pull *away from hegemonic masculinities* and the complex negotiations that occur along the way that many compensatory theorists forget when theorizing the violence of subordinate masculinities.

How then might we understand Matchee and Brown? First, it is important to note that their responses should not be conflated into one, nor is it necessary to assign to each a definitive label for all time of warrior or humanitarian, as Miller and Moskos use these terms. Instead, we might consider that both endured the racism that the Inquiry would later show to be endemic in the Canadian military. Their responses were not the same. As we thread our way through the little that is available about their experiences of Somalia, we might then examine their contradictory impulses – towards participating in the colonial encounter and keeping away from it. We can, in this way, acknowledge their subordinate status without making them exceptional and come closer to appraising the systemic practices and constraints that produce violent men of all races and classes in specific situations. While the evidence indicates that a compensatory dynamic might have been operating, as I discuss below, this must be considered within the larger context in which the degradation of Somalis and the violence against them were so widespread as to almost be routine aspects of the peacekeeping encounter.

Little information is available about Matchee to confirm his responses in Somalia. Major Seward recalled that he thought highly of Matchee, to the point of feeling 'smug' that he had promoted him before he left for Somalia.[100] Sergeant Boland considered him to be the soldier with the best field skills in all of 2 Commando.[101] In many of the court-martial proceedings, an admiration for Matchee's brand of aggressive masculinity emerges and some soldiers concede that Matchee was only doing what everyone else was doing. Master Corporal Giasson testified that Matchee knew that what he was doing would be unlawful in Canada, but he felt that an order had been given to abuse the prisoners.[102] Although much would be made later of Matchee's involvement in incidents at the regiment's base at Petawawa in Ontario, involving members of the Airborne Regiment burning a sergeant's car, there is little to suggest that Matchee was in any way different from the rest of his unit. His experiences of racism in the unit were the only thing that set him apart.

From articles written by the *Toronto Star*'s Peter Cheney, we know that Matchee came from an Indian reserve, just outside a very small prairie town. The Matchees are Cree and Matchee's father is a councillor of the band, descended from an ancestral chief. The family taught their children pride in their heritage. Cheney, basing his information on interviews, describes a young Matchee becoming a jockey and attending thoroughbred racing shows with his father. In 1983, with the blessing of his parents, a seventeen-year-old Matchee, who had grown to six feet four inches and was over 80 kilos (175 pounds), left his remote reserve to join the military. He returned five years later to marry a young white woman who used to board at his parents farm. Shortly after the birth of their daughter, Matchee joined the Airborne Regiment and he and his young family were posted to the Petawawa military base. In the military, he was given the nickname Geronimo, which he privately hated. He was taunted by a sergeant who called him an 'Indian Welfare bum.'[103] His unit had several card-carrying members of white supremacist groups, including Matchee's friend Matt MacKay. Although he complained to his parents in a letter that the racial abuse was beginning to get to him and that he wanted to quit, Matchee's father encouraged him to stick it out, arguing that sooner or later the unit would run out of names to call him.[104]

At least one possible strategy to survive in this environment is to fit in, a compensatory practice. The more that minority members are isolated, and Aboriginal members of the entire regiment numbered only ten, the more likely it is that they overidentify with the dominant group.[105] Matchee was known as an aggressive hazer of new recruits, so much so that in his transcripts, Corporal Brady MacDonald recalled him as 'a bully type of person,'[106] and Kyle Brown maintained that he feared Matchee.[107] Both MacDonald and Brown, of course, had something to gain from this characterization. A character witness for Kyle Brown recalled that when she first saw news of the torture and killing and heard Matchee's name, her husband, a military man, commented that 'he couldn't believe this didn't happen sooner to this man.'[108] Private Brocklebank recalled a question he posed to Matchee about whether he felt bad that the prisoner had died. Matchee's response was: 'Ah, the guy was weak.'[109] Brocklebank appeared to think that this answer was typical of Matchee, presumably because the latter valued physical prowess and performed an aggressive masculinity. There is some evidence as well that Matchee called upon his racial background to mark himself as strong. He had a tattoo of a teepee, the symbol of his band. In Somalia, Matchee apparently posted an emblem of his tribe on the notice board accompanied by the words 'White men fear the Indian.'[110] Matchee also apparently boasted the morning after the killing, 'Indians two, white man nothing.'[111]

What are we to make of these responses in situating Matchee within the argument I have been making about the colonial nature of the encounter and the contradictory impulses present in subordinate men as well as majority men? While there is evidence of compensatory practices, it is difficult to find the evidence for fitting Matchee into a character such as Bigger – a young man in search of belonging who is the main character in Richard Wright's novel *Native Son*. Bigger is a Black man whose response to racism and to the hopelessness of inner-city poverty is to engage in crime beginning with theft and assault and ending with the rape and murder of a white woman. Bigger grew out of his own encounters, first with Black boys who terrorized other Black children, then with Black teenaged boys who would openly confront whites by engaging in criminal behaviour (such as stealing), and finally with Black men who took their rebellion to such heights that extreme violence (including rape and murder) soon ensured that they were jailed, shot by police, executed, or confined to an insane asylum. Such men were the only ones 'who consistently violated the Jim Crow laws of the South and got away with it, at least for a sweet brief spell.'[112] In their 'childish ideas' of violently confronting the conditions of their own subordination, ideas Matchee might be said to have expressed in his count of 'Indians two, white man nothing,' Wright identifies 'a deep hunger' for inclusion – an inclusion secured through violence.[113]

In an afterward to his 1940 novel, Wright describes Bigger as a man produced by racism, a man who possessed 'the tensity, the fear, the hate, the impatience, the sense of exclusion, the ache for violent action, the emotional, the cultural hunger.'[114] These powerful emotions fuel Bigger's violent impulses; violence makes him feel temporarily whole and in control. Bigger 'lived by violence, through extreme action and sensation, through drowning daily in a perpetual nervous agitation.'[115] He knew of the rights guaranteed in the American Constitution and knew that 'every man and woman should have the opportunity to realise himself, to seek his own individual fate and goal, his own peculiar and untranslatable destiny. Bigger knew these things as much as he knew that he did not have access to them.'[116]

Certainly, we could speculate that as an Aboriginal man, Matchee would have shared some degree of Bigger's sense of exclusion. The unrelenting racism of his life would have led him to no other conclusion. Equally, Matchee's response, to make himself a subject through violence, is something we can just glimpse through the thin details of his actions in Somalia. To argue, however, that Matchee is simply Bigger, outwhiting the white guys by being more violent, is to ignore how *unexceptional* his violent responses were in Somalia. To suggest that Matchee was a version of Bigger is to turn Matchee into a monster, as so many tried to do. It may well have been his experience of racism that prompted him to violence but a far more powerful force at work was the colonial shape of the encounter, something that all the men, for different reasons, were drawn into, and which many opted to perform. Matchee seemed to have accepted the prevailing norm that Somalis were to be treated as potential enemies and as morally inferior.

What, then, of Kyle Brown? His one-quarter 'Aboriginality' was nonetheless apparent to a journalist who described his 'flat Brown face,'[117] and to his lawyer who sought to have evidence about Matchee's racial pride in the torture discounted because he feared that the impression would be left that Matchee and Brown could be conflated into the same type of person – presumably, Indians on the rampage.[118] (The evidence concerning Matchee's statements about Indians was ultimately ruled inadmissible, the judge being persuaded by the defence's argument that 'the inference could be that because they share a common heritage Brown would be more likely to join in a common enterprise' with Matchee than any other soldier.)[119] In Brown's account, there is also a sense that he believed that disciplining Somalis was a part of everyday operations, even though more than any other participant, it is Brown who appeared to be the most troubled and who took the most initiative in 'blowing the whistle.' When Brown first encountered the prisoner, he thought of teaching him a lesson. As he put it at his court martial: 'I looked at the prisoner and I called him a thief in Somali and I struck him across the jaw.'[120] Brown maintained that Somalis were aggressive towards Canadian troops and that he was very concerned to discouraging thievery because he remained quite disturbed by the shooting of a looter two weeks earlier on 4 March.[121] As he put it, '[T]hings seemed to be getting out of hand since the March 4th killing. I thought things were getting out of hand. He [Arush] was putting himself in danger by coming into our compound [and] possibly he could be killed if he came back.'[122] Brown kicked the prisoner a few times but then began to be worried by the ferocity of Matchee's responses.

When he went off duty that night, Brown thought of reporting Matchee but wondered how to do so when there were orders to abuse the prisoners.[123] He talked to Captain Hillier whose response was that if the prisoner died, there would be trouble. When Hillier followed up on Brown's concerns a short time after, Shidane Arone was already dead. It only remained for Captain Sox to order Matchee and Brown, the only two soldiers still up, to prepare the body for transport downtown. The next morning Matchee woke Brown and told him not to say anything about the sticks.[124] Significantly, the unit had a holiday that day and everyone participated in the fun and games, including Matchee and Brown, although the latter did try to talk to other soldiers and higher-ups about the night's events.

In Brown's account, even though he presents himself as being worried about the violence directed against Somalis, he does not dispute that Shidane Arone needed to have been taught a lesson. He also seems to have shared the view that the soldiers had of being in the position of colonizers, who posed for pictures with their bound captives. Although Brown maintained that his picture-taking (discussed earlier), was done simply out of fear and a desire to save Arone from further violence, and that he was in shock that night, in fact he took the opportunity of Corporal Biddy's visit to the bunker to ask him for film for his camera. As Brown asserted at his court martial, 'I wanted to take pictures.'[125] Being absolutely ordinary in Somalia clearly meant recording the degradation of Somalis.

While Matchee's and Brown's 'ordinariness' must be acknowledged, to do so seems to open the door for the argument that each bears limited responsibility for his actions. This was indeed the line of argument taken by Brown's defence counsel, who forcefully articulated that the 'most remarkable thing about Trooper Brown is that there was nothing remarkable about him.'[126] Brown was 'simply a young man who had witnessed an event which got out of hand, which he didn't know how to control, which he ultimately made a decision, perhaps too late, to try to stop it and was overcome by what he had seen and wanted to do the right thing and to do so in the face of at least indirect threats emanating from his peers.'[127] Inevitably, if Brown was simply the same as everyone else, then 'common sense and principles of fairness dictate that if Trooper Brown is guilty of murder, or torture, or manslaughter, so are half of 2 Commando and many others.'[128]

Indicting everyone was not, of course, likely to be an accepted alternative to finding Brown guilty. To steer a path between the argument that Brown was simply acting like everyone else and that everyone participated in the violence, Brown's defence counsel relied on two strategies. Since somebody had to take the rap, the first strategy consisted of demonizing Matchee as a 'mean bully.'[129] The second strategy demonized Somalis and Somalia, a strategy also evident in the defences prepared by the lawyers for the white soldiers. Duplicating the strategy of Captain Rainville's lawyer at his court martial over the 4 March incident, Brown's lawyer argued that in such a 'strange and frightening, and even hostile land,' Canadian troops were intensely vulnerable and simply had to defend themselves against Somali aggression.[130] In his words:

> It is my submission, gentlemen, that there is ample evidence before this court that there was a general understanding amongst the troops that it was OK to rough up the prisoners a little bit for a deterrent purpose ... And I say that for this reason, that the troops were in a lawless country. There was no civil institutions, there was no civil authority. There was nothing that could be done to those looters who were captured. They could not be turned over to anybody who could effectively deal with them such as happens in most civilized countries. They could not call the police and have them arrested and expect that he [sic] would be taken to court and dealt with according to the law. At the same time the soldiers were very vulnerable. They're out in the field. They had no locks. They had valuable kit and they are obviously particularly concerned about the security of their weapons.[131]

The idea of vulnerable innocent soldiers frustrated and forced to go beyond the limit of lawful and civilized behaviour, which would become a central line of argument for the Inquiry, relies intrinsically on a colonial logic: the natives can only be kept in line through force. Indeed, it is the natives who are said to drive the colonizers to violence. Deployed in tandem with the idea that Matchee was the real culprit, it served to normalize Private Brown's actions, as it did Private Brocklebank's. While the strategy worked for Brocklebank, however, it did not work for Brown who received a sentence of five years in prison and dismissal from the Armed Forces. We can only speculate on the reasons for this outcome. For the journalist Peter Worthington, who wrote an account of Brown's role in collaboration with Brown himself, the army 'betrayed Kyle Brown' in making him take the rap for something Matchee did.[132] Others reason that the Somalis simply had to be kept in line through violence, and to discipline Somalis through engaging in acts of humiliation and violence was only patriotic duty. Ironically, it is in sharing this belief that Brown's complicity is most clearly evident. Unexceptional to the end, Brown was simply as complicit as everyone else, and therefore responsible for his own acts of violence and for acquiesing to the violence.

Conclusion

It has been difficult to explore the origins of Matchee's and Brown's behaviour. I feared that in the process of doing so I was bound to confirm the opinion of those who saw men of colour as inherently given to violence. Rather than rein-stall the stereotype of the man of colour as a criminal, or as insane, it was tempting to simply adopt the position that racism drove them to do what they did. This position, however, as I have shown in my critique of compensatory practices, ultimately reproduces the idea that the two men were exceptions because they were burdened by racism. The compensatory argument exoner-ates them for what were clearly acts of inhumanity. Most of all, a compensatory argument takes the focus away from the structural conditions of what was in essence a colonial encounter. It *individualizes* the violence and makes it look like the property of specific men. Without an understanding of the colonial terms of the peacekeeping encounter, we are also too easily led to the place described by defence lawyers, a lawless land where the immoral natives drove ordinary soldiers to commit acts of violence in self-defence. Ironically, the explanation that racism drove men of colour to commit acts of violence against Somalis parallels in significant ways the explanation that the natives them-selves and the brutalities of the climate drove the men to violence. Each line of argument confines the violence to bodies and landscapes abstracted out of con-text and each has the effect of limiting responsibility.

The idea of compensation clearly cannot bear the weight of the complexi-ties of the colonial situation. For instance, while it seemed clear that at least some compensatory behaviour was in operation, it is equally probable that repudiation, to use Chen's descriptions of strategies, was present – for exam-ple, in Matchee's efforts to assert racial pride and possibly in Brown's explana-tion that he hoped to discourage Shidane Arone from stealing because it would ultimately cost him his life. It is possible that Matchee and Brown felt the same way as some Black American soldiers in Somalia – deeply conflicted between hearing a familiar racism directed at Somalis and the national mis-sion to civilize Somalis and keep them in line. A Black American soldier interviewed by Miller and Moskos expressed his own conflict this way: 'I am cross-pressured between disgust when my troops beat up [Somalis] and when Somalis act like savages.'[133] Black American soldiers reported feeling ashamed whenever Somalis acted in a 'barbaric' manner in front of whites, but they also reported feeling manipulated by Somalis because they had the same colour of

skin and were ridiculed by Somalis who called them 'n—' and expressed contempt for their broader facial features.[134] (Somalis might have positioned
Black Americans who did not share their own predominantly aquiline features
as 'Bantus,' who are inferiorized and degraded in Somalia.) Although Miller
and Markos document that the majority of Black American men (and both
white and Black American women) adopted a humanitarian rather than a
warrior approach, some Black soldiers felt shame, anger, betrayal, and disap-
pointment and did turn to violence. Brown clearly disapproved of his unit's
racism as they chased Somalis with guns on the night of 4 March, but he also
believed that Somalis had to be taught a lesson for their own good. Matchee
responded to racism in his environment by performing a masculinity that was
as aggressive as some of the white men, in particular those who had executed a
Somali infiltrator.

Although it is difficult to prove, we cannot discount these possible connections between the Aboriginal men's racially subordinate status within their
unit and the violent strategies they may have adopted to negotiate the conflicts
and contradictions. In hindsight it seems significant that the videotape depicting white soldiers uttering racial slurs against Somalis showed a quiet Kyle
Brown, sitting a little distance from the others and not participating in the
display of bravado for the camera. Matchee's defiant bulletin-board posting
and wearing of Aboriginal symbols, and even his announcements of the score
of Somalis killed by white men and by 'Indians' – done in a unit where some
members were card-carrying white supremacists and where the U.S. Confederate flag openly proclaimed racist views – also seem, in hindsight, to indicate
an environment overdetermined by race well before the troops found themselves involved in peacekeeping efforts to help and 'instruct' Africans in
democracy. Any explanation for Matchee's and Brown's behaviour has to
include both compensatory and repudiating practices, but more than this, it
has to make room for the colonial violence operating in the peacekeeping
encounter.

Many of the soldiers named in the various military legal proceedings were
ordinary men. Most were white and working-class men who displayed an
astonishing degree of ignorance about the world and about Africa. Few of
these soldiers had 'seen' the world, often leaving small, rural communities to
go directly into the military, living life within its narrow confines. Sergeant
Boland, for instance, joined the military at seventeen. He left a small farming
community to join up. Private Brocklebank left his small community after
completing grade twelve and went directly into the army. Matchee and Brown
followed similar pathways. There was minimal chance that any of these men
would have had the opportunity to encounter African men before Somalia,

and when they did encounter African men, they each operated with the racist assumptions of Canadian popular culture. More than this, I would argue, both the non-elite men and the elite men were deeply invested in the idea that men of the North who are peacekeepers go to the South to use their superior skills to clean up after wars, make Africans behave, and help them survive. More education, worldliness or cultural information could barely compete against the colonial investments that the peacekeeping encounter both produced and relied upon.

The systemic racial underpinnings of the encounter between Somalis and Canadian troops are very much in evidence in the men's recollections of the torture and murder of Shidane Arone. What is evident more than anything else is how absolutely unremarkable the violence seemed to be to the men who enacted it, witnessed it, or simply heard that it was happening. If we remain enmeshed in theories of compensatory subordination and exceptional men, we will miss the racial violence that was enacted by many soldiers and military leaders in the name of self and nation. We will also miss that while racially subordinate individuals may seek respectability through engaging in violent practices against other subordinate groups, they are more likely to reject such violence. Rather than a theory of compensation, a theory of masculinity that places white supremacy at its centre might better account for the violence of both men of colour and white men. Matchee and Brown and many of the white men were each enacting, in different ways, a colonial encounter. It is this that the legal processes would not examine. As chapter 4 shows, the nation and the commissioners of the Inquiry averted their gaze each time an opportunity arose to consider how race shaped what happened in Somalia between Canadian troops and the local Somali population.

CHAPTER 4

Bad Apples and a Nation Wronged: Public Truth and the Somalia Affair

A national narrative is born in and from chaos. Its purpose is to restore or imitate order and to minimize confusion about what is at stake and who will pay the price of dissension. Once, long ago, these stories developed slowly. They became over time national epics, written, sung, performed and archived in the culture as memory, ideology and art.

In some modern nations the construction of a national narrative is given over to a government agency and their uniformed enforcers ... In other nations the manufacture of a public truth is harder – cautioned and delayed by a free press, an openly dissident citizenry, a reversible electorate.

Toni Morrison, 'The Official Story'[1]

In *Somalia Yellow*, a play written by Blake Brooker about war artist Allan Harding MacKay's experience of the Canadian peacekeeping mission in Somalia, the characters Denise and Clayton muse aloud along two parallel tracks about their memories of bad apples:

DENISE: I thought I would not be affected by the events in Somalia.
I ignored the news when it came out.
I refused to believe it had anything to do with me.
I thought it was the work of a few bad apples.

CLAYTON: Halloween was a favourite time, eh.
And apples was our favourite fruit.
There was one crabapple tree on the rez.
Not bad since there was only three trees on the rez.
I mean, three trees near where the houses were.

DENISE: But later, when I saw on the news
A video made during a Canadian Airborne hazing ritual
even before they left for Somalia
when I saw the images of racism,
the hidden hatred in my country's military,
then the degradation this Somali boy had to suffer –

CLAYTON: I ate too many green crabapples
and sicked all over my dad's work socks
He scared the living shit out of me.[2]

The scene between Denise and Clayton ends with the character Andy remembering the war artist Allan MacKay:

Allan was more concerned about his anxiety
than the suffering of the Somali people
It was disturbing to understand
that that was what being a human meant.
When he saw their suffering
he knew it had nothing to do with him.[3]

How does the nation come to know that what happened in Somalia has nothing to do with us? How do we reassure ourselves that we will not be affected by these events, that the Somalia Affair did not change us from a good, peace-keeping people into a nation of racists? These questions are the focus of this chapter and help us to look at how the Somalia Affair entered our cultural memory.

In a nation where racism is so vigorously denied, the Somalia Affair posed an enormous challenge to Canadian confidence. The chaos brought on by the pictures of Arone's torture, the videotapes, and the trophy photos of captured children was too much to bear. We needed to believe that those images of racism and violence could have nothing to with us, yet Matchee and Brown could not endure the weight of our shame. Even as we relied on the theory of bad apples who had somehow contaminated an otherwise good barrel, we remained haunted by shadows at the edge of our national memory: Matchee's bad apples on the 'rez,' the kind that make him sick; white soldiers yelling racial epithets and a Black soldier with the letters KKK sprayed on his back. Were we haunted by the 'rez' itself, the people we confined to a place where there are only three trees? This was the nation's struggle, which began the morning we saw the first images: we believed in our national innocence yet feared that we did in fact possess 'hidden hatred.'

A national narrative minimizes confusion and restores order. In the Somalia Affair, the confusion was about race and brutality. Was there widespread racism in the military? Did it come from us? Did it cause the brutality? The images contradicted who we knew ourselves to be; they touched a nerve. It seemed possible that we were not after all a nation of peacekeepers who had gone to Africa to save Africans from themselves. The job of a national narrative is 'the production of belief' and spectacle; in this case, images of brutality supply 'the raw material from which a narrative emerges – already scripted, fully spectacularized and riveting in its gazeability.'[4] What we do with these bodies, 'the agreed upon interpretation of the events that is sold and distributed as public truth,' must confirm who we are as a nation and as a people. The bodies must reassure us that we had nothing to do with it. In the case of the Somalia Affair, how was this possible?

The photos and the videotapes so shocked the Canadian public that the government responded with the disbandment of the Canadian Airborne Regiment in January 1995 and with the creation of a Commission of Inquiry. Two judges, one French Canadian (Gilles Letourneau) and one English Canadian (Robert Rutherford), and a journalist (Peter Desbarats) were appointed to report on the organization and management of the Canadian military. The Inquiry's focus on institutional and systemic issues nonetheless required an examination of the pre-deployment, 'in-theatre,' and 'post-theatre' conduct of the Canadian Armed Forces – a mandate which soon took commissioners into the treacherous waters of Arone's and Aruush's deaths (among others), military cover-up, and a growing body of evidence that the encounter had been rife with 'incidents.' Although the Inquiry catalogued these events exhaustively (until it was prematurely shut down), and provided an alarming and close-up view of the debacle in Somalia, its conclusion – a searing indictment of military leaders – was only that as a nation we had been betrayed. Racism became the smallest of problems, overtaken by the larger issue of incompetent and careerist generals. In the official script of public memory, we insisted on remembering ourselves as a wounded nation, a remembrance that vitally depended upon the erasure of wounded, tortured, and killed Somalis, on the erasure of racism, and on the reinstallment of an innocent, peacekeeping nation.

In parts one and two of this chapter, I sift through the Inquiry's discussions about race, first with interveners who tried to argue for its salience and then with scholars. I identify those 'alchemical'[5] tricks – principally the containment of racism in overt acts of hatred only and racism's disappearance into culture – tricks that cordon off the violence and transform it into gold. The frustrated soldier, pushed to the brink by Africa and Africans, emerged from under the rubble of community and scholarly deliberations; what was left nat-uralized and undisturbed was the violence on Black bodies, bodies seen as nec-essarily absorbing the anger, frustration, and hardships endured by Canadian troops. The troops, the Inquiry concluded, were 'ill-prepared and rudderless.'

In part three, I show how the soldiers' innocence, and correspondingly, the corruption and irresponsibility of their generals (which was courageously named by the commissioners) enabled the nation to reaffirm its innocence; to come to know, that is, that the Somalia Affair had nothing to do with us. We turned in relief to the comfort of our national mythology, a mythology in which we are a non-imperial power without dreams of conquest. I explore this national dream of innocence as it is revealed in a personal account of the inquiry, in a book written by one of the Inquiry's commissioners, Peter Des-barats. This account is only one expression of the national dream, but it is an instructive one because it conveys so clearly the 'structure of feeling' around Canadian nationalism and how this feeling helped us construct a public truth about the Somalia Affair.[6] Desbarats illustrates how everyday beliefs in our superiority (our niceness, our penchant for democracy, our modesty) achieve coherence only if we stand outside history and within a racial story of civilized and savage peoples. We went to Africa handicapped by our niceness and naïveté, and we were taken advantage of by our own unscrupulous military leaders. Made vulnerable by our own morality, we could either stay at home or risk trauma, the kind that comes when civilized peoples encounter a savagery for which they are unprepared. This is the final political use to which we put those images of violated Black bodies: we imagined a world in which we were not implicated.

I. The Disappearance of Race

Media Responses

If we experience ourselves as a nation through public-sphere accounts, as Lau-ren Berlant suggests,[7] the media's rendition of the West's intervention in Somalia in 1992 prepared us to see ourselves as civilized Canadians who were forced to save Somalis from themselves. Long before Canadian peacekeepers arrived in Africa in 1992, media stories prefigured the encounter as one of biblical dimensions. In *Maclean's*, the country's national news magazine, Somalia was inexplicably 'stalked by famine,' 'beyond hope,' and living through a 'holocaust of war and famine.' By late December, just in time for Christmas, 'deliverance' was at hand. Operation Deliverance (the Canadian mission) and Operation Restore Hope (the U.S. mission) were both launched to bring

Somalia 'back to life.' Canadian press mimicked American presidential rhetoric in its presentation of Somalia as a primitive society helplessly caught in the
backwardness of its own traditions.[8] Yet our domestic lessons in citizenship
were no less colour coded. During March 1993, around the same time that
Shidane Arone was tortured and Matchee allegedly tried to hang himself, the
suicides of Aboriginal youth and alcoholism in Native communities were two
of the major stories breaking in Canada. In side columns and back pages,
another story peeped through of Aboriginal peoples protesting police brutality
and the occupation of their lands.[9] Eerily, these news stories helped us to make
sense of an alleged suicide attempt of an Aboriginal soldier on duty in Somalia.
Perhaps they also prepared us for the media reports that would explain why a
young Somali man ended up dead.

It was perhaps the already scripted story of Somalia as 'savagery overtaken by
civilization'[10] and the familiar domestic racial scripts that made it easy for us to
accept uncritically military explanations for the 4 and 16 March killings of
Somalis. One day after the 4 March incident, the media reported Colonel
Labbé's assessment that the shootings had been the response of 'well-trained
soldiers' to possible saboteurs of important military equipment such as the
American Black Hawk helicopters (a possibility that the Commission established as highly unlikely and contrary to the facts). Journalists never questioned
Labbé's explanation that 'a great deal of equipment had been stolen from the
compound.'[11] Nor did the shooting of a Red Cross guard by Canadian soldiers
attempting to quell a 'riot' raise alarm bells. The media again reported without
comment the military's version of events that 'armed bandits' were a constant
threat and that one had to defend oneself.[12] Indeed, well into March, after
Arone's murder, journalists were still reporting with sympathy the animosity
Canadian soldiers were feeling towards rock-throwing Somalis. 'Many soldiers
say privately they wish they could shoot more often,' Paul Watson of the *Toronto Star* wrote in an article devoted to describing the 'rough life' soldiers
endured in Belet Huen.[13] We can only speculate on whether the public would
have learned anything further about peacekeeping violence had reporters on a
pre-planned visit to the Canadian camp at Belet Huen not witnessed the confusion as an unconscious Matchee was taken away in an ambulance, an incident Jim Day of the *Pembroke Observer* pursued upon his return to Canada.[14]

While the violence against Somalis did not greatly interest the media, the
cover-up of that violence by the military did. By the first week of April, the
arrest of various soldiers in connection with Arone's murder, the defence minister's bid for leadership of the governing Conservative party, and the immi-
nence of an election, all conspired to turn the death of Arone and the alleged
suicide of Matchee into a story about a military and political cover-up, an

emphasis it would never really lose. The key concern, as *Globe and Mail* columnist Geoffrey York identified, was 'why the military waited more than two
weeks to reveal the death and the attempted suicide.'[15] On 20 April 1993, sur-
geon Barry Armstrong's letter to his wife, describing the execution and wounding of unarmed Somalis, was leaked to the media, providing further fodder for
the story of a cover-up. Few news analysts asked questions about the violence
itself, and none raised the issue of racism.

An in camera internal military inquiry (known as the de Faye Inquiry)
begun in May 1993 concluded that the violence had simply been the work of a
few bad apples, men witnesses described (as a lawyer for the Inquiry later
summed up) as 'rambunctious young men who get into trouble on R&R.'[16]
Most officers and soldiers, a research study for the de Faye Inquiry later concluded, were willing to accept this theory until it became clear at the conclusion of the military trials, that the only men convicted of wrongdoing were
men of the lower ranks.[17] One question would hang in the air: Where were
the leaders? It would not become a compelling one, however, until the publication of the photos and the videotapes and the subsequent establishment of
the Inquiry in November 1994.

If the incidents in Somalia failed to arouse attention (their racial underpinnings having been hidden), the photos and videotapes changed everything.
Private Kyle Brown's sixteen photographs of the Arone murder were the blast
of media messages which, according to Toni Morrison, were the spectacle that
rapidly enforced the national narrative.[18] The photos were released to the
media in November 1994, following the completion of the court martial proceedings, but most were still restricted from publication. The few photos that
were initially allowed to go to press, however, were graphic enough to provoke
widespread public condemnation of the newspapers that had chosen to pub-
lish them. There could be no denying 'Canada's shame' and its principal
image: a tortured Black man's head held in place with a baton wielded by a
soldier who at first appeared white.[19] The racial storyline supported by the
image seemed self-evident, but it was nevertheless soon displaced. Matchee
and the Canadian Airborne became aberrations, products of a peculiar *military*
subculture. As the *Ottawa Citizen* dramatically announced to its readers upon
publication of the full set of photos, they revealed 'the culture of members of a
military unit who treated killing as a sport.'[20] There could be no question that
the violence had anything to do with us, that is, the nation as a whole. When
Barry Armstrong added fuel to the fire by revealing that his superior had
ordered the destruction of evidence relating to the 4 March killing of Aruush
and the wounding of Hamdare,[21] the possibility of rogue leaders was added to
what we already knew was a rogue regiment. One day later, the government

announced the creation of the Commission of Inquiry into the deployment of Canadian Troops to Somalia.

Race could not be so easily dismissed, however. Soon two more 'sudden blasts of media messages' pushed the idea of a national inquiry to the forefront of the political agenda. Canadians watching the evening news on Sunday, 15 January 1995, saw video clips of the soldiers on peacekeeping duties in Somalia drinking and making a number of violent and racist comments about Somalis. Barely three days later, the release of a second video depicted domestic 'scenes of racism and degradation so vile' within the military that the television networks thought it advisable to forewarn viewers about the graphic brutality of the images. Military analyst Scott Taylor, who made the videotapes available to the media, reminded viewers that the racist hazing ritual they were observing had, in fact, taken place in Canada in broad daylight and was obviously officially sanctioned. Unidentified soldiers confirmed that racism against the only Black soldier in the regiment was commonplace.

While the photographs had suggested that Matchee (with Brown's help) had been the sole villain, the videotapes depicted a more widespread and definitively racist complicity, and they connected what had happened in Somalia to prior events in Canada. Few observers could deny the racism evident in the tapes, although some tried. A member of Parliament of the then Reform Party considered the tapes degrading but not racist, for example,[22] and military experts deplored what they nevertheless deemed to be merely hazing practices of a more degrading variety than others. Experts emerged to explain that the 'group bonding' revealed by the first videotape, and the hazing rituals of the second, were what soldiers turned to in order to survive the perils of military life. Whether 'sophomoric silliness'[23] or a 'military wide problem of racism,'[24] the two videos were so shocking that the media began to seek fuller explanations for the violence they depicted.

The 'silliness' had to be explained. Reporters began to uncover the white supremacist affiliations of some of the soldiers of the Canadian Airborne Regiment, although they were not all the same soldiers most directly implicated in the torture and killings in Somalia.[25] The problem of racism remained clearly confined to the Airborne Regiment, however, and companion articles on other more heroic troops enduring low pay and being forced to turn to food banks helped to further isolate a regiment increasingly described as a rogue one.[26] By the spring of 1995, when the Inquiry began, with graphic images of overt racism and card-carrying white supremacists firmly embedded in public memory, the most available framework for understanding the Somalia Affair was still one about a few bad men and their possible racist affiliations, but the video images had pushed the question of accountability to the forefront. To the question 'What went so wrong?' there was now another possible answer: a widespread breakdown in the military chain of command and a cover-up.

Some shared journalist Allan Thompson's assessment that when 'historians chronicle the Somalia Affair, they may well devote as much attention to cover-up plots hatched in Canada as to the tragic events of early 1993, when Somalis were killed and abused by Canadian peacekeepers.'[27] Linda Goyette, who agreed with his assessment, wrote that we simply couldn't continue to call the Somalia story by its name anymore because it had now become a story about a military cover-up.[28] For most of 1996 and 1997, until the Inquiry was abruptly curtailed, Canadians heard mostly of the military's alteration and shredding of documents and computer records. 'The plight of the generals,'[29] a plight involving incompetence and even irresponsibility but not involving racism, had fully replaced the death of Arone and other Somalis. The journalist who reminded his readers that the Somalia Inquiry's central issue should have been a simple one of 'Canadian soldiers abusing Somalis' was a lone voice crying in the wilderness.[30] By the time the Inquiry was shut down in January 1997 (and ordered to issue its report by June of that year) and the last witness, Major Barry Armstrong, had taken the stand, it was too late to investigate the events of 4 and 16 March. A national memory of rogues and unscrupulous men had come fully into its own, and we no longer had to think about 'hidden hatred.'

The progress of the story from acts of racist violence against Somalis to a story about a few bad soldiers and white supremacists, and ultimately about bad leadership, cleared a path for establishing who the real victims were. As a senator commented in reaction to the shutting down of the Inquiry, a cruel joke had been played on the Canadian public.[31] For many, as the Inquiry's deliberations seem to drag on, Canadians became victims of 'our penchant for spare-no-expense navel-gazing and the country's naive, but unshakable belief in the perfectability of mankind.'[32] What was important about us was our own overdeveloped sense of morality. If the final report of the Inquiry failed to shock us, it was only because we were a people endlessly 'ferreting out the sins of those in government,' sins 'more imagined than real.'[33] It was most certainly not because we were a nation unwilling to confront racism. Our relentless focus on cover-up and collusion confirmed an unhealthy national obsession with self-criticism. Journalists sometimes saw the irony of forgetting the original crimes but understood it as a casualty of our national virtue of self-deprecation. As *Toronto Star* columnist Rosie DiManno put it: 'How typically Canadian that we become more animated and reactive, and outraged over the chain of responsibility, or the chain of collusion, or the chain of concealment, than we did over the original crimes and deplorable conduct of Canadian peacekeepers.'[34] It is this aspect of the official story, our mythological virtues as a nation that is somehow too gentle, too bureaucratic, and too given to navel-gazing, that seemed to have enabled us to look at racism in the Somalia Affair and still not really see it. The same pattern of self-congratulatory nationalism was repeated in the Inquiry itself.

Community Responses: The Struggle over the Meaning of Race

The disappearance of race in the Inquiry was not a foregone conclusion, despite the public framing of events as one about leadership and a nation betrayed. Both antiracism and Jewish advocacy groups contested the position that racism had little to do with events in Somalia. As a lawyer for B'nai Brith summed up, 'It should not be necessary to remind the military that you don't kill people because of theft, you don't kill people because they're black and when such killings occur you don't cover them up.'[35] From the moment the Inquiry began, these advocacy groups lobbied commissioners to examine the role that racism played in Somalia. For the two groups representing Jewish Canadians (the Canadian Jewish Congress and B'nai Brith), racism was conceptualized as white-supremacist group or hate-group activity. Antiracism advocacy groups representing Somali Canadians, African Canadians, and people of colour (the Coalition of Somali Canadian Organizations, the African Canadian Legal Clinic, and the Urban Alliance on Race Relations) stressed racism's historical roots in slavery and its contemporary manifestations in immigration policy. They also urged the Inquiry to investigate allegations of multiple incidents of violence against the Somali population. More sympathetic to the views of Jewish advocacy groups (and having more opportunity to hear these views since Jewish groups had been established for a much longer time and therefore had better resources), commissioners accepted interventions that shed light on the activities of white supremacists in the military but declared all other aspects of racism to be too broad to be relevant. At the outset, then, a framework was put in place that limited how the encounter between the people of Belet Huen and Canadian peacekeepers could be understood in terms of its racial dimensions. The focus became hate-group activity and there was little room left for appreciation of the encounter's colonial character and the racial underpinnings of so many peacekeeping operations in the Third World.

There was, of course, much to say about hate-group activity in the military. On 23 January 1993, CBC Radio aired an investigation into the activities of right-wing extremists in the Canadian Armed Forces. The program concluded that white-supremacist groups saw the military as an attractive prospect for two reasons: first, because it afforded an opportunity for weapons training and, second, because it was mostly white and was therefore a potentially fertile ground for recruitment of members. The military had begun to investigate white-supremacist activities within its ranks (Project Siros) in 1991. By the time the program aired, a military report concluded that over sixty-five members of the Armed Forces could be shown to have involvement in white-supremacist organizations. Approximately nineteen of these came from troops stationed at Petawawa, the base of the regiments who went to Somalia. It is not surprising, then, that in preparing to examine issues of racism, the Inquiry should have assembled a series of document books on racism (which were made available to interveners), including military responses to the issues of white supremacy within its ranks.

Policy documents indicated that there had been a casual attitude towards and a tolerance of white-supremacist activity in the Forces. For instance, quite remarkably, although the military concluded that a significant number of the sixty-five men were members of the Ku Klux Klan, many were deemed to be curious followers rather than serious activists.[36] It is not surprising that B'nai Brith and the Canadian Jewish Congress, two advocacy groups with considerable expertise in white-supremacists groups (such groups target both Jews and people of colour), should have considered it critical to intervene in the Somalia Inquiry on the issue of hate group activity. Karen Mock, the then national director for the League for Human Rights of B'nai Brith and a specialist in race-relations training, pointed out that hate groups had 'Nazi ideology at their very core' and Jewish advocacy groups had long made it their business to know as much about their activities as possible.[37] B'nai Brith's first major concern was that the military reflected a culture that tolerated white supremacists and that this tolerance was a highly dangerous practice. As counsel for B'nai Brith carefully explained, 'Not every soldier, and it is not my suggestion, is a potential Nazi or a potential racist, but every hard core adherent to neo-Nazi groups sees themselves as a soldier ...'[38] If neo-Nazis were the problem, then racism became an issue of 'a blessedly small number of individuals and incidents,'[39] primarily a few bad apples who spoiled the entire barrel.

The appropriate antiracist response to the problem of a few bad apples was to screen out racists and ensure that those who 'slipped through the cracks' were not in any way condoned or encouraged through a tolerance for hate speech.[40] Hate speech incited violent practices, Jewish advocacy groups argued, and had to be vigorously condemned.[41] The Somalia Affair revealed a 'negative race relations climate' in the military and an urgent need to consider not only the recruitment and training of soldiers but also the attitudes of senior officers.[42] In particular, B'nai Brith asked the Inquiry to explore the poisoned atmosphere it felt might have prevailed among the troops in Somalia and which might have profoundly affected racial-minority soldiers.[43] With

Matchee and Brown in mind, B'nai Brith's Karen Mock explained to commissioners that soldiers who are feeling vulnerable themselves because of the existence of racism do not see themselves as fitting in and do not easily rely on others.[44]

As warranted and useful as the focus on hate-group activity was, particularly given the Inquiry's aim to examine systemic policies and practices such as recruitment and training and the military's own shocking tolerance for white supremacists, it was not an approach that could shed much light on the actual incidents involving discrimination and harassment against racial-minority soldiers nor on the torture, executions, and everyday acts of brutality against Somalis. For one thing, few self-declared white supremacists were involved in the key incidents and two key participants were of Aboriginal origin, men who were themselves the targets of racism. For another, to look for exceptional and overtly racist acts was to miss the absolute ordinariness and pervasiveness of racist attitudes and practices both in the military generally and among the troops deployed to Somalia. The tension between the extraordinary and the everyday was evident in the Inquiry whenever commissioners tried to grapple with the role that race played.

Commissioners Grappling with Race

The Inquiry began by trying to establish whether the incidents on the hazing video were an indication of widespread racism in the military, or at the very least in the Airborne Regiment. To this end, the Black corporal on the videotape, Christopher Robin, was questioned at length about his experience in the military and at the hazing party, in particular. Disappointing the commissioners and a host of lawyers who questioned him in this regard, Corporal Robin would only repeat that he did not feel that he was the victim of racist treatment. It was clear that things were done to him that were not done to others, but Robin steadfastly refused to indict his fellow soldiers. Ironically, he defended his fellow soldiers by noting that, as a Black child growing up in a white community, he had endured many racial slurs and that he had occasionally heard the same slurs in the military as well.[45] They were perhaps uttered at the initiation, Robin acknowledged, but he viewed it as simply part of the initiation where many unpleasant things were said.[46] Pressed (to acknowledge that racist comments were made during the initiation) by the lawyer representing B'nai Brith, Robin responded earnestly: 'Les choses qui sont dites, Monsieur, à cette organisation-là, ils disaient pas tout ça du fond de leur coeur, il faut que vous comprenez' ('The things that were said, sir, within this organization, were not said with malicious intent, you have to understand').[47]

People were drinking, Robin explained, and said things that they would not otherwise say. There was little the commissioners could conclude from this adamant stance. The very ordinariness of Corporal Robin's experience made it difficult to connect what had happened to him to a few specific white-supremacist individuals.

Looking for evidence of hate-group activity, commissioners and Jewish advocacy groups repeatedly ran into the problem that racist acts were considered harmless and were merely a part of building esprit de corps. Like Corporal Robin who insisted that racist slurs were not intended to harm, the military officers cross-examined by counsel for B'nai Brith and the Canadian Jewish Congress, staunchly maintained that the presence of overt signs and symbols of membership in hate groups did not indicate that there was racist *activity*. For instance, Captain Patrick Koch maintained that, even if an individual soldier was associated with a neo-Nazi movement, he would only be disciplined if he actually incited a riot.[48] Major Anthony Seward considered the displaying of the Confederate flag (a popular white-supremacist symbol) as simply an expression of 'young men trying to find out who they are in life.'[49] Sergeant Major Clarence Jardine astonished commissioners when he declared that he would even tolerate a soldier wearing a swastika because the type of tattoo one wore was a matter of personal choice.[50] If racism consisted of the displaying of such symbols, then the military was clearly not prepared to condemn it. As Commander Paul Jenkins asserted, those who were 'racist in belief' did not pose a security threat.[51] Racist jokes and slurs were also considered harmless. While several officers simply denied ever hearing any racist slurs,[52] Sergeant Major Jardine confidently declared that he himself had indulged in telling racist jokes, passing them on because 'some of them are good.'[53] There appeared to be few regrets about sending soldiers like Matt MacKay, a member of a white supremacist group, to Somalia.[54] An internal military report had even concluded that the video of soldiers making racist remarks about Somalis was simply 'a sort of travelogue meant for families at home.'[55]

When he took the stand, the presence of white supremacists within the military troubled the deputy minister of defence as little as it had the senior officers. If there were racists in the military, Robert Fowler told the Inquiry, it was no more than the percentage of racists in Canadian society as a whole. At any given time, both in the military and in Canadian society, Fowler declared, 'you're going to have a low number of child molesters, wife beaters and murderers as well as racists.'[56] Commander Jenkins went further: there were likely to be fewer racists in the Canadian Forces than in the general population.[57] Unintentionally, Fowler and Jenkins remind us why we cannot attribute what happened in Somalia solely to the presence of and official tolerance for hate-group activity. Reprehensible as the tolerance for such attitudes and practices was, these patterns of behaviour did not appear to occur with any greater frequency in the military than they did in the general population. What went wrong in Somalia had its origins in something much more widespread than the activity of a hate group. What that something was remained difficult to name in a context where racism took on the meaning of overt and extreme displays of white supremacist activities.

On the question of the participation of Matchee and Brown in violence against Somalis, the emphasis on hate-group activity and the notion of a poisoned environment for racial-minority soldiers also bore little fruit. Early on it was suggested that Brown had been linked with racist skinheads, an unsubstantiated suggestion made by Keith Landy of the Canadian Jewish Congress. As Brown's lawyer protested in a written submission, Brown never got a chance to clear his name on this point since the Inquiry was never able to investigate the 16 March incident. Not only was he not involved with such groups, his counsel wrote, but Brown had also once belonged to a group that had promoted racial harmony, and he himself had been the target of racist comments and conduct.[58] Commissioner Letourneau, troubled by the operation of race in the case of Matchee and Brown, put the issue of their participation in racist acts to B'nai Brith:

> The next question is a difficult one, and you may want to speak to it today or you may want to reflect on it. It has to do with racism by people who are themselves members of visible minorities or cultural minorities. My question is: Is there a different dimension to the problem? ... Could there be, for example, a compounding effect in being a member of a visible minority subject to racism and being in a unit where racism is tolerated if not prominent and, as a result, having to live up to the standards of the unit. You would try to show that you are just as capable of racism as anyone else, and perhaps even more, to be part of the group.[59]

In response, Rubin Friedman of B'nai Brith explained: 'In the culture of trying to fit in, it is well known that there are many tests for belonging to a group. If one of the tests is expressing overt hatred to some other targeted group, we know that this is quite often how hate groups work.'[60]

Karen Mock expanded on his argument suggesting that in such a context 'victims themselves become victimizers.'[61] As I argued in chapter 3, Brown and Matchee need not have been compensating for their own powerlessness in order to participate in brutal acts against Somali prisoners. They were simply doing what everyone else did. The disciplining and inferiorizing of Somalis were part of the everyday of peacekeeping. What remained unaccounted for, and indeed unacknowledged altogether in these exchanges about Matchee and Brown's special investments in expressing overt hatred, was the widespread participation of many soldiers in violence and acts of degradation against Somalis, and an even broader acquiescence to these practices among both the troops and the leaders.

Anti-Racism Groups and the Push for a 'Race Inquiry'

Interveners who tried to present a broader view of the meaning of racism found the Commission less receptive to them than they had been to advocacy groups for whom racism was primarily about overt or extreme racist acts. Counsel for the Urban Alliance on Race Relations (a broad-based anti-racist advocacy group), in making his application for standing, began by asserting that the Somalia Affair 'was not about singling out or targeting the military as an institution that is so drastically different than any other Canadian institution.'[62] Racism was a problem in many Canadian institutions, Julian Falconer commented, and it could not be understood 'as simple matters of factual inquiry.' Instead, understanding racism required 'years of close monitoring of social and historical events' and specific expertise in 'race inquiries.'[63] Questioned by commissioners as to the meaning of the term 'race inquiries,' Falconer replied that a race inquiry: 'involves the ferreting-out of racist acts, racially-motivated acts, or acts that are race-related. On a broader systemic level, the race inquiry involves ferreting out systemic racism or institutional racism. Finally, the race inquiry is directed at how to resolve and create anti-racist strategies.'[64] In a race inquiry, he continued, it was important to keep one central principle in mind: racism was not just an issue of overt acts but could manifest 'itself at very different levels.'[65] In the case of the deployment of Canadian troops to Somalia, one had to first 'microscopically analyse the facts, determine if there [was] misconduct of one form or another, including misrepresentations or lying in terms of accounts of events.'[66] If misconduct was found, the next step would be to examine motive. Cautioning the Inquiry that the racial motives behind Arone's death were unknown, Falconer maintained that even though the Inquiry was clearly not a trial, one still had to look into the facts of the deaths and alleged atrocities.[67] At this latter suggestion, the Inquiry's chair, clearly irritated, interrupted Falconer and reminded him, 'I have been listening to you for some time now and giving you some leeway, to some extent.' The hearings, the chair reiterated, were not to discuss the terms of reference of the Inquiry, but to discuss policy.

Later, in its application for intervener status, the Urban Alliance met with further resistance when it requested government funding of an amount that would adequately cover the salaries of its personnel while they participated in the Inquiry. The Urban Alliance saw this as a justified request – its members would bring an expertise about racism and antiracism education to the Inquiry process and because, as a non-profit organization, it could not afford to volunteer its members' time. Commissioner Desbarats implied that this might be a conflict of interest, and that if the Urban Alliance were to be funded, other organizations in similar positions would also be lining up for such funding. Falconer replied to this 'flood gates' argument by pointing out that anyone with something valuable to contribute should be rewarded for their time and knowledge.[68] The Urban Alliance was granted standing but did not receive the amount of funding it needed to cover its costs of participation in the Commission, and did not participate further.

The African Canadian Legal Clinic, a community-based legal agency representing African Canadians, brought before the Inquiry its expertise in 'the identification, analysis and redress of racial discrimination with a focus on, but not limited to, anti-Black racism.'[69] Sharing the view of the Urban Alliance that racism 'is fundamentally at the core of the vast majority of institutional and structural problems in mainstream Canadian society,'[70] the ACLC began its application for standing by noting the immensity of the role of racism in the events in Somalia. The Clinic's brief reminded commissioners of the West's 'collective amnesia' about slavery, an amnesia that enables Western nations 'to continue to portray Africans as inherently inferior; it allows them to speak the language of charity and hand-outs, instead of compensation and reparations, with respect to both Africans and Africans in the New World; it allows Western nations in fact to be racist with an easy conscience.'[71] The Somalia Affair was consistent with Canadian history in that racism and white supremacists were allowed to flourish in the military. The white powder thrown on Corporal Robin during the hazing rites was intended to remind him that he had to submit to white supremacy or face the consequences.

Proposing a historicized and contextualized understanding of the encounter between Canadian troops and Somalis, the ACLC suggested some of the ways in which a critical race analysis might be applied. First, white supremacy was not merely an overt form of racism. Racism also manifested itself culturally as the 'elevation of Western culture over other non-Western cultures, including African cultures.'[72] Racism was evident when Canadian media accused Somalis of being a drain on the welfare system. Both anti-Black racism and cultural racism were evident in the treatment of the Somali people by members of the Canadian Armed Forces. Citing, among other things, the use of racist terms to refer to Somalis, the alleged statement of Colonel Labbé that he would offer a case of champagne to the first person who killed a Somali, the rumour that Sergeant Major Jardine had told other soldiers to point machine guns at Somali citizens, and Lieutenant Colonel Mathieu's orders to shoot between the 'skirts and the flip-flops,' the ACLC concluded that 'racism led to violent and deadly treatment of some Somalis.'[73]

For the ACLC, there was clearly interplay between racism and the use of force. The rules of engagement had to be examined in terms of 'the location in which the mission will take place.'[74] Since Africans were often not understood or respected and were viewed as 'primitive,' 'uncivilized,' or 'underdeveloped,' racism informed how Canadian soldiers made sense of where they were. For example, Somalis obliged to travel long distances for water were automatically classified as unknown individuals engaging in risky activities far from home.[75] Referring to the incident of 17 February 1993 when Canadian soldiers fired directly into a crowd of Somalis who were said to be throwing rocks, the ACLC noted how similar behaviour on the part of the population of the former Yugoslavia did not provoke a parallel aggressive response from Canadian peacekeepers, a point Somali Canadians would also make. Recalling that a disproportionate number of Blacks were shot by police, the ACLC submitted that the same process takes place when soldiers make decisions regarding the use of force. These racist ideologies characterize Black men in particular, as more threatening and violent than white men As discussed in the ACLC's submissions, this ideology was used to justify the excessive use of force against African slaves.[76]

Canadian soldiers possessed non-violent means of de-escalating the threats they faced but did not do so possibly because there were some soldiers 'who arguably *wanted* to injure and kill Somalis.'[77] When protesters and unarmed men were shot, and Arone among others were tortured, the issue was 'a human rights concern, a criminal concern and potentially a war crime concern.'[78] The ACLC's strong position on the role and meaning of racism in the Somalia Affair had little impact on how the Inquiry conducted its proceedings and how it reached its final conclusions, as I discuss below. Notwithstanding the fact that it was prematurely shut down before it could investigate the events of 4 and 16 March, there was little to indicate that racism had any other meaning for commissioners than extreme and overt acts associated with a small group of white supremacists.

From Humanitarians to Conquerors

The community that tried hardest to turn the Inquiry's gaze to the multiple violent events in Somalia was also the newest advocacy group and the one possessing the fewest resources. The Coalition of Somali Canadian Organizations (COSCO) sought standing (and funding) in order to bring to the Inquiry's attention the total number of Somalis killed (six) as well as the Canadian Forces' treatment of the entire community of Belet Huen. For many members of the Coalition, the matter was a straightforward one. As COSCO member Ahmad Hashi put it, Canadian peacekeepers had 'crossed the bridge of being humanitarians to the bridge of being conquerors.'[79] The Coalition wanted to bring evidence of Canadian misconduct during the 17 February incident when soldiers fired at an unarmed crowd. They also had accounts from the people of Belet Huen of the shooting of a Red Cross guard and of Canadian peacekeepers driving through the town shooting at the local population.[80] It was important, COSCO's lawyer Isaac Sechere told the Inquiry, that the truth should come out: 'There are two different versions of these events, two truths if you will. One of them is here, and the other is back in Somalia. How are we going to get to know this?'[81]

In their application for standing, COSCO noted that Arone's family and others were willing to come forward to testify as to the facts as they saw them, a prospect which commissioners seemed to feel amounted to a retrial. Arguing at first that the costs of taking the Inquiry to Somalia would be excessive, the commissioners then had to respond to COSCO's suggestion that testimony could be videotaped. (One of COSCO's members, Abdullahi Godah Barre did in fact go to Belet Huen to videotape witnesses and he made the videotape available to the inquiry.)[82] At the very least, COSCO proposed, the Commission should hear from the key Somali interpreter for the Canadian Armed Forces, and even set up the arrangements for the Commission to interview him by telephone. Little came of these suggestions and COSCO's two central arguments, that race was central to what happened and that adequate compensation ought to be paid to the families, failed to get any consideration.[83]

In COSCO's legal brief and in its oral arguments for standing, Belet Huen became a real place, with specific conflicts and characteristics that had to be explored if the full story of the Somalia Affair were to come to light. Not prepared to investigate the actual events, commissioners were initially open to the idea that COSCO offer expertise on the culture, norms and social practices in Belet Huen. Invited to illustrate this aspect of their contribution, Isaac Sechere began by describing the political make-up and cultural practices of the different clans and rulers in Somalia. The Hawadle of Belet Huen, he suggested, had strong traditions of dispute resolution and compensation. They were renowned throughout Somalia for their peaceful relations with neighbouring clans. The Hawadle had defied General Aidid and his clan and welcomed UN and Canadian peacekeepers. For their trouble, Canadians confiscated Hawadle weapons, leaving them defenceless. Shortly after the Canadians left, Aidid invaded Belet Huen and it took the Hawadle nine months to liberate themselves. The Hawadle, Sechere told the Inquiry, had 'a sense or feeling that they made mistakes in entrusting their lives to foreigners who had come and gone.'[84]

The idea that Canadian peacekeepers, in their ignorance of local politics and custom, had made a greater mess of things than existed before seemed to offend commissioners. Commissioner Desbarats, for example, seemed to bristle at the suggestion that (as he put it) 'the Canadian occupation was a disaster for the people of Belet Huen' and that it left the people of Belet Huen worse off than before. Commissioner Rutherford was also incredulous when Sechere stated that the Coalition's information had come from the elders of Belet Huen, information that challenged the view that there was a state of famine and lawlessness prior to the Canadians' arrival, as Canadian media had reported. Famine and lawlessness prevailed elsewhere in Somalia, COSCO's sources confirmed, but was not so evident in Belet Huen. Questioning Sechere as to his sources of information, Commissioner Rutherford appeared to dismiss the information COSCO had obtained from one of its members who had gone to Somalia to gather information.[85] Commissioners seemed to feel that any Somali source of information was inherently suspect because of clan rivalries. Commissioner Desbarats, for instance, wondered if the Armed Forces had accepted the invitation of a Somali national to brief them on the culture and practices of Belet Huen, if they would have been offered a one-sided view of things.[86] Even on cultural issues, it seemed, COSCO would have had as little to offer as any other Somali. It was not knowledge of this kind with which the Inquiry was principally concerned.

An important feature of COSCO's argument was the linking of the treatment of Somali Canadians to the treatment of the people of Belet Huen,[87] an unwelcome and incomprehensible analytical framework in a context where the spaces of here and there had to be clearly demarcated as politically and culturally different. For example, during the Inquiry, medical officer Major Barry Armstrong testified that it was official practice to dispense with paperwork when a Somali died; since Somalia was without a government and few Somalis had birth certificates, there was little need for death certificates.[88] In Canada, at the same time, the government introduced legislation denying permanent resident status for five years to Convention refugees who did not possess identity documents. This measure, known as the 'documents rule,' principally affected Somalis and Afghanis and prevented them from accessing the full benefits of citizenship, such as the right to pay the local rate for university tuition and the right to student loans.[89] COSCO – already engaged in lobbying on this issue and indeed initially formed to deal with it – would have exposed these kinds of contradictions to the Inquiry, as its application for standing clearly proposed to do. Its brief included information on the documents rule and on COSCO's response to allegations made by a Member of Parliament that the Somali community had engaged in collective social-assistance fraud.

By linking racist laws and practices in Canada to the events in Belet Huen simply by their own existence as a coalition, COSCO undermined the idea that Somalia and Canada were distinct and separate spaces, an argument also proposed by the African Canadian Legal Clinic and the Urban Alliance on Race Relations. This was an anti-racist approach the Commission was unwilling or unable to consider. Without funding, none of the groups representing people of colour could continue to press their arguments and, for the duration of the Inquiry, what had happened to the people of Belet Huen at the hands of Canadian peacekeepers remained largely unconnected to racism in Canada. Race would all but disappear in the Inquiry and culture would take its place. The notion of Somalia as a frustrating, wild, and culturally incomprehensible land of warring tribes would remain in place alongside the idea that Canadian troops were simply defeated by its challenges.

The commissioners read and heard the advocacy communities' submissions and issued a decision on 3 August 1995. The Inquiry would investigate unreported incidents if sufficient evidence confirmed that they had taken place, but the Inquiry would not go to Belet Huen to obtain evidence. With respect to racism, the Inquiry would not investigate racism in the Canadian military as a whole. Instead, it would maintain a focus on the deployment of troops to Somalia and would consider the issue of racism to be one element of a broader question of the extent to which cultural differences affected operations in-the-atre. As the chair explained in his decision, the 'terms cultural differences are broader in scope than the issue of racism or human rights itself. They refer to all these sociological, anthropological, political, economic, intellectual and human characteristics which define a culture and serve to differentiate it from another.'[90] The knowledge that would be required, then, would not come from Africans themselves. Instead it would come from anthropologists and sociologists who could lend scientific credibility to the notion of cultural difference.

It is difficult to talk about racism when the testimonies and knowledge of those most affected by it are excluded or limited from the start. When racism is understood to be overt expressions of hate involving a few pathological individuals, and if it is about flaws in character or training and not about the systemic dehumanization of the Other, then its occurrence is treated as an aberration. The containment of the definition of racism to mean the presence of a few white supremacists or official tolerance of hate speech dislodges another explanation – one about a sustained, historical, and deeply embedded 'hidden hatred' of Black bodies and the material and ideological systems that thrive on it. To open the door for this second explanation, the personhood of racial Others must be the premise. The knowledge that groups representing Africans and other people of colour sought to bring – knowledge of their dehumanization – was not recognized as knowledge but as emotion – bias that might even have originated in clan rivalries. In contrast, the knowledge of scholars of culture – knowledge that nearly always presumes racial Others to be *objects* of study – garnered respect. If in the end we came to know that the Somalia Affair had nothing to do with us, it was a knowledge born out of our own epistemology: who counts and who does not; who can know and who cannot.

II. Race as Culture

The move from race to cultural difference carries with it a profound risk. As Said writes, imperialism has always depended on the view that peoples to be dominated are culturally (rather than biologically) inferior.[91] Difference, as I have shown for other contexts, always smuggles in hierarchy.[92] A difference framework suggests that peoples possess certain cultural characteristics, in the case of Somalis, tendencies towards clannishness, for instance, and in the case of Canadians, an apparently inborn niceness and civility. These cultural characteristics have their basis in national mythology and they emerge out of an underlying racial hierarchy in which Canadians of European origin are positioned as superior to people of colour. When cultural difference became the focus of what needed to be understood about the encounter, it discouraged a more self-critical, historical approach and it limited accountability.

If what went wrong in Somalia could be attributed to the difficulties the West had in understanding Somalis, blame was easily laid at the Somalis' door. Thus it was Somali clan rivalries and complexities, and not the West's tendency to stereotype and oversimplify the Somali situation, or its implication in colonial domination in Somalia and Western racism, that made things go wrong. Canadian troops and leaders, overwhelmed by what surely defied understanding (the clannish tribes and their warlords), could not help but make the mistakes they did. Who could blame them? These risks of talking culture are especially acute when political rhetoric about Somalia, for example American presidential rhetoric, repeatedly drew on an image of savagery, as several scholars have shown.[93] As John Butler has convincingly argued, such political rhetoric drew upon the imperial idea of a people as savage, more than it did on the modern idea of individual leaders as savage, although both ideas were present in political discourses about Somalia. In public narratives, the primary evil in Somalia was Somali culture, an imperial notion that omitted Somalia's colonial and pre-famine history as well as the local impact (in particular the loss of civilian lives) of U.S. efforts to capture General Aidid.[94]

Some of the difficulties that emerge when we begin with difference and not dominance, and with culture rather than racism, were evident in the exchanges between commissioners and Dr Kenneth Menkhaus, an anthropologist and adviser to the United Nations on the politics, history, and culture of Somalia. In his presentation, Menkhaus walked a fine line between pointing out where the Canadian Armed Forces, in their ignorance of Somali society, had possibly gone wrong and conveying his appreciation for the challenges peacekeepers faced in negotiating Somali society. Somali society, Menkhaus began, 'developed in an environment of considerable scarcity and competition for pasture land and wells.'[95] There is a great deal of conflict in such an environment and Somalis rely upon a complex clan structure to navigate their environment. The clan structure serves Somalis well but is 'a source of tremendous frustration for outsiders.'[96] Clans look after the interests of their own members over those of other Somalis, for example. It was thus understandable that clans would divert aid to their own members whenever they got the chance.

Yet, while the society was full of violent conflict, Menkhaus stressed that clans had 'complex and sophisticated systems of conflict management.'[97] It would be a mistake, he suggested, to confuse such conflicts with 'anarchy' and to presume, as the media regularly did, that Somalia was innately given to chaos and fighting. Somali culture had specific rules, was highly democratic (in spite of the exclusion of women from politics), and often had entirely legitimate hostile responses to peacekeepers, which Somalian history made more comprehensible. For instance, although Somalis did not rely on the idea that land was owned, they operated with a notion of clan-based zones or spheres of control. Clans therefore felt it legitimate to demand a toll from outsiders passing through their zone of control, whether or not they were humanitarians, a practice peacekeepers found to be reprehensible. One of the last anti-colonial armed resistance movements, Somalis remained bitter that their peoples were divided up between the colonial powers, splitting clans across different territories. Because they retained their anticolonial orientation, they did not automatically welcome foreigners. Indeed, Menkhaus noted, Somalis by and large did not view the U.N. intervention as a humanitarian one, but as European self-interest and interference into their affairs. It was not surprising, therefore, that they were not overwhelmingly grateful for aid.

Urging commissioners to reject common-place myths that the Somalis have always been a society of warriors and warring tribes (Menkhaus noted that he had felt safe to walk anywhere in Mogadishu in 1988), he offered his analysis that the society had experienced a rapid decline during its civil war.[98] Somalia had descended into 'Mad Max anarchy' and adopted 'a whole economy of plunder.'[99] Pirates, drug smugglers, and Mafiosos took over and many places became 'very, very dangerous.'[100] Food became the main item over which the war was fought, making humanitarian intervention a perilous thing.[101] Alternating between the view that Somalis 'were not just a bunch of maniacs' but people who 'had compelling cultural reasons or social reasons' for what ever they did and the view that anarchy had taken over, Menkhaus was questioned as to whether the Canadians were indeed surrounded by danger and whether they themselves might have had compelling reasons to do what they did. Unable to comment specifically about Belet Huen (which he suggested was more peaceful than many other places), Menkhaus acknowledged the activities of roving bands of teenage militia – youth, he felt, who tested U.N. soldiers on how far the rules of engagement went. Nevertheless, he observed, to adopt too defensive a position became a self-fulfilling prophesy. If every Somali was a potential threat, then it was an easy move from there to violence. In fact, peacekeepers needed the skills of social workers and diplomats, and not the skills of soldiers.[102] Canadians were welcome in Belet Huen, he concluded, but the potential for misunderstanding was great between them and the local population, given internal clan rivalries and Canadian inability to understand and negotiate them.

It was certainly possible to conclude from Kenneth Menkhaus's presentation that Canadians bore some responsibility for their ignorance of Somali society, but ignorance alone does not fully explain why so many troops saw Somalis as thieves and ungrateful liars who needed to be taught a lesson. In the end, it was not only expert opinion on Somali culture that commissioners needed in order to appreciate what had gone wrong but also expert opinions on Canadians. Who were the soldiers and which cultures and histories did they come from? To answer these questions, the Inquiry needed to consider the history of regiments such as the Airborne and the history of race relations in Canada. Criminologist Jean-Paul Brodeur's study on violence and prejudice, prepared for the Inquiry, attempted to fill this gap.

Violence and Racial Prejudice in the Context of Peacekeeping examined how Canadian Armed Forces were exposed to and reacted to 'ethnic and cultural differences as well as the various reactions to this exposure – acceptation [*sic*], positive valuation, xenophobia and racism.'[103] Possessing a background in issues of police brutality, Brodeur did not shy away from naming the important role that racism played in the events that unfolded in Somalia. Addressing racism as an international phenomenon (but concluding strangely that the literature on colonialism was of little help since the encounter was not a colonial one), Brodeur asserted at the outset that racism was often 'misguidedly represented as intolerance towards differences.' Intolerance, he noted, can take very different forms. 'People different from us can be rejected, when they are seen as a threat to our own identity and even to our own being, or they can be forcibly cloned, as it were, when we feel confident enough to assimilate them.' Peacekeepers were vulnerable, he continued, to feeling that the population they had come to protect were not only different and inferior but a threat to their identity. Soldiers easily fell into racism 'because of a false perception that an ethnic community has no institutions at all, when its institutions are simply different from our own.' Significantly, Northern peacekeepers in Third World countries were particularly at risk of falling into racism through such perceptions.[104]

Armed with these premises, Brodeur explored racism in the military and in the Canadian Airborne Regiment and concluded that we could not attribute peacekeeping violence simply to the presence of an 'Airborne mystique' of an elite unit, or to 'manly feelings' present in warriors. For one thing, the Airborne was not really an elite unit, never having served in combat (except once in 1974 in Cyprus). For another, there was plenty of evidence to suggest the prevalence of racist attitudes throughout the unit. Finally, the Airborne had engaged in similar acts of violence as had the Belgians, acts primarily committed against youth and children who were thought to be stealing. Both Belgian and Canadian activities were at first permitted and even encouraged. Only much later were they condemned. All of these factors, Brodeur concluded – combined with little or no training in mediation and negotiation, a tolerance for white supremacists, and little information about Somalis – easily resulted in violent and racist behaviour. The Inquiry, drawn as it was to the view that what happened in Somalia had more to do with a few white supremacists and incompetent leaders and with the challenges of a culturally different and 'lawless land' than with a more generalized phenomenon of racism or colonialism, paid scant attention to *Violence and Racial Prejudice in the Context of Peacekeeping*. Instead, it turned to the research on the Airborne conducted by anthropologist Donna Winslow, a study commissioned by the Inquiry and it is Winslow's work that appears to have had the most influence on the Inquiry's final report.

Racism is excluded from the start in Winslow's study. On the very first page of the acknowledgments, she clarifies that her research examines 'not racism but culture – military culture, and particularly the Canadian Airborne Regiment's culture.'[105] The military and the Regiment are studied as a special 'tribe' in modern society, a distinct subset. In the context of a subculture, it can be argued that the warrior image, so evident in the interviews with fifty men, has no relationship to Canadian society or to its history. The encounter in Somalia is a fresh one, between two culturally distinct entities: military and non-military groups. Framing the story as one of cultural difference neatly transforms the problem in Somalia from violence to cultural misunderstanding. Problems arise because the parties are different, not because they are enacting relations of domination and subordination.

The paradigm of cultural difference limits accountability for violence, racism, sexism, and homophobia in the military. As chapter 2 discussed, military violence and the hypermasculine world of militaries are both naturalized as arising from the conditions of combat, an explanation Winslow accepts. In the special subculture of the military, Winslow tells us, killing has a unique place: 'When military men are telling me that they can be asked to lay their life down for their country, they are also saying that they will be asked to kill for their country.'[106] Men of this subculture see the world as a mean and dangerous place.[107] One can even understand why military men would worry that esprit de corps is damaged when women and minority groups are given special treatment and allowed to enter the military. Winslow writes quoting Jack Granatstein and agreeing with him that the '"single most" serious problem faced by the CF is that the 'politically correct' and safe way of doing things is not the best way to prepare a military that can fight and win wars.'[108] As both B'nai Brith and the African Canadian Legal Clinic argued in their applications for standing, esprit de corps cannot require racism; the military clearly needed to rethink how it understood the interaction of esprit de corps and individual human dignity.[109] Karen Mock of B'nai Brith pointed out to commissioners that esprit de corps 'needs to be enhanced in a way that people know that they can rely on each other.'[110] Neither women nor sexual and racial minorities would experience such trust in racist, sexist, and homophobic environments.

Warrior identities, Winslow writes, are useful things to have in combat, provided of course that they do not become exaggerated.[111] Seen in this light, the disturbing and apparently raced and sexualized hazing rituals are 'anthropologised' as revealing only the classic stages of separation, liminal inversion, and reintegration. The point of such rituals, to build membership in a group whose lives are often in each other's hands, may seem 'incomprehensible to an outsider' who does not fully understand the extreme need to build trust among soldiers.[112] The 'Zulu ritual,' for example, in which a soldier drops his pants and has a length of toilet paper inserted in his buttocks and the paper is then lit on fire, illustrates danger (the soldier has to down a beer and pull the paper out), anal fascination, and homoerotic behaviour. Strangely, it is not seen to reveal racism, even though the soldiers watching must chant 'Zulu' chants. In such rituals, Winslow sees only a 'primitive aesthetic' unconnected to the white settler society in which it occurs.[113]

The cultural difference of the military as a subgroup, their extreme group bonding, helps Winslow to explain why Native Canadians may have felt pressure to be more aggressive than white members of the group, that is, because they had a greater burden of proof to show their belonging, a compensatory line of argument that ignores the aggressive actions of others. Paradoxically, it does not interest Winslow that non-white groups did in fact encounter severe racism in the military. When the Black soldier in the hazing ritual did not complain, and testified repeatedly that the ritual was not racist, Winslow concludes that he simply understood and recognized the inversion and parody for what it was – a rite of belonging. Cultural rites, without their context and histories in a white settler society, cannot then be interrogated for their impact on real Black bodies. We are invited to forget, as the African Canadian Legal Clinic noted, what the sprinkling of white powder on Black bodies has usually meant.[114]

Violence is culturalized by Winslow when she analyses the soldiers' beliefs about Somalis (discussed in chapter 2). These beliefs are accepted as being fixed and are used to lay out why we ought to understand the frustration of such a culturally distinct group as the military. This rationale was certainly in use during the military trials by lawyers defending the soldiers charged with violence, as Winslow reminds us: 'Canadians were particularly frustrated by theft of property. The idea of theft is abhorrent to an Airborne soldier whose training puts emphasis on building trust and teamwork since you may one day have to trust a comrade with your life.'[115] The fact that members of the Airborne were themselves thieves (in separate incidents, Canadian soldiers stole a revolver, a ceremonial sword, and money from Somali households, and approximately $1,400 from their own canteen),[116] and that the thievery of Somalis was the thievery of children and teenagers drawn to the food and water of the camp, passes unnoticed. The cultural difference, innate to the Airborne and by extension to the military, replaces any interrogation of actual behavioural and social relations between dominant and subordinate groups.

It is a short step from cultural difference to naturalized violence, as Winslow's final analysis demonstrates. The violence is ignited, she concludes, when an officer gives an order to abuse Somalis. This order 'caused everything to line up – the frustration from the heat, dust, food, living conditions, insults and stealing by Somalis, and particularly the rebel image and the hyper investment in aggressivity in 2 Commando. This combined with excessive alcohol (and perhaps other drug) consumption resulted in an explosive cocktail.'[117] Ostensibly, if the soldiers 'lost it' in Africa, it is only because, given their own (military) culture, they were pushed too far by the Africans, their own leaders, and the cruelties of the land itself. This relationship between violence and frustration in a military subculture became the central containment strategy for the Inquiry. Winslow, relying on the traditional concepts of her discipline to reframe the violence in Somalia, illustrates a scholarly technology of domination; wrapped in scientific neutrality, the explanation of cultural difference masks oppression and white complicity. It enables the telling of a story of white innocence.[118]

III. Ill-Prepared and Rudderless Soldiers and a Nation Wronged

The inquiry heard from 116 witnesses, examined thousands of documents, conducted its own research studies, and drew on a number of submissions between April 1995 and April 1997, at which point the Liberal government ordered that the hearings be concluded. When it issued its report in July 1997, Canadians were given a detailed catalogue of what had gone wrong. We learned about soldiers whose behavioural suitability for peacekeeping was questionable, about white supremacists whom military screening procedures had failed to catch, about a regiment so poorly prepared that few soldiers knew the rules of engagement concerning the treatment of detainees and the use of force. There was a breakdown in discipline and leadership well before the troops had even left Canada, commissioners concluded, and the stage was set for the full-scale debacle that ensued. Commissioners did not flinch from naming just how badly the mission had failed. They concluded, for example, that the Somalis who were shot in the 4 March incident did not breach the wire as the military had maintained, and that bait had been used to entrap them.[119] The one man reported killed at the Bailey bridge where crowds were fired upon was only one-sixth the number of actual deaths reported; the military's actions of blocking the bridge in the first place might have incited the riot that ensued.[120] A number of beatings of detainees and humiliation of Somali children had occurred.[121] Significantly, Somalis had posed little threat and Belet Huen was a relatively stable environment. Although the commissioners noted the scale of the debacle, in their opinion, the trails clearly led to frustrated soldiers and ultimately to their incompetent, careerist, and immoral leaders as being the reasons why 'the mission went badly.'[122]

Acknowledging that Canadian soldiers had acted badly, including engaging in racially motivated conduct prior to going to Somalia (in the hazing incident, for example) and while on duty there (for instance in the use of racist slurs as shown in one of the videotapes), commissioners were clear that the troops were not to blame for the debacle. Culture and climate accounted for many of their failings. Relying on the arguments made in Winslow's study, their final report describes the frustrated soldier in a unique subculture, a man pushed to the brink by the conditions prevailing in Africa. Peacekeepers were stressed by the incidents of petty thievery, overwrought and demoralized by the lack of good food, infrequent mail, inadequate information, culture shock and, most of all, the unforgiving climate.[123] Such 'pent-up frustration' could only 'boil over' and lead, in the case of the 4 March incident, to 'death by ambush' for unsuspecting Somalis.[124] Poorly prepared, confused about the rules, and knowing little about Somali culture, it was not surprising that the stresses of the mission proved too much for the troops.

If culture and climate played their part, however, blame lay mostly else-where. The frustrated soldier to whom fate had dealt such a harsh blow in Somalia makes his appearance in the opening lines of the Inquiry's report, alongside the real culprits of the Somalia Affair:

> From its earliest moments, the operation went awry. The soldiers, with some notable exceptions, did their best. But ill-prepared and rudderless, they fell invari-ably into the mire that became the Somalia debacle. As a result, a proud legacy was dishonoured. Systems broke down and organizational discipline crumbled. Such systemic or institutional faults cannot be divorced from leadership responsibility, and the leadership errors in the Somalia mission were manifold and fundamental ... Our soldiers searched, often in vain, for leadership and inspiration.[125]

The wrongdoers are military leaders who failed to plan, train, and discipline and who failed to accept responsibility for the breakdown of the systems. The extent of leadership breakdown documented in the Inquiry was unprece-dented and utterly damning, beginning with the cover-up of violent incidents by senior officers almost immediately after they occurred and continuing throughout the Inquiry's deliberations. Commissioners denounce, for example, Colonel Labbé's explanation to the media that the 4 March incident was one involving trained Somali saboteurs.[126] They note that trophy photos were ordered to be destroyed.[127] Documents required by the Inquiry were shredded and key information was withheld or altered, delays that caused the Inquiry to twice ask for extensions. On the witness stand, senior officers often gave testi-mony 'characterized by inconsistency, improbability, implausibility, evasive-ness, selective recollection, half truths, and even plain lies.'[128] The final straw was the government's decision to shut down the Inquiry just when it had moved closer to the 'key centres of responsibility,' the upper ranks in the chain of command.[129]

Terrible silences have remained. As the Inquiry itself noted, had it contin-ued, it would have examined the torture and murder of Arone in detail, including probing into the alleged severe beatings of Somalis immediately prior to 16 March, the mysterious disappearances of Matchee's camera and a document he wrote amounting to a confession, and the circumstances surrounding his alleged suicide. The Inquiry would have looked for patterns between the plans for the 4 March mission and the 16 March mission, which culminated with the arrest of Arone, including the possibility that bait to entrap Somalis was used on both nights. Finally, they would have explored the possibility of a cover-up of the circumstances surrounding both incidents. Had they continued, commissioners concluded, their profound questions would have been these:

> What was the motive for the torture and killing of Arone? How could the values and culture of the Canadian military and its leadership have allowed the atrocities in Somalia to occur and tolerate subsequent attempts to cover them up? Why did so many soldiers look the other way in relation to the incidents of March 4th and March 16th? Why did any ethical sense or sense of compassion for the victims appear to be almost totally absent during the deployment and its aftermath?[130]

How would these questions have been answered, questions posed at the end of the Inquiry rather than at its beginning? They are questions that begin at the epicentre of the violence itself and move outwards in circles of complicity, from those who committed brutal acts, to those who watched, condoned, and covered them up. They require that we understand the Somalia Affair as an encounter with multiple points of violence, an encounter in which ethics, compassion, and respect were pervasively absent. Racism, so narrowly confined in the Inquiry to white supremacists and to acts of hate speech and dislodged by the focus on culture, would have been an important place to start and end. How else could the near total absence of ethics and compassion be understood? But racism, understood more broadly as colonialism or imperialism (that is, not simply the acquisition of lands but also 'impressive ideological formations'[131] that continue on into the present), was the very place that the Inquiry would not go. Why? The answer can be found in our pursuit of redemption.

A Nation Wronged

In *Culture and Imperialism*, Edward Said describes what an imperial attitude looks like today. It begins with the idea that the present state of the Third World, its 'barbarities, tyrannies, and degradations,' originates in its own histories, 'histories that were pretty bad before colonialism and that reverted to that state after colonialism.' Perhaps the West should have 'remained true to its civilizational responsibilities' and kept the subjected races in check. Now having descended into chaos, the Third World is inexplicably ungrateful for Western handouts. Said poignantly observes:

> How easily so much could be compressed into that simple formula of unappreciated magnanimity! Dismissed or forgotten were the ravaged colonial peoples who for centuries endured summary justice, unending economic oppression, distortion of their social and intimate lives, and a recourseless submission that was the function of unchanging European superiority. Only to keep in mind the millions of Africans who were supplied to the slave trade is to acknowledge the unimaginable cost of maintaining that superiority.[132]

Imperial attitudes towards Africans begin with taking ourselves outside of this history. As Canadians we do not see ourselves in imperial history; after all, we say, we did not have African colonies and if we have profited in any way from those histories, we believe that it is only accidentally. We imagine ourselves as coming to the encounter in Belet Huen marked only by our good intentions. If events did not unfold as they should have, it is only because we were unprepared and duped.

To understand the peacekeeping encounter in Somalia as a colonial one, a claim I make throughout this book, we would first have to abandon the idea so crudely expressed in the media, but so deeply internalized by soldiers, leaders and the public, that we were in Somalia as innocent people with a special gift for peacekeeping, a people outside of history. Underpinning this apparently harmless fantasy is an insidious racial hierarchy: Somalis are a primitive peoples, beset by warring tribes, a society that mysteriously descended into chaos; Canadians can bring them gifts of order, democracy, and civilization. We cannot feel respect for a people we have cast as imperial savages. We especially cannot feel respect when we have cast ourselves in comparison as a good people, with good intentions and good traditions, and when our goodness and vulnerability is so evidently the story we want to tell. When the Inquiry concluded of the Somalia Affair that the 'victim will be Canada and its international reputation,'[133] it signalled our national investment in making the battered bodies disappear into this story of goodness.

Practices of empire, Said comments (drawing on Raymond Williams), are supported by structures of feeling, ways in which we come to know ourselves that depend upon, even as they produce, a racially ordered world.[134] Along with references to our national goodness come attitudes that are bound up with an identity that 'imagines itself in a geographically conceived world.'[135] Canadianness as a structure of feeling stands in the way of our pursuit of accountability. It is a way of knowing ourselves that discourages those hard questions about what men from the North are produced historically to feel about Africans and, significantly, about themselves in the world.

The structure of feeling underpinning Canadian national mythology is particularly in evidence in the published recollections of one of the commissioners. The only non-lawyer appointed, journalist Peter Desbarats published his reflections in part as a response to the premature shutting down of the Inquiry by the Canadian government (hence his focus on the cover-up). For Desbarats, who continues the line of argument from the Inquiry, there is no question that the violence in Somalia was the outcome of corrupt leadership, both political and military. If the leaders are corrupt, however, the people are good and innocent and it is this story of national goodness that dominates the pages of his book, *Somalia Cover-Up: A Commissioner's Journal.*

The Canadian national story, as Desbarats tells it, is above all what Mary Louise Pratt has termed an anticonquest story. In *Imperial Eyes*, Pratt writes of the innocence of European naturalists in the age of empire, who saw themselves as unsullied by conquest and imperial rule, men who proclaimed their innocence even as they asserted their hegemony. Self-effacing, and possessing 'an aura not of authority but of innocence and vulnerability,' the anticonquest man acquires his innocence only 'in relation to an assumed guilt of conquest, a guilt that the naturalist tries to escape, and eternally invokes, if only to distance himself from it once again.'[136] Both non-elite and elite constructions of Canadian nationalism are usually deeply inflected with comparisons between Canadian innocence and American guilt.

Canadians, Desbarats begins predictably, are a non-militaristic people whose recent misfortune it has been to learn that we have a corrupt military.[137] Until Somalia, the nation had believed in its honest and virtuous fathers, men like Desbarats's own father who returned as a hero from the Second World War.[138] Of his own generation, Desbarats writes: 'We collaborated with our neighbours to respect property divisions, to help one another, and, on a widening scale, to organise clubs, churches, and local political associations.' But we went too far and built bureaucracies that forgot human values.[139] Nonetheless, we remained a people dedicated to peace, order, and modesty. Unlike Americans who went off to Vietnam, Canadians 'took a perverse delight in welcoming American draft dodgers' and preferred to be 'uncontroversial, unobjectionable, unspectacular, [and] gentlemanly ...'[140] Canadians are not flag-wavers and consider a noisy display of patriotism to be un-Canadian; they are more given, or at least they used to be, to quiet family picnics and modest displays of fireworks.[141] Above all, Canadians are unsure of their national identity, as Americans clearly are not.[142] Such a modest and peaceful people, it goes without saying, were shocked and appalled by the events in Somalia. Desbarats describes the people in the street who commiserate with him when he tells them that he has to immerse himself in the grisly details of Somalia[143] – the veterans who pump his gas and urge him to 'get all those bastards'[144] (the corrupt military leaders) and indeed the entire nation for whom the tale of Somalia became a kind of 'horrifying addiction.'[145]

A Canada so described is mostly populated by noble, hard-working, unassuming white people, who are nonetheless from the elite of Central Canada and not from the working class or from the more peripheral regions of the country. Judge Rutherford, Desbarats' co-commissioner, is one such 'quintessentially Upper Canadian,' a nineteenth-century term for the mainly British-origin settlers in what became the province of Ontario and a term that intentionally reminds us of the Rutherford's rootedness in Canada: 'His great-grandfather was the first settler to reach the Owen Sound area, travelling by Indian trail in the early 1800's from Galt. Judge Rutherford has a cottage there amid other cottages and a farm owned by his close relatives. The Rutherfords of Owen Sound must be something like the Kennedys of Hyannisport on a smaller scale.'[146]

In a masterful act of forgetting, we do not see in this portrait the bloody history of dispossession and colonization. Owen Sound and the entire peninsula on which it is located were the last lands to be seized by white settlers in southern Ontario. The Saugeen (Ojibway) nation found itself starved out and evicted by Judge Rutherford's ancestors to the more desolate lands of Cape Croker.[147] Similarly, we learn of that Judge Gilles Letourneau, his other co-commissioner, comes from 'generations of Quebec farmers and workers' whose roots are 'deeply embedded in the rocky soil of Quebec's south shore.'[148] If Rutherford and Letourneau are 'symbolic of Canada,' Desbarats himself, as the third commissioner, personifies the anticonquest man. With a French name and Scottish ancestors, and only 'haltingly bilingual,' he stands in the middle of 'the eternal Canadian dialogue between the Letourneaus and Rutherfords.'[149]

Of course Canada is not entirely without Black and Aboriginal bodies and these circulate in Desbarats's account like shadows in the national dream, emerging into full form only as 'fetishized bodies juxtaposed against white or superior male minds.'[150] The first of the few Black bodies[151] to trouble Desbarats's white settler landscape is Christopher Robin, the Black corporal of the hazing video, who in his testimony steadfastly refused to incriminate his fellow soldiers and who insisted that things were not as racist as they seemed. Constituting himself as the authority on Robin's experience, albeit a tentative one, Desbarats interprets Robin's silence as the corporal's need to believe that he really was accepted in the white community, an interpretation that adroitly sidesteps all the material consequences facing a Black man who indicates that he believes otherwise. For Desbarats, Robin is only understandable through the figure of the second Black person to appear in the narrative, Mairuth Hodge, a Black woman with whom Desbarats worked twenty-five years ago. Mairuth, like Robin, is described as not believing that there was racism in Canada (and indeed the world), so benign were her experiences growing up Black in Montreal. Mairuth learns the truth from Desbarats and her white colleagues, who teach her not about Canadian racism but about Black power in the United States.[152] As Anne duCille writes of similar textual strategies by white writers, 'the privileged white person inherits a wisdom, an agelessness, perhaps even a racelessness that entitles him or her to the raw materials of another's life and culture, but, of course, not to the Other's condition.'[153]

Black figures slide into one another in Desbarats's narrative and become the landscape on which white knowledge is profiled. The Haitian maid Nella who cleans his hotel room in Ottawa provides Desbarats with a fortuitous experience of peasant wisdom. Depicted as foreign (she has rigid moral standards on single motherhood in comparison to Desbarats's more liberated niece), and underprivileged compared with him (her own niece died of cancer as a child), Nella answers Desbarats's question about the reason for life by looking towards heaven and 'saying something about God knowing.'[154] His conversation with Nella provides only the setting, however, in which we see Desbarats at his computer terminal, pondering the end of the Inquiry at the hands of the Canadian government.[155] Walking the streets of Ottawa, Desbarats notices 'swarthy Lebanese' and 'a black Haligonian in flowing white linens' distributing pamphlets, the latter standing as proof to Desbarats (in his own 'bureaucrat's blue suit') that Canadians maintain a social harmony even with figures who look like 'Lawrence of Arabia.'[156] Black Haligonians, of course, are mostly the descendants of slaves who came to Canada as free servants of American loyalists in the late eighteenth century, well before some of Desbarats' own ancestors, and who today continue to live primarily in Halifax.

Aboriginal bodies inhabit Desbarats's book as embodiments of savagery who highlight white anticonquest innocence. Discussing Matchee who some alleged tried to take his own life, Desbarats notes that Canadians were 'confused' by Matchee's suicide attempt because he reminded us of the high suicide rate of Aboriginal peoples in Canada's prisons. This strange comment seems to suggest either that Aboriginal peoples are prone to taking their own lives when imprisoned or that Aboriginal peoples in Canadian prisons are similar to Matchee who was violent, or both.[157] Aboriginal people next appear when we learn that in sending the Airborne Regiment to Somalia, Canada left itself dangerously unprotected in the event the country was faced with another Oka.[158] In the summer of 1990 the deployment had witnessed an armed confrontation between Aboriginal peoples and the Canadian military over the use of Mohawk burial grounds in Oka, Quebec, for the development of a golf course.[158] There can be little doubt from this storyline who belongs to the nation and who does not.

What such a configuration of bodies enables for the dreamer is an understanding of what happened in Somalia as a 'virus of rebellion' that contaminated an otherwise pristine Northern land. As Desbarats explained,

> I use the term 'virus' to describe the regiment's recurring strain of defiance of authority − a virus of rebellion that seemed immune to treatment and whose immunity grew stronger as it survived a series of challenges. Colonel Morneault preferred to call it a 'cancer' that would remain in remission for months and years before exploding. In the end, it was shown to have the potential to destroy the entire regiment, but no one ever seriously tried to eradicate it.[159]

Like the social construction of AIDS as an African disease that has contaminated North America and Europe,[160] the violence of Canadian peacekeepers in Somalia is not indigenous to the Canadian military or indeed to Canada. The unruly elements in the Airborne Regiment, elements that developed under the hot sun and spread like a cancer, contaminated otherwise professional troops. Innocent Canadians would learn from the Somalia Affair about the virus of rebellion contaminating their land. They would also learn, as anticonquest figures must, that 'we understand almost nothing about the political and tribal complexities of African countries' and 'should not try to resolve them through short-term military interventions.'[161] If we failed in Somalia, it is because of our national naïveté coupled with our historical desire to do good. We did not fail because we were violent or racist, or both. Desbarats's dreams of innocence are national dreams. The dreamer must forget the very violence that has enabled him to know himself.

Desbarats has continued to be haunted by the tragedy of the Somalia Affair, suggesting in an article published in 2000 that in many respects the Somalia Affair was worse than the massacre of Vietnamese civilians by American soldiers at My Lai.[162] At least at My Lai, Desbarats observes, the Americans were in the midst of a bloody war against guerrilla forces and often had trouble distinguishing civilians from guerrillas.[163] Canadians were in Somalia as peacekeepers. The comparison with My Lai is always a shaky one, given the different contexts, but if there is one place in which the two stories come together, it is at the place of race. Both American soldiers and Canadian peacekeepers saw their victims as racially inferior, and both felt immensely threatened and pushed to teach the natives a lesson. It is this impulse and its historical underpinnings that we must question without retreating to the terrain of national mythology. As Peacekeeping Watch (a network formed by the Centre for the Strategic Initiatives of Women, the Women's Caucus for Gender Justice, and the Women's International League for Peace and Freedom) noted about the violence of peacekeepers, what has been least discussed is 'the effect of utilizing troops from former colonial powers in decolonized territories as well as the prevalence of racist attitudes and beliefs among the troops when deployed to communities about which they have little knowledge or understanding.'[164] To discuss such things, we will have to move beyond our dreams of innocence, dreams in which naïveté is what marks us as a people.

Conclusion

'Our children and loved ones,' Canadians of colour have commented in the aftermath of the Somalia Affair, 'are asking questions about their value as persons in this country in view of the atrocious events in Belet Huen.'[165] What would have made colonial relationships and colonial violence visible and provided an answer to citizens of colour? Certainly an acknowledgment of the violence and its origins in racism would have gone a long way to reassuring us that as citizens we are not standing outside the nation. I argued in this chapter that a national dream of innocence precluded an examination of what men from a white settler state thought they were doing in Africa. It is not surprising that law, in the form of inquiries or in its more conventional forms, arranges the tryst that enables the story of innocence to continue on the backs of Black bodies.[166] For law is a party to the original forgetting and is itself (to borrow Stoler's paraphrase of Foucault) 'the consequence of massacres, conquests, and domination.'[167] It was the colonizers who later appointed the law's impartial commissioners and vigilant lawyers[168] to judge what happened in Somalia. The starting premise was one of national innocence: a proud legacy dishonoured; a history of innocence remembered. From this point, we could only interpret the encounter as a fresh moment standing in the time of this dreamed history. To truly challenge such national stories in the law, we need to appreciate how deeply the stories shape the subjectivities of the dominant group.

Somali and other African Canadians offered a possibility of rupturing these dreams of innocence. They linked the spaces of Somalia and the spaces of Canada in their own bodies, and their perspectives contested the view that the clean snows of Petawawa and the hot desert exist, if at all, as discrete spaces. In linking the legacy of slavery, anti-Black racism, and repressive immigration measures to the violence visited on Somali bodies in Belet Huen, they attest to the lack of innocence both here and there. Finally, they remind us that the fight for accountability and democracy has to be 'denationalized' in the sense that its pursuit requires us to move both inside and outside the boundaries of nation.[169] As Canadians, we need to examine our complicity towards Aboriginal Canadians and Canadians of colour as well as towards the citizens of Somalia. This does not mean that we should stay home when genocides are in progress. Rather, it means that we leave behind our national dreams of innocence and practice what Liisa Malkii calls a 'historicized humanism,' one that is not constituted on the simple basis that we go to Africa to save Africans from themselves.[170]

Violence, absorbed into the story of white nation-states watching helplessly or intervening militarily as the Third World succumbs to tribalism (they did it to themselves), has become the narrative of choice. These are the cherished notions not only of Canadians but of the West on the whole. They have been used, for example, in connection with the Rwandan genocide and the massacres in the former Yugoslavia. When a counterstory is released, such as when the International Federation of Human Rights Leagues noted in its report that the genocide in Rwanda was not motivated by ancient tribal hatreds but instead 'was organised by an enlightened elite who studied in our (European) schools and universities,' it becomes quickly absorbed by the larger cultural narrative of innocence.[171] Human rights abuses, abstracted out of context and history, work ideologically and materially to support the dominance of white Western nation-states. To contest the analytical frame that surrounds these abuses, particularly when they are taken up in the law, requires that we begin by unravelling national mythologies. In the Canadian context, the Somalia Inquiry shows how these mythologies deeply shape dominant subjects who, in turn, entrench them further.

It has been difficult to call Northern countries to account for their acts of peacekeeping violence against racialized/Third World peoples. An Italian Commission of Inquiry into Somalia concluded that overall the conduct of Italian troops in Somalia had been good. Several incidents of the brutal rape of girls and children, the beatings of Somalis, and the torture of Aden Abukar Ami through the application of electric shocks to his genitals were confirmed, even though the Commission did not deem it necessary to travel to Somalia for evidence. The Commission found that only rank-and-file soldiers had carried out these abuses and that some lower-ranking officers had sometimes condoned it. At the highest levels, there was only 'an inability to foresee that certain events might occur.'[172] Reprimands and temporary suspensions followed the conclusion of various military courts. The systemic answer, for the Italian Commission, was simply to educate troops on the principles of democracy.[173]

A Belgian inquiry into acts of peacekeeping violence, undertaken by the military itself, concluded that isolated instances of human rights violations had occurred and that there existed a small group of soldiers belonging to a political party holding extreme views.[174] Furthermore, troops needed to be better trained in human rights law and the problem of alcohol abuse needed to be addressed. As in the Italian case, in separate military trials, Belgian peacekeepers were either acquitted or given suspended sentences of a few days.[175] Appeals lodged in the case of the paratrooper who had force-fed a Somali child pork, had tied another to a military vehicle and ordered the vehicle driven off, and had forced a Somali girl to perform a strip show, resulted in twelve-months imprisonment and the payment of a fine.[176]

We can attribute this lack of accountability on the part of Western nations to something as general as a belief in the non-humanity of the peoples of the South. What I have tried to show in this chapter is the minutiae of how such a general proposition unfolds in the law. If the legal inquiries into peacekeeping violence tell us anything at all, it is surely that racial superiority disguises itself in the law as a story about hapless men from the North, obliged to civilize and keep Africans and other Third World peoples in line. Historically, of course, the white man's burden has always required violence.

Postscript

As a nation we remain uneasy about the Somalia Affair, an unease that sometimes swirls around the figure of Matchee. For Marj Matchee, the wife of Matchee, a disturbing question remains. In 1998, denied a disability pension on his behalf because the military concluded that Matchee wounded himself, Matchee's wife publicly questioned 'how a six-foot-four man could hang himself in a seven-foot-high cell and why he had cuts and bruises and a big hole in the back of his head.'[177] Insisting that her husband was always a strong-willed individual who vehemently opposed suicide and who communicated to her through gestures that he did not try to kill himself, Mrs Matchee has spoken of Matchee's pronounced agitation and fearfulness whenever anyone wearing a military uniform enters his room. The possibility that someone tried and succeeded in preventing Matchee from testifying hints that others were involved in peacekeeping violence and had something to gain from his silence. For her part, Mrs Matchee attributes her husband's aggressive behaviour in Somalia to the antimalaria drug mefloquine, a matter she is pursuing in a federal court.

In 2002, a 'pale and gaunt Matchee,' his hair 'flecked with gray,' was led into a Saskatoon courtroom by his mother for a hearing that is held every two years in order to determine whether or not he is fit to stand trial for the murder of Arone. Then thirty-seven years old and unable to walk properly, chew his food, or be left alone, Matchee was once again declared unfit to stand trial. His father still finds it necessary to explain to journalists that his son is truly incapable of standing trial and is not merely hiding behind his illness.[178] Unable to find closure through Matchee, Canadian media wonder regularly whether or not mefloquine might in fact have had the side effect of increasing aggression and impairing judgment of soldiers in Somalia. In one such television program, a soldier, Robert Prouse read from the diary he kept while on peacekeeping duties in Somalia: 'I walk around drunk with a loaded pistol to my head. The cold steel pressure against my temple feels good. I hold a pistol to a child's head in a macabre game, eenie, meanie, miny, moe. His friends laugh at the joke of it, but scatter when I point it at them. It is my mind, not the Somalis, who will destroy me here.' The show's host comments, 'Prouse prevailed. Master Corporal Matchee did not.'[179]

At similar moments of national trauma, such as when an epidemic of domestic violence resulted in the murders of several military spouses by their soldier partners, or when an American pilot accidentally dropped a bomb on Canadian soldiers on peacekeeping duty in Afghanistan, a mefloquine-like explanation emerges. American media speculated that the soldiers who killed their wives were suffering from 'gulf-war syndrome.' Some commentators explored the possibility that the pilot who accidentally killed Canadian soldiers might have been high on amphetamines.[180] What such speculations achieve is a determined looking away from anything systemic. We must look away if we are to preserve our innocence. Our efforts to look away, to remember the Somalia Affair as something we can live with, have been unflagging. But the silences haunt us, even as they make us who we know ourselves to be. Perhaps in this tension lies the hope.

CONCLUSION

Acting Morally in the New World Order: Lessons from Peacekeeping

> They went there because there was a belief that there were humans who needed help and found themselves totally incapable of providing that help and they come back with this new generation of injury called post-traumatic stress syndrome that in fact affects the brain because those moral dilemmas not being solved remain ...
>
> You've got to start wondering about the depth of your belief in the moral values, the ethical values, and your belief in humanity. All humans are humans. There are no humans more human than others. That's it.
>
> General Roméo Dallaire, 'A Good Man in Hell'[1]

> We will lift this dark threat from our country and from the world.
>
> President George W. Bush,
> 'Speech to the 2002 Graduating Class
> at the United States Military Academy'[2]

General Roméo Dallaire's direct and compelling words, pronounced in an interview with Ted Koppel of the American Broadcasting Corporation on the occasion of the general's appearance at the Holocaust Memorial Museum in Washington in 2002, convey the depths of feeling into which we are plunged when we consider the question of acting morally in the New World Order. Ours is an age of genocides and mass murder. Traumatized by his inability to prevent the genocide in Rwanda, and made into a national icon representing our collective frailty and middle-power incapacity to act against the amorphous 'evil' that lives in the Third World, General Dallaire nonetheless insists that we find a way to act morally and help those who need our help. For him there is no question that we could have, and should have, intervened more forcefully and responsibly in Rwanda. He remains angered by the failure of

Western states to intervene militarily and has wondered aloud if the colour of the people being murdered made a difference to how much the West cared.[3]

An equally passionate appeal for humanitarian intervention comes from the former president of Doctors Without Borders: 'Our responsibility as human beings – and as what Albert Camus called "doctor as witness" – was and is to speak out, to witness authentically to the reality of inhumanity and to speak out against the moral hollowness of political inaction.'[4] Against such appeals, a non-intervention position seems automatically immoral. However, the speaker of these words, Dr James Orbinski also makes clear the enormous challenge of sorting out what is humanitarian intervention and what is not. As he and other speakers on CBC Radio's *Ideas* all agreed, 'Humanitarianism by military intervention is a dangerous response and one that can be legitimate only under extremely restricted conditions.'[5] It is the perils of humanitarianism by military intervention that mostly preoccupies us in this world of peacemaking, as we attempt to discover what acting morally means today.

In practice, those advocating war and those advocating humanitarian intervention can sound the same. For example, President's George W. Bush's war cry, his plea for intervention against 'the dark threat,' comes couched in the language of peacekeeping and humanitarian intervention. His speeches are peppered with the oxymoron, 'We fight, as we always fight, for a just peace – a peace that favours human liberty.'[6] Significantly, the argument 'Peace through War' is expressed as a universal and timeless morality in language that is meant to convince us that when we support President Bush, we are acting morally out of a shared belief in the humanity of all peoples, as he implores us to do:

> Moral truth is the same in every culture, in every time, and in every place. Targeting innocent civilians for murder is always and everywhere wrong. (Applause) Brutality against women is always and everywhere wrong. (Applause) There can be no neutrality between justice and cruelty, between the innocent and the guilty. We are in a conflict between good and evil, and America will call evil by its name. (Applause) By confronting evil and lawless regimes, we do not create a problem, we reveal a problem. And we will lead the world in opposing it. (Applause)[7]

It is useful to remember that some of the worst atrocities have been undertaken in the name of human rights. King Leopold of Belgium, whose nineteenth century exploits in Congo contributed to the loss of ten million African lives, was known as a great humanitarian in his day.[8] How, then, do we thread our way through the politics of 'helping those who need help'? How do we gauge what it means to act morally? Most of us on the Left think we know. We believe that we can tell the difference between a war cry and a cry for peace.

The lesson from this study of peacekeeping is that we should not be so complacent, so confident of our ability to tell wrong from right. How do ordinary, caring, thinking people, come to believe in a world of 'dark threats' and white knights, how do we come to support the knight as he sallies forth, even while believing that we are anti-war and come from a deeply peace-loving people? Two interrelated responses are offered here. First, as the preceding chapters show, we are seduced into the modern story of dark threats and white knights through racism. Second, in this moral universe, whole categories of human beings are declared superfluous, as Hannah Arendt remarked of the totalitarian world of the Nazis. As in that world, we in the New World Order are propelled into a similar moral universe where the choices appear stark and limited: either we stop the evil or we do not. In the totalitarian world, either one obeys the law of eliminating unproductive beings – beings Hitler characterized as an 'evil principle'[9] – or one is eliminated. Acting morally within such limited choices becomes irrelevant, useless, or, most of all, undertaken in the belief that large numbers of human beings *are* superfluous. In these final pages, I want to reflect on what we are up against when we try to think outside such moral universes.

I. The Role of Racism in the New World Order

An up-close look at peacekeeping reveals that we are drawn into the showdown between good and evil referred to in George W. Bush's speeches, or in peacekeeping and humanitarian encounters, because they offer us a sense of self and belonging – an identity that is profoundly racially structured. We are being hailed as civilized beings who inhabit ordered democracies, citizens who are called upon to look after, instruct or defend ourselves against, the uncivilized Other. In this fantasy, we enter a moral universe that limits the extent to which we can even begin to think about the humanity of Others; our very participation depends on consigning whole groups of people into the category of those awaiting assistance into modernity. We can even believe, as Roméo Dallaire does, that there are no humans more human than Others, and still understand the world as made up of those needing assistance and those providing it. True on one level, the paradigm of saving the Other nevertheless precludes an examination of how we have contributed to their crises and where our responsibility lies. It is a paradigm that allows us to maintain our own sense of superiority. With its emphasis on pity and compassion, saving the Other can be a position that discourages respect and true belief in the personhood of Others.

If racism is how we enter into the contemporary story of the First World assisting the Third World into modernity, it is surely because it works so handily to secure First World dominance. The argument presented in this book, that contemporary peacekeeping is first and foremost a colonial project, reveals three important things about the alliance between racism and First World dominance. First, Northern peacekeepers imagine themselves as going to the Third World to sort out the tribalisms, ethnic hatreds, and warring tribes that now characterize so much of Africa and Eastern Europe. They go as members of a family of civilized nations, nations that understand themselves to be carrying the traditional white man's burden of instructing and civilizing the natives. In Canada, we understand our own middle-power role as one of bearing witness to the great evil that dwells in the South, an evil that traumatizes and overwhelms us. It is important to note that in the cultural story we tell about our international role, we always go to the South as innocent parties who are not implicated in the terrible histories we confront there.

Second, such narratives have remarkable power. As mythologies they are enacted whenever individual peacekeepers, regardless of their colour or countries of origin, go to Africa intent on a civilizing mission. As George W. Bush directly put it, Western militaries must currently operate as did Eisenhower, MacArthur, Patton, and Bradley, 'as commanders who saved a civilization.'[10] I suggest in this book that there is a strong relationship between masculinity and the making of the nation. Masculinity becomes 'a racial imperative,' as George Mosse observed for the Nazi period in Germany.[11] Men who achieve manhood through a national obligation to instruct less advanced Others perform a hegemonic masculinity in which they imagine themselves to be cowboys in 'Indian country,' surrounded by an 'alien race' that threatens to overwhelm. Violence helps establish who is, in fact, in control.

Third, ordinary citizens enter into these fantasies of racial superiority in small, quotidian ways: through our national mythology, for example, and through a casual belief in the non-humanity of Others. It is not as monsters that we collude in these brutal acts, but as 'nice' people, living in the nicest place on earth, and as compassionate people traumatized by brutality. It is the strangest of ironies that we come to know ourselves as superior, civilized beings through narratives about our special vulnerabilities and talents at keeping the peace. In the media, and through official acts of remembrance, we weave around us fictive worlds in which we are the only civilized beings, a story, it goes without saying, that is dependent on the presence of uncivilized Others. When the violence of peacekeepers erupted, we learned through our media and through a national inquiry that we, and not the Somalis who had been tortured and killed, were the real victims. We were victimized by unscrupulous soldiers and incompetent generals, and our reputation as a peace-loving and peacemaking people was tarnished, perhaps forever. We remember the Somalia Affair as a story about a few bad apples, and uneasily insist that they did not spoil the whole bunch. We were sure that the Somalia Affair had nothing to do with us. On an international scale, as Linda Polman shows, when things go wrong in peacekeeping we seek refuge in the story of an incompetent UN, forgetting that the UN is us, that five states determine if peacekeepers are dispatched, and that the UN's budget is profoundly affected by the refusal of its member states, and in particular the United States, to pay its dues. Perhaps, Polman specu-lates, we believe that the UN has a life of its own because we really want to believe 'a world in which firm but fair blue helmets turn out to eliminate evil.'[12]

There is a particular, bounded, moral universe discernable in these sto-rylines of showdowns between good and evil. Peacekeeping narratives are decontextualized and dehistoricized. They are full of archetypes whose popu-lar rendition we see in movies such as *Lord of the Rings* when the hobbits set out in the company of other civilized peoples to save middle earth (the free world) from the evil of the dark lord Salron. The story of peacekeeping and humanitarian intervention imports race into the very meaning of morality, an epistemological move which David Goldberg and others have suggested is a feature of modernity. Morality requires that we intervene to stop the evil, that we bear witness to it but within this conception of morality, there are autono-mous moral subjects capable of intervening, and Others who, in Goldberg's words, 'should be directed.'[13] Race contaminates morality through infecting the very premise of personhood. Taken to its extreme, racism's role in the project of modernity can mean what it did during the Third Reich: 'Such noble ideals as freedom, equality and tolerance would become reality only if the race were preserved and its enemies defeated.'[14] Concealed in an appar-ently universal framework in which there is good and evil is a small piece of history – the history of imperialism, fascism, and racism.

Contemporary talk of evil merely repeats what Edward Said has described as 'the moral epistemology of imperialism.' In the case of Palestine, to which Said applies the phrase, Britain's justification for determining that Palestine should belong to the Zionists (in the famous 1917 Balfour Declaration) rested on the notion that the desires of the country's 700,000 Arabs were absolutely irrelevant. Located outside modernity, they simply could not be permitted to stall the march of progress.[15] Like the Africans encountered by peacekeepers, the Palestinians have no personhood to disturb the simple frame of who is good and who is evil. The moral universe of imperialism, as in the moral uni-verse of peacekeeping mythologies, is a universe of those who must be saved and those who must do the saving.

It must be acknowledged that moral universes structured by the principle that large groups of people are evacuated from humanity nonetheless vary. It is a long road from discrimination against peoples and the occupation of their lands to mass murder. Race, while certainly not tangential to these moral universes, is not the whole of it. As Mosse explored in his history of European racism, it took a special set of conditions for racism to climax in the Holocaust, chief among them nationalism. Racism began the journey to the Holocaust by giving 'everyone a designated place in the world, defining him as a person and, through a clear distinction between 'good' and 'evil' races, explaining the puzzling modern world in which he lived ... Who could ask for more?' comments Mosse.[16] Providing unity, and annexing itself to every important idea including a marriage to middle-class ideals of respectability, racism required only 'nationalist fury' in Germany to create the world it imagined, and to work in service of totalitarianism.[17] Germans animated by a belief in their national superiority could consider the annihilation of Jews as both moral and necessary for the nation's survival since Jews existed outside the nationalist German's moral universe.

Mosse's insights regarding the alliance between racism and nationalism and their compatible moralities should give us great pause as we consider the rhetoric of an 'axis of evil' and the West's easy categorizing of peoples outside humanity, either through characterizing them as evil (as George W. Bush does) or through understanding them as people awaiting help into modernity (as Roméo Dallaire does). What does racism require to climax today, and have we in the West begun to walk down the path we so readily identify in the Third World, where evil is policy and we become unable to think outside of its narrow confines? An examination of the moral parameters of the totalitarian universe suggests that we have.

II. Superfluous Human Beings and Evil as Policy

Hannah Arendt's well-known formulation of the banality of evil developed in her early work on the nature of totalitarianism[18] was revised when she was confronted with what was both a legal and a moral problem. While covering the trial of Adolf Eichmann (responsible for arranging the deportation of Jews and their transport to concentration camps) in 1961 in Jerusalem, Arendt was struck by the extent to which the law kept looking for Eichmann the monster. What kept confounding everyone, Arendt noted, was the way in which Eichmann was absolutely ordinary, though importantly, no less culpable. Eichmann repeatedly insisted that he had acted morally in following orders. He claimed that he did not hate Jews, that he even admired and respected them. At the trial, psychiatrists said he was normal – although afterwards the diagnosis changed. In a much quoted passage, Arendt describes the problem Eichmann revealed:

The trouble with Eichmann was precisely that so many were like him, and that the many were neither perverted nor sadistic, that they were, and still are, terribly and terrifyingly normal. From the viewpoint of our legal institutions and of our moral standards of judgment, this normality was much more terrifying than all the atrocities put together, for it implied – as had been said at Nuremberg over and over again by the defendants and their counsels – that this new type of criminal who is in actual fact *hostis generis humani*, commits his crimes under circumstances that make it well-nigh impossible for him to know or to feel that he is doing wrong.[19]

To ignore how Eichmann understood his own actions is to miss something crucial about the moral universe of totalitarianism. What, then, did Eichmann's normality consist of? Eichmann was neither simply a cog in a machine, a faceless bureaucrat, nor a virulent anti-Semite. Arendt, Dana Villa writes, was deeply concerned to show that 'extreme wickedness was not necessary to aid in the performance of evil.'[20] Eichmann willingly participated in crimes legalized by the state and commented often during his trial that he had simply obeyed the law. His conscience did not so much tell him what was right and what was wrong as it did what was his duty and what was not, a conflation of morality with legality.[21]

For Arendt, Eichmann was 'thoughtless' and it is this 'thoughtlessness' or inability to make a moral judgment, and his emotional remoteness from the horror, that is conveyed in the phrase 'the banality of evil.' His thoughtlessness lay not so much in his failure to consider Jews as persons but more in his deeply held belief that he was caught in a moment in history in which their annihilation was justified. Taking up Arendt's notion of the banality of evil, Wayne Allen describes the banal mind as one that 'seems to lack calculation beyond the procedure requisite to carrying out certain acts. It has no goal, no future state of affairs beyond the acts assigned to it. It is literally thoughtless and has no long-term objectives in whose light it seeks fulfilment.'[22] Thoughtlessness, however, is not emptiness. As Allen clarifies, Arendt's notion of thoughtlessness is 'the heedless recklessness and hopeless confusion or complacent repetition of "truths," which have become trivial and empty.'[23] It bears much thinking, I believe, to examine the 'truths' that are so often repeated in our context. Here what I have in mind are not only George W. Bush's 'axis of evil' but other far less-dramatic pronouncements about our special middle-power capabilities in the New World Order.

How does an ordinary man commit acts of evil, paying heed to the trivial and empty truths and acting on them? In coming to terms with this question, Arendt can see the self-making practices at work in Nazi structures, the way in which, for example, someone who was once a mediocre travelling salesman gains an opportunity for a grander self through his activities in the SS. Deporting Jews and organizing their transport to extermination camps gave Eichmann an importance in his own eyes that seemed to obscure everything else. It is for this reason that Eichmann does not recall discussions about extermination but remains struck by insignificant details of things that were a novelty to him, for example, the fact that he once went bowling at one of the places where a meeting was held. Arendt is not, however, arguing that a simple relationship exists between Eichmann's powerlessness and his participation in violence. Instead, totalitarianism gave men like Eichmann, as well as many other types of individuals, an entire moral universe in which they could come to know themselves as whole, a universe in which the extermination of Jews was not a moral issue. Men such as Rudolf Hoess, commandant of Auschwitz, regarded the question of why Jews should be exterminated as irrelevant and beyond his obligation to think about. Arendt asks why. At his trial, Eichmann insisted that no one around him, not even the Zionists he often dealt with, objected to anything. Although many would later argue that they were 'inwardly opposed,' few openly rejected the basis of the Nazi regime. The killing of Jews was simply the rule of law. Arendt makes the important point for which she is most remembered: 'Evil in the Third Reich had lost the quality by which most people recognize it – the quality of temptation.'[24] To do evil was to obey the law. The temptation was *not* to murder. Evil in the Third Reich is, in this sense, banal.

In the totalitarian universe revealed in Eichmann's testimony, a world where evil is 'policy,'[25] everyone is invited to come to know himself in the way that Hoess and Eichmann do. Dana Villa notes that for Arendt the 'the unique horror of totalitarianism was that it created a system in which 'all men have become equally superfluous,' equally deprived of their individuality and equally suited to the role of executioner or victim.'[26] To focus on tyrants or megalomaniac leaders, then, is to miss the point. Evil in such a universe cannot be personalized or exceptionalized. It is a world in which there can be no obstacles to the laws of Nature or History, laws that rendered Jews as superfluous and maintained that they were, irrevocably, the architects of their own destruction. Villa summarizes Arendt's initial insight into the nature of totalitarian evil: 'Totalitarian evil is radical or absolute, not because it is a prideful denial of God, but because it seeks to assimilate man to the laws of nature (or nature temporalized as History), expunging his contingent freedom in the name of a determinist ideology.'[27] The totalitarian world is not distinguished by its mass killings of human beings as much as it is by its organized attempt to eradicate the concept of human being altogether, replacing it with the idea of an irrevocable progress towards the eradication of superfluous human beings.

The concentration camps were key to the production of a moral world without human beings. The camps cannot be understood in terms of their instrumentality (they were sometimes not efficient in that they used transport required to win the war) and, for Arendt, it is not their scale on which we ought to focus. Rather, their worst evil was not the killing but the 'creation of a self-imposed universe where human dignity no longer exists.'[28] The camps demonstrate 'that there are no limits to human power, and that there is nothing built-in or permanent about human dignity.'[29] They teach their inmates and others who know of their existence that there is nothing the individual can do in the wake of the powerful natural law of the superiority of the Aryan race and the superfluity of Jews. We would do well to remember at this point, as Villa reminds us, that Arendt presents us with the thesis that totalitarian terror is radically different from other forms of terror. Unlike revolutionary power, which comes to an end when its opponents are destroyed, totalitarian power demands 'an unending supply of innocent victims, but also the thorough dissolution of the relative permanence and stability created and preserved by positive law.'[30] The class of enemies is constantly being revised, the law is revised, there are no boundaries. Everyone must internalize his or her own superfluousness, as the machine of History or Nature rolls on.[31]

The camps make the world into a place where a system is installed that functions according to its logic, where one group of people is dehumanized and the others, the killers, are 'programmed' to kill without thinking. Importantly, dehumanization is done in three steps, red flags already hoisted in our time. First, dehumanization begins with the destruction of the juridical subject: with the relegation of entire categories of people to spaces outside the protection of the law. People outside the law are not criminals and a concentration camp is different from a prison. No rule of law applies to its inmates since they are not juridical subjects. Second, the camps then efface the moral person because anonymous mass death is the only possibility. There is no possible moral course of action. Conscience is inadequate or irrelevant. The choice is between murder, death, or betrayal. Human dignity may have survived in the camp, Villa notes, defending Arendt, but the camps were successful and it is this that Arendt insists that we face.[32] Third, individuality is destroyed when there is no point to free will. For Arendt, Villa writes, the most shocking implication of these three stages of dehumanization was not 'the loss of specific rights, but the loss of a community willing and able to guarantee any rights whatsoever.'[33] The camps represented the destruction of the moral subject. Arendt's conclusions are chilling:

Evil has become banal because its justification (its purpose) lies, or is claimed to lie, outside the actions of men: Nature defined in terms of race, and History determined by economics. Therefore, its source cannot be intentionality but helplessness, *an abject responsibility for having been caught in a certain moment in History.* The instrumentalization of man now assumes a spurious grandeur as doctrines of historical progress conclude by methodizing human thought. Ideologies then set thoughtlessness to motion.[34]

New World Order mythologies and the practices that sustain and are sustained by them can take us in the horrifying direction so carefully mapped by Arendt. It can do so by its production of 'thoughtlessness,' the repetition of simple truths meant to convince us that we are locked into a moment in history when the 'axis of evil' must be defeated at all costs. In a global showdown between good and evil, there is simply not much to consider in terms of what acting morally means, and whose side one is on. The dark threat must simply be lifted by any means and anyone who suggests otherwise is probably protecting Osama bin Laden, as we are led to believe in the rhetoric of the war against terrorism. The world is as simply divided as in Nazi Germany, between those who kill and those who must be killed. Today, too, dehumanization has also begun with the destruction of the juridical subject. Large numbers of people simply stand outside the law (in Guantanamo Bay, in Iraq, in Palestine), spaces where their personhood need not be an issue for consideration. As I write this, execution posts are being constructed in Guantanamo Bay for prisoners not accorded their civil and political rights. Their numbers are growing daily (those who look Muslim, for instance).[35]

Arendt reminds us that we require an arrogance and an insistence on independence of thought to refuse the totalitarian moral universe. If the Holocaust was able to happen because large numbers of Germans found it morally defensible, what enabled them to function in the totalitarian moral universe was the conviction, strengthened at every turn and in law in Nazi Germany, that destiny, the destiny of a superior race and a superior nation, could not be halted. Like Eichmann, we can become caught up in the vision, believing in its legality and understanding our participation in it as a patriotic, moral duty. The pages of such publications as the *New York Times* and the *New York Review of Books* are regularly filled with favourably reviewed recent publications arguing that the invasion of Iraq was a moral imperative, liberal interventionism that is 'about saving minorities from death and persecution, not about spreading revolution.'[36] Invasions, these pages proclaim, are really about answering the call of a higher civilization.

If it took nationalist fervour to enable racism to climax in the Holocaust, we must begin to subject contemporary expressions of it to critical scrutiny. In the West, we have critiqued what we name as ethnic nationalisms and tribalisms elsewhere but we have not examined our own domestic versions of them nor have we often enough shone the spotlight on the wars the West has waged or on its own weapons of mass destruction. Resisting self-scrutiny, we enter the edges of a totalitarian moral universe through the portal of national mythology. In the West, and in Canada specifically, we are interpellated as moral, civilized beings who should help those less fortunate or less advanced than ourselves, people at the mercy of evil dictators. A study of peacekeeping reveals that we understand ourselves as swelling the flood sweeping through the globe, a flood that is our own law of Nature and History. We can even deeply believe in the personhood of racial Others, as Dallaire evidently does, and as Eichmann claimed he did, but still find ourselves caught up in History. Under such circumstances, we will be unable to respect racial Others, understanding them as existing outside the boundaries of morality as beings who are acted upon.

As ordinary people, we succumb to 'thoughtlessness' when we believe that we are mysteriously imbued with values of democracy and peace, more so than anyone else. This is the equivalent to saying, 'We are not like them. They are not like us.' The sentiment has dozens of everyday versions to be found in our media, in general and in intimate dinner table conversations. Included in this list are such claims as there is nothing but madness there, we confront absolute evil when we go there, and so on. We find the beginnings of 'thoughtlessness' in claims that the 'malevolence of the environment' drove peacekeepers to madness in Somalia, that democracy just hasn't taken root in Africa, a problem we have to fix. 'Thoughtlessness' is there when we intervene on these grounds, when we go unprepared, not knowing where countries are on a map yet feeling that we can actually do some good. It is an ignorance and nationalist fantasy of the most dangerous kind.

What national fantasies provide, as it so clearly did with Eichmann, is a ready-made identity.[37] When we consider that we experience something as intimate as our own (gendered) identities through peacekeeping and humanitarian interventions (women can feel themselves to be 'good women' and middle-powers can view themselves as diplomats), then the emotional pull towards 'thoughtlessness' will be intense indeed, as intense as it was for Eichmann. Thinking critically about national mythologies will feel deeply destabilizing. It will feel as though we have lost our sense of self. The body, we should remind ourselves, expresses the colour line in the extreme violence we saw in Somalia and in the instructional impulses white people feel towards people of colour. Colour-line mentality is not simply a mentality but a practice, an ontology and an epistemology achieved through physical engagement with the Other. 'We ignore the sensual aspect of colorlined space at our peril,' warns Anthony Farley in his insightful discussion of race as a form of pleasure.[38] Beatings, torture, the tying up of children under the hot sun: these convince the soldier of *his* proper place providing memories 'of white race-pleasure, of voluptuous white pleasure-in-cruelty.'[39] Even the soldier who has himself been the one to be beaten up as the Other is not immune to race pleasure. He like everyone else, is lured into the fantasy of the colonizer. More than anything, it is the ordinariness of the violence that strikes one about the peacekeeping encounter in Somalia and the way in which the men's sense of self was so intimately bound up with dominance. We should find no violence ordinary.

The claims that I make here about our everyday participation in a moral universe of imperialism will frustrate those seeking a 'quick fix'[40] to the problems of peacekeeping. Should we send peacekeepers of colour, for example? Any peacekeepers who go on their missions imbued with the sense of a civilizing mission will soon find themselves knee-deep in colonial fantasies and will, I argue here, soon resort to the violence that convinces colonizers that they are whole. Perhaps we can simply train our own peacekeepers better, others suggest, imagining as General Dallaire himself does, that courses on mediation, and even courses on anthropology (presumably to be able to tell a Hutu from a Tutsi), will suffice. Mastering an arsenal of practical skills will not be able to compensate for the limitations of soldiers and leaders either unable to see the personhood of Others or unable to see their own implication in their histories. An antiracist training (or at least a more critical and extensive cross-cultural training and 'contextual sensitization'),[41] suggested by Jean-Paul Brodeur, will also encounter obstacles. As Brodeur himself recognized, similar training initiatives with police, for example, often run aground when the police deeply resent and therefore resist any implication that they might be racist.[42] More important, such training initiatives come to nought when there is no institutional commitment to reorganize peacekeeping activities to conform with an anticolonial approach, one that begins with the premise that we are not bearing the white man's burden.

In the face of all these obstacles, it is most tempting to say that we should stay home, a position shared by those who think we should stay home until we are better armed and prepared for war. Staying home at a moment of crisis like the Rwandan genocide, the refusal to supply UN troops to General Dallaire, is, in my view, immoral. At such moments of crisis, we must go, but *how* we go is critical. We can do very little good if we go equipped with nothing beyond information from an encyclopaedia. Equally, we are unlikely to thread our way through the complexities of what must be known if we go convinced that ours is a civilizing mission. The challenge in the long term is to think beyond these moments of acute crisis. To see our choices as starkly as a choice between going and not going is again to remain within the moral universe of imperialism.

A more critical look at how we are implicated in the crises we purport to solve would reveal that there are long-term strategies that we have been loathe to consider, among them foreign aid and a refusal to support practices such as those promoted by the World Bank and the International Monetary Fund that further impoverish the Third World. To take just one small example, before we go to Congo as peacekeepers (a prospect that seems imminent at the time of writing), we should consider, as one letter to the editor noted, that we share the blame of what is happening there. Canadian registered mining companies in Congo are involved in numerous illegal mining operations, Helen Silbiger informed readers of the *Toronto Star*, operations that 'lead to gross violations of human rights and plundering of minerals and other forms of wealth.'[43] Peacekeeping is as mired in these realities as are invasions. Our implication in various contemporary conflicts may be hard to trace; after all, obscuring these details remains a priority for both corporations and governments.

At the very least we know, however, that we cannot take refuge behind the stock phrases about how nice we are.[44] Pressed by audiences anxious to solve peacekeeping once and for all, I have often disappointed in my inability to provide the solution for Rwanda, Bosnia, Somalia, and so on. What I have tried to insist upon in this work is that we develop great vigilance about those attitudes and practices that flow from a universe structured by a civilized North and an uncivilized South and so tightly morally bounded between the lines of citizens and non-persons. I emphasize this vigilance most of all when we believe deeply that all humans are humans.

What has been most striking in public conversations about peacekeeping, as indeed in the Somalia Affair itself, is our relentless collective pursuit of redemption, a sure-fire indicator of the degree to which colonial fantasies and practices are about the making of self. When we hear stories of police brutality or racial profiling, we insist on the madness of those who make such claims. Prominent Canadians find it necessary to write that we are not the worst racists in the world.[45] To whom is this refrain a comfort and who gains a sense of self from it? Certainly it is no comfort to the victims of our brutalities. Similarly with peacekeeping, I have heard often that we are not the worst. While this might be true, we have lent support to the worst.

Perhaps the most disturbing aspect of the fantasy of the white knight is what he does with the suffering of others. In her thought-provoking article comparing Arendt's plea that we not mythologize evil with Charlotte Delbo's passionate cry that we resist domesticating suffering (Delbo was a non-Jewish French member of the resistance who survived Auschwitz), Jennifer L. Geddes reminds us of Delbo's concept of useless knowledge. For Delbo, her extreme suffering at Auschwitz, a place where 'you can watch your mother die and not shed a tear,' is the kind of knowledge that destroys. No good can come of it and those who did not suffer cannot redeem themselves through coming to share in this knowledge. Those who did not suffer cannot know in the same way and will be tempted to sentimentalize suffering. We will be tempted to find something good that can come of it. Even as she writes *Auschwitz and After*,[46] so that we might feel and taste 'the physicality of her suffering,' Delbo, as Geddes points out, insists that 'there is a gap between her experience of extreme suffering and our ability to understand that experience.'[47]

As outsiders, Delbo's writings tell us that we have an obligation to listen to those who have suffered, resisting the temptation to redeem suffering. Whenever we have considered peacekeeping, indeed whenever we have contemplated any intervention into the crises of the Third World, we have generally not listened to those who are suffering. Instead, we have used their suffering to reconstitute ourselves as white knights and as victims, taking ourselves out of their histories. We have indulged in what Susan Sontag describes as 'the pleasure of flinching,' wanting to weep and to collectively remember but not wanting to probe too deeply into the difference between looking on and direct suffering. Collective memory has really been 'collective instruction' in who we are.[48] Let us then look critically at who we are.

Notes

Introduction. 'Savage Wars of Peace'

1 W.E.B. Du Bois, *The Souls of Black Folk* (1903; reprint, New York: Fawcett Publications, 1962), 23.
2 From a new preface written in 1953, ibid., xiii.
3 President George W. Bush, 'Speech to the 2002 Graduating Class at the United States Military Academy' (1 June 2002) West Point, New York. Retrieved from <http://www.ashbrook.org/articles/bush_02-06-01.html>. 23 June 2003.
4 Allan Thompson, 'War Wounds,' *Toronto Star*, 15 December 2001, K1, K2.
5 Rudyard Kipling, 'The White Man's Burden,' *McClure's Magazine* (February 1899), in *Anti-Imperialism in the United States, 1898-1935*, ed. Jim Zwick. <http://www.boondocksnet.com/ai/kipling/kipling.html>. 23 June 2003.
6 CBC, *Sunday Report*, 15 January 1995
7 CTV, *Canada A.M.*, 19 January 1995.
8 Peter Worthington, 'Chaplain Left in DND Chill,' *Toronto Sun*, 9 July 1996, 11; Allan Thompson and Sonia Verma, 'Investigator Linked to Somalia Furor,' *Toronto Star*, 29 August 1999, A1, A6; Allan Thompson, 'Chaplain in Somalia Affair Keeps Job,' *Toronto Star*, 30 August 1999, A1.
9 Commission of Inquiry into the Deployment of Canadian Forces to Somalia, *Information Legacy: A Compendium of Source Material/Commission of Inquiry into the Deployment of Canadian Forces to Somalia. Héritage documentaire: recueil des ressources/ Commission d'enquête sur le déploiement des Forces canadiennes en Somalie* [CD-ROM] (Ottawa: Minister of Public Works and Government Services Canada, 1997), hereafter '*Information Legacy*.' My citations follow *Information Legacy*'s categorization of materials: 'Exhibits and Documents,' 'Hearings Transcripts,' 'Written Submissions,' 'History of the Commission,' 'Research Studies,' 'General Courts Martials,' and 'de Faye Inquiry.' In addition, 'Dishonoured Legacy: The Lessons of the Sama-

lia Affair – Report of the Commission of Inquiry into the Deployment of Canadian Forces to Somalia' is also on the CD-ROM where it is referred to as 'Commission Report,' a format followed in the citations.

General Beno's memo can be found in 'Miscellaneous Breach of Service Regulations,' 14 October 1994. Document No. DND016453, Control No. 001179, Document Book No. 40A, Tab 3, Somalia III: Summary Reports and Related MP Reports, 'Exhibits and Documents,' *Information Legacy.*

10 'BGen Beno Report to Commanding Officer CDN AB REGT, CFB Petawawa, Operation Cordon-Training Direction,' 22 September 1993, Document No. DND000179, Control No. 000104, Document Book No. 13, Tab 20, Pre-deployment General Documents, 'Exhibits and Documents,' *Information Legacy.*

11 Michel Rainville, Interview, 'Somalie-armée canadienne,' *Le Point*, Radio-Canada 7 February 1996.

12 Corporal Purnelle, Interview, 'Somalie-armée canadienne,' *Le Point*, Radio-Canada 7 February 1996; Commissioner Letourneau, Public Hearing Transcripts, vol. 66, 29624 (9 May 1996), 'Hearings Transcripts,' *Information Legacy.*

13 'Miscellaneous Breach of Service Regulations,' 14 October 1994. Document No. DND016453, Control No. 001179, Document Book No. 40A, Tab 3, Somalia III: Summary Reports and Related MP Reports, 'Exhibits and Documents,' *Information Legacy.*

14 Worthington, 'Chaplain Left in DND Chill,' 11.

15 Toni Morrison, 'The Official Story: Dead Man Golfing,' in *Birth of a Nation'hood: Gaze, Script, and Spectacle in the O.J. Simpson Case*, ed. Toni Morrison (New York: Pantheon Books, 1997), xv.

16 Chinua Achebe, 'An Image of Africa: Racism in Conrad's *Heart of Darkness*,' in *Hopes and Impediments: Selected Essays, 1965–1987* (London: Heinemann, 1988), 8.

17 Arundhati Roy, *War Talk* (Cambridge, MA: South End Press, 2003), 83–4.

18 Anthony Farley, 'The Poetics of Colorlined Space,' in *Crossroads, Directions, and a New Critical Race Theory*, ed. Francisco Valdes, Jerome McKristal Culp, and Angela Harris (Philadelphia: Temple University Press, 2002), 99.

19 Edward Said, *Culture and Imperialism.* (New York: Alfred A. Knopf, 1993), xvii.

20 Ibid.

21 Roy, *War Talk*, 109.

22 Anson Rabinbach and Jessica Benjamin, foreword to *Male Fantasies*, Vol. 2, *Male Bodies: Psychoanalyzing the White Terror*, by Klaus Theweleit, trans. Erica Carter and Chris Turner in collaboration with Stephen Conway (Minneapolis: University of Minnesota Press, 1989), xxi; originally published in German as *Mannerphantasien*, Vol. 2, *Mannerkorper: Zur Psychoanalyse des weissen Terror* (Frankfurt am Main: Verlag Roter Stern, 1978).

23 Renato Rosaldo, 'Imperialist Nostalgia,' *Representations* 26 (1989), 107.

24 See Sherene H. Razack, ed., *Race, Space and the Law: Unmapping a White Settler Society* (Toronto: Between the Lines, 2002).

25 Homi Bhabha, 'A Good Judge of Character: Men, Metaphors, and the Common Culture,' in *Race-ing Justice, Engendering Power: Essays on Anita Hill, Clarence Thomas, and the Construction of Social Reality*, ed. Toni Morrison (New York: Pantheon Books, 1992), 233.

26 Roy, *War Talk*, 36. Emphasis in original.

Chapter 1. Those Who 'Witness the Evil'

1 President George W. Bush, State of the Union Address, 29 January 2002. Ashbrook Center for Public Affairs, Ashland University. Retrieved from <http://www.ashbrook.org/articles/bush_02-01-29.html>. 23 June 2003.

2 Gerry Bellett, 'Traumatized Former Peacekeepers Will Be Offered Counselling in B.C,' *Vancouver Sun*, 7 July 2000, B5.

3 William Walker, 'Frum No Longer one of the president's men,' *Toronto Star*, 26 February 2002, A11.

4 Gill Anidjar, introduction to *Acts of Religion*, ed. Jacques Derrida and Gil Anidjar (New York: Routledge, 2002), 3.

5 Richard Slotkin, *Gunfighter Nation: The Myth of the Frontier in Twentieth-Century America* (New York: Atheneum, 1992), 6.

6 Ibid., 3.

7 Michael Ignatieff, *Blood and Belonging: Journeys into the New Nationalism* (Toronto: Penguin, 1993), 2.

8 Ibid.

9 Jan Nederveen Pieterse, 'Sociology of Humanitarian Intervention: Bosnia, Rwanda and Somalia Compared,' in *World Orders in the Making: Humanitarian Intervention and Beyond*, ed. Jan Nederveen Pieterse (New York: St Martin's Press, 1998), 244.

10 Slotkin, *Gunfighter Nation*, 6.

11 See chapter 2 of this book.

12 Inderpal Grewal, 'On the New Global Feminism and the Family of Nations: Dilemmas of Transnational Feminist Practice,' in *Talking Visions: Multicultural Feminism in a Transnational Age*, ed. Ella Shohat (Cambridge: MIT Press, 1998), 502.

13 In a search of the *New York Times* for 2001, no articles were found referring to peacekeepers as traumatized, whereas Canada has consistently featured them.

14 Slotkin, *Gunfighter Nation*, 15.

15 Kali Tal, *Worlds of Hurt: Reading the Literatures of Trauma* (New York: Cambridge University Press, 1996), 6.

16 Renato Rosaldo, 'Imperialist Nostalgia,' *Representations* 26 (Spring 1989), 107–122.

17 Tal, *Worlds of Hurt*, 3.

18 Lauren Berlant, 'The Subject of True Feeling: Pain, Privacy, and Politics,' in *Feminist Consequences: Theory for the New Century*, ed. Elisabeth Bronfen and Misha Kavka (New York: Columbia University Press, 2001), 128.

19 Ibid., 131.

20 Ibid., 132.

21 Ibid., 133.

22 Ibid.

23 Roméo Dallaire, 'Death and Duty: Interview with Roméo Dallaire,' Interview by Brian Stewart, CBC Television, *This Magazine*, 3 July 2000. Retrieved from <www.cbc.ca/news/national/magazine/dallaire/index.html>. 23 June 2003.

24 George Koch, 'The Cross,' *Saturday Night*, September 1996, 64–8, 70, 72, 83, 84.

25 Peter Worthington, 'Editorial: Turning Grief into a Growth Industry,' *Toronto Sun*, 11 May 1999, 17.

26 Jocelyn Coulon, 'Massacre de Casques bleus au Rwanda,' *Le Devoir*, 6 December 1997, A5.

27 *The Unseen Scars: Post Traumatic Stress Disorder*, CBC Television, *This Magazine*, 25 November 1998. Retrieved from <www.tv.cbc.ca/national/pgminfo/ptsd/wounds.html>. 23 June 2003.

28 *Dying to Tell the Story* (Toronto: Turner Original Productions, 1998). First aired on *The Passionate Eye*, CBC Newsworld, 31 January 1999.

29 See Patricia R. Zimmerman, *States of Emergency. Documentaries, Wars, Democracies* (Minneapolis: University of Minnesota Press, 2000).

30 Ibid., 63.

31 Ibid., 64.

32 Indeed, for Dallaire himself, and for some journalists and historians, the trauma narrative became quickly harnessed to cutbacks in military spending. As one military psychiatrist after another attested, Canadian soldiers would not have experienced so much trauma if the military had been better resourced. See Norma Greenaway, '"Bankrupt" Forces Need $2B: Dallaire,' *Ottawa Citizen*, 14 November 2002, A5.

33 Dallaire quoted in Monique Giguere, 'Le général Dallaire ne va pas mieux,' *Le Soleil*, 14 October 2000, A19.

34 Liisa H. Malkii, 'Speechless Emissaries: Refugees, Humanitarianism, and Dehistoricization,' *Cultural Anthropology* 11, no. 3 (1996), 392–3.

35 Ibid., 397.

36 Ibid., 390.

37 Dana Nelson, *National Manhood: Capitalist Citizenship and the Imagined Fraternity of White Men* (Durham, NC: Duke University Press, 1998), 10–11.
38 Mary Louise Pratt, *Imperial Eyes: Travel Writing and Transculturation* (London: Routledge, 1992), 60–1.
39 Malkii, *Speechless Emissaries*, 390.
40 Carol Off, *The Lion, The Fox and The Eagle: A Story of Generals and Justice in Rwanda and Yugoslavia* (Toronto: Random House Canada, 2000), 29.
41 Ibid.
42 Edward Said, *Culture and Imperialism* (New York: Alfred A. Knopf, 1993), 25.
43 Chinua Achebe, 'An Image of Africa: Racism in Conrad's *Heart of Darkness*,' in *Hopes and Impediments: Selected Essays, 1965–1987* (London: Heinemann, 1988), 8.
44 Nelson, *National Manhood*, 10–11.
45 Ibid., 16.
46 'Tabernacle' is the area on an altar where consecrated hosts are kept. The word is used by French Canadians as a curse.
47 Allan Thompson, 'Nightmare of the Generals,' *Toronto Star*, 5 October 1997, A14.
48 Robert Howard, 'Dallaire: U.S. Troops a Liability,' *Hamilton Spectator*, 17 March 2001, D04.
49 Roméo Dallaire, 'Broken Soldier: A Peacekeeper's Nightmare: Interview with Roméo Dallaire.' Interview by Ted Koppel, ABC News, *Nightline*, 7 February 2001. Retrieved from <http://abcnews.go.com/sections/nightline/nightline/transcripts/nl010207_trans.html>. 23 June 2003.
50 Dallaire, 'Death and Duty Interview with Roméo Dallaire.'
51 Finbarr O'Reilly, 'Price of Waging Peace: Roméo Dallaire's Collapse Symbolizes a New Type of Stress Afflicting Soldiers,' *National Post*, 15 July 2000, B1, B5.
52 Gil Courtemanche, *A Sunday at the Pool in Kigali*, trans. Patricia Claxton (Toronto: Alfred A. Knopf, 2003), 12.
53 *The Last Just Man* identifies the UN's refusal to let Dallaire act and the United States' 'gun-shy' responses after the killing of eighteen American soldiers in Somalia as powerful reasons why General Dallaire was unable to stop the genocide and why, as one reviewer of the film put it, he has personally paid the price of their 'vanity.' See, Travis Hoover, review of *The Last Just Man* (Directed by Steven Silver, 2001), *Capsule Review*, 30 April 2002. Retrieved from <http://www.filmfreakcentral.net/hotdocs/hdapr30capsules.htm#just>. 23 June 2003.
54 Brad Evenson, with files from Ron Corbett, 'Broken Dallaire, Haunted by Rwanda, Lies Drunk in Park,' *National Post*, 29 June 2000, A1, A8.
55 Francois Billet, 'Au secours du général Dallaire,' *La Presse*, 9 July 2000, A15.
56 Graham Fraser, 'In Support of Canada's Role on World Stage,' *Toronto Star*, 17 September 2000, A11.
57 Ibid.

58 Anna Hudson, Handout, distributed by Propeller Gallery, Toronto, 11 September 2002. Available on-line from <www.propellerctr.com>.
59 Malkii, *Speechless Emissaries*, 389.
60 Ibid.
61 G. Passey, 'Psychological Consequences of Canadian UN Peace-keeping Duties in Croatia and Bosnia 1992–93' (paper presented at the Fourth European Conference on Traumatic Stress, Paris, France, May 1995). Cited in Lars Mehlum and Lars Weisaeth, 'Predictors of Posttraumatic Stress Reactions in Norwegian UN Peace-keepers 7 years After Service,' *Journal of Traumatic Stress* 15, no. 1 (2002), 17–26.
62 André Marin, 'Systemic Treatment of Canadian Forces Members with Post Trau-matic Stress Disorder,' *Special Report*, 2000. Retrieved from the Government of Canada's National Defence Web site: <http://www.ombudsman.forces.gc.ca/reports/mceachern_e.htm>. 23 June 2003.
63 Ben Shepherd, *A War of Nerves: Soldiers and Psychiatrists in the Twentieth Century* (Cambridge, MA: Harvard University Press, 2001).
64 Marin, 'Systemic Treatment of Canadian Forces ...'
65 Alexander Panetta, 'Soldiers Sue Military over Stress Syndrome,' *Toronto Star*, 27 May 2003, A24.
66 Shepherd, *A War of Nerves*, 397.
67 Linda Polman, *We Did Nothing: Why the Truth Doesn't Always Come Out When the UN Goes In*, trans. Rob Bland (Toronto: Viking, 2003), 8. Originally published in Dutch as *'k Zag twee beren* (Amsterdam: Atlas, 1997).
68 Lars Weisaeth, 'Preventative Intervention' (paper presented at the North American Treaty Organization Conference, 1994). Cited in C.D. Lamerson and E.K. Kello-way, 'Towards a Model of Peacekeeping Stress: Traumatic and Contextual Influ-ences,' *Canadian Psychology/ Psychologie Canadienne* 37, no. 4 (1996): 195.
69 Lars Weisaeth, 'Armed Conflicts,' in *International Responses to Traumatic Stress: Humanitarian, Human Rights, Justice, Peace, and Development Contributions, Collab-orative Actions, and Future Initiatives*, ed. Yael Danieli, Nigel S. Rodley, and Lars Weisaeth (Amityville, NY: Baywood Publishing, 1996), 269–70.
70 Brett T. Litz, 'The Psychological Demands of Peacekeeping for Military Person-nel,' *Clinical Quarterly* 6, no. 1 (Winter 1996), 275. Article available on-line from The National Center for Post-Traumatic Stress Disorder Web site: <http://www.ncptsd.org/publications/cq/v6/n1/litz.html>.
71 Krista Foss, 'Military on Guard for Signs of Stress as Soldiers Return,' *Globe and Mail*, 31 July 2002, A5; David Wood, 'Suspect Showed Signs of Gulf War Syn-drome,' *Toronto Star*, 25 October 2002, A6.
72 Litz, 'The Psychological Demands of Peacekeeping for Military Personnel.'
73 Mehlum and Weisaeth, 'Predictors of Posttraumatic Stress ...' 24.
74 Tracy Xavia Karner, 'Engendering Violent Men: Oral Histories of Military Mas-

culinity,' in *Masculinities and Violence*, ed. Lee H. Bowker (London: Sage, 1998), 200.

75 Toni Morrison, *Birth of a Nation'hood: Gaze, Script, and Spectacle in the O.J. Simpson Case*, ed. Toni Morrison and Claudia Brodsky Lacour (New York: Pantheon Books, 1997), xxvi.

76 Brett T. Litz, Lynda A. King, Daniel W. King, Susan Orsillo, and Matthew J. Friedman, 'Warriors as Peacekeepers: Features of the Somalia Experience and PTSD,' *Journal of Consulting and Clinical Psychology* 65, no. 6 (1997), 1001–10. Article available on-line from the National Center for Post-Traumatic Stress Disorder Web site: <http://www.ncptsd.org/topics/active_duty_military.html>.

77 Ibid., 1006. Emphasis added.

78 Ibid.

79 Ibid., 1002.

80 Geoffrey Hayes, 'Canada as a Middle Power: The Case of Peacekeeping,' in *Niche Diplomacy: Middle Powers after the Cold War*, ed. Andrew Cooper (New York: St Martin's Press, 1997), 73.

81 Ibid.

82 Donald Gordon, 'Canada as Peacekeeper,' in *Canada's Role as a Middle Power: Papers Given at the Third Annual Banff Conference on World Development*, ed. J. King Gordon (Toronto: Canadian Institute of International Affairs, 1965), 51.

83 Ibid.

84 Alfred Legault, in collaboration with Manon Tessier, *Canada and Peacekeeping: Three Major Debates* (Clementsport, NS: Canadian Peacekeeping Press, 1999), 67.

85 Gordon, *Canada as Peacekeeper*, 54.

86 Ibid., 58.

87 Roy MacLaren, *Canadians on the Nile, 1882–1898* (Vancouver: University of British Columbia Press, 1978), 159.

88 J.L. Granatstein and David J. Bercuson, *War and Peacekeeping: From South Africa to the Gulf – Canada's Limited Wars* (Toronto: Key Porter Books, 1991), 1.

89 Ibid., 2–3.

90 Ibid., 201.

91 Ibid., 220.

92 Ibid., 232.

93 Ibid.

94 Gregory Wirick, 'Canada, Peacekeeping and the United Nations,' in *Canada among Nations, 1992–1993: A New World Order*, ed. Fen Osler Hampson and Christopher Maule (Ottawa: Carleton University Press, 1992), 94.

95 Ibid., 95.

96 Granatstein and Bercuson, *War and Peacekeeping*, 224, 231.

97 Ibid., 225.

 98 Ibid., 234.
 99 Quoted in Kathleen Kenna, 'Canucks "Ultimate Boy Scouts" – and Other U.S. Theories: 500 Academics in U.S. Puzzle Over Elusive Canadian,' *Toronto Star*, 18 November 1999, A14.
100 Ibid.
101 Sherene H. Razack, 'Simple Logic': Race, the Identity Documents Rule and the Story of a Nation Besieged and Betrayed,' in *Journal of Law and Social Policy* 15 (2000), 181–209.
102 Carl Berger, 'The True North Strong and Free,' in *Nationalism in Canada*, ed. P. Russell (Toronto: McGraw-Hill, 1966).
103 Quoted in Stanley Fogel, 'Decolonizing Canadian Literature: The Deconstructive Paradigm,' in *Unequal Partners: A Comparative Analysis of Relations between Austria and the Federal Republic of Germany and between Canada and the United States*, ed. Harald von Riekhoff and Hanspeter Neuhold (Boulder, CO: Westview Press, 1993), 235.
104 Pierre Martin and Michel Fortmann, 'Canadian Public Opinion and Peacekeeping in a Turbulent World,' *International Journal* 50 (1995), 370–99.
105 Andrew Cohen, *While Canada Slept. How We Lost Our Place in the World* (Toronto: McClelland and Stewart, 2003).
106 Keith Krause, 'Canadian Defence and Security Policy in a Changing Global Context,' *Canadian Defence Quarterly/Revue Canadien de Defense* 23, no. 4 (1994), 11.
107 Ibid., 11–12.
108 Dan G. Loomis, *The Somalia Affair: Reflections on Peacemaking and Peacekeeping*, rev. ed. (Ottawa: DGL Publications, 1997).
109 Ibid., xxiv.
110 Ibid., 390.
111 Martin and Fortmann, 'Canadian Public Opinion,' 391.
112 Ibid., 389.
113 Michael Ignatieff, 'A Bungling UN Undermines Itself,' *New York Times* OP-ED, 15 May 2000, A25; Michael Ignatieff, *Virtual War: Kosovo and Beyond* (New York: Henry Holt, 2000), 213.
114 J.L. Granatstein, 'What's Wrong With Peace-keeping?' in *Canada and the New World Order: Facing the Millennium* (Toronto: Irwin, 2000), 45–54.
115 Gail Bederman, *Manliness and Civilization: A Cultural History of Gender and Race in the United States, 1880–1917* (Chicago: University of Chicago Press, 1995).
116 Nelson, *National Manhood*, 63.
117 David Savran, *Taking It Like a Man: White Masculinity, Masochism, and Contemporary American Culture* (Princeton, NJ: Princeton University Press, 1998), 240.
118 President George W. Bush, quoted in Savran, *Taking It Like a Man*, 241.

119 Noam Chomsky, *Rogue States: The Rule of Force in World Affairs* (Cambridge, MA: South End Press, 2000), 11.

120 Edward Mortimer, 'Under What Circumstances Should the U.N. Intervene Militarily in a "Domestic" Crisis?' in *Peacemaking and Peacekeeping for the New Century*, ed. Olawa A. Otunnu and Michael W. Doyle (Lanham, MD: Rowman and Littlefield, 1998), 117.

121 Cited in Noam Chomsky, *The New Military Humanism: Lessons from Kosovo* (Vancouver: New Star Books, 1999), 62.

122 Denise Ferreira Da Silva, 'Towards a Critique of the Socio-Logos of Justice: The Analytics of Raciality and the Production of Universality,' *Social Identities* 7, no. 3 (2001), 421–54. See also Linda Martin Alcoff, 'Philosophy and Racial Identity,' *Radical Philosophy* 75 (1996), 5–14.

123 Marc Milner, 'Defence Policy for a New Century: Report of the University of New Brunswick Workshop on the Defence Review,' *Canadian Defence Quarterly* 23, no. 4 (1994), 18.

124 Ibid.

125 Ingrid Lehmann, 'Peacekeeping, Public Perceptions and the Need for Consent,' *Canadian Defence Quarterly* 25, no. 2 (1995), 17–19.

126 Jocelyn Coulon, *Soldiers of Diplomacy: The United Nations, Peacekeeping, and the New World Order* (Toronto: University of Toronto Press, 1998), x.

127 Kofi Annan, *The Causes of Conflict and the Promotion of Durable Peace and Sustainable Development in Africa; Report of the Secretary-General* (April 1998), paragraph 10. Retrieved from <www.un.org/ecosocdev/geninfo/afrec/sgreport/report.html>. 23 June 2003.

128 Ibid.

129 Ibid.

130 Ibid.

131 Wirick, 'Canada, Peacekeeping and the United Nations,' 104.

132 Paul Johnson, 'The United Nations Should Foster Self-Government in Africa,' in *Interventionism*, ed. Paul A. Winters (San Diego: Greenhaven Press, 1995), 88.

133 Ibid., 92–3.

134 Ibid., 94.

135 Ibid., 89.

136 Barbara Crossette, 'The World Expected Peace. It Found a New Brutality,' *New York Times*, 24 January 1999, sec. 4, 1, 16.

137 Ibid., 16.

138 Ignatieff, 'A Bungling UN Undermines Itself,' A25.

139 Ibid.

140 Walter Clark, 'Failed Visions and Uncertain Mandates in Somalia,' in *Learning*

from Somalia: The Lessons of Armed Humanitarian Intervention, ed. Walter Clarke and Jeffery Herbst (Boulder, CO: Westview Press, 1997), 17.

141 Ibid.,16.

142 Ibid., 4.

143 Jarat Chopra, 'Introducing Peace-Maintenance,' in *The Politics of Peace-Maintenance*, ed. Jarat Chopra (London: Lynne Rienner Publishers, 1998) 1–18.

144 Jonathan Goodhand and David Hulme, 'From Wars to Complex Political Emergencies: Understanding Conflict and Peace-building in the New World Disorder,' in *Third World Quarterly* 20, no, 1 (1999): 14, 15.

145 Ibid., 17.

146 Phillipe Guillot, 'France, Peacekeeping and Humanitarian Intervention,' *International Peacekeeping* 1, no. 1 (1994): 30–43.

147 Gerard Prunier, 'The Experience of European Armies in Operation Restore Hope,' in *Learning from Somalia*, ed. Clarke and Herbst, 135–47.

148 Marie-Claude Smouts, 'The Political Aspects of Peace-Keeping Operations,' in *United Nations Peacekeeping Operations: A Guide to French Policies*, ed. Brigitte Stern, trans. David Boyle (Paris: United Nations University, 1998), 7–39.

149 Guillot, 'France, Peacekeeping and Humanitarian Intervention,' 40.

150 Paolo Tripodi, 'Mogadishu versus the World,' in *The Colonial Legacy in Somalia, Rome and Mogadishu: From Colonial Administration to Operation Restore Hope* (New York: St Martin's Press, 1999), 164.

151 Chopra, 'Introducing Peace-Maintenanced,' 9–10.

152 François Debrix, *Re-Envisioning Peacekeeping: The United Nations and the Mobilization of Ideology* (Minneapolis: University of Minnesota Press, 1999).

153 Ibid., 216.

154 Ibid., 217.

155 Ibid., 8.

156 Ibid., 8–9.

157 Ibid., 97–8.

158 Pieterse, *World Orders*, 236.

159 Ibid., 237.

160 Ibid.

161 Ibid., 256.

162 Mel McNulty, 'France's Role in Rwanda and External Military Intervention: A Double Discrediting,' *International Peacekeeping* 4, no. 3 (1997): 24–44.

163 Mahmood Mamdani, *When Victims Become Killers: Colonialism, Nativism, and the Genocide in Rwanda* (Princeton, N.J: Princeton University Press, 2001), 10.

164 Off, *The Lion, the Fox and the Eagle*, 30.

165 Mark Steyn, 'What the Afghans Need Is Colonizing,' *National Post*, 9 October 2001, A1, A10.

166 Pepe Escobar, 'Commentary The New Imperialism,' *Asia Times*, 6 November 2001. Retrieved from <http://www.atimes.com/c-asia/ck06aG01.html>. 23 June 2003.

167 Razack, 'Simple Logic.'

168 Slotkin, *Gunfighter Nation*, 4.

169 Ibid., 5.

170 Mamdani, *When Victims Become Killers*.

171 Said, *Culture and Imperialism*, xi.

Chapter 2. Men from the 'Clean Snows of Petawawa'

1 Peter Desbarats, *Somalia Cover-Up: A Commissioner's Journal* (Toronto: McClelland and Stewart, 1997), 63.

2 Christopher R. Browning, *Ordinary Men: Reserve Police Battalion 101 and the Final Solution in Poland* (New York: HarperCollins, 1992), 160.

3 Details in the diary of Robert Prouse. *The Somalia Affair*, directed by Christine Nielson (Toronto: Barna-Alper Productions, 2002).

4 Associated Press, '3 U.N. Soldiers Die in Somali Ambush,' *New York Times*, 3 July 1993, A3.

5 Donatella Lorch, 'Marines Begin Somali Shooting Inquiry,' *New York Times International*, 5 March 1993, A6, and 7 April 1993, A6.

6 David Pugliese, 'Military Scandals Plagues Italy, Belgium,' *Halifax Daily News*, 23 June 1997, 18.

7 The Italian Inquiry was referred to as the 'Gallo Commission Report' in the English media because it was headed by former Constitutional Court Judge Ettore Gallo.

8 Commissione Governativa d'Inchiesta, *Relazione Conclusiva sui fatti di Somalia* (Rome: Ministro della Difesa, 8 August 1997), 9. See also, 'Torture in Somalia condonnato Ercole,' *La Republica*, 13 April 2000. Retrieved from <http://www.republica.it/online/cronaca/somalia/ercole/ercole.html>. 23 June 2003.

9 Giovanni Porzio, 'Somalia. Gli italiani torturavano i prigionieri: ecco le prove,' *L'Ecomancia*, 6 June 1997. Reproduced in *Panorama* magazine. Retrieved from <http://www.ecomancina.com/somalia1.html>. 23 June 2003.

10 Rene Pollett, 'Italy Reopens Somalia Inquiry,' *Globe and Mail*, 29 August 1997, A1.

11 Amnesty International Report, 'Belgium: (January–December 1997,' 2. Retrieved from <http://www.amnesty.org/ailib/aireport/ar98/eur14.htm>. 23 June 2003.

12 Allan Thompson, 'Army Chief Is Recalled for Drinking in Kosovo,' *Toronto Star*, 2 October 1999, A1.

13 Canadian Forces, Haiti – Board of Inquiry into Leadership Relationships with the

Military Police and Events Surrounding Mistreatment of Haitian Detainees.' *Final Report* (Ottawa: Department of National Defence, April 1999).

14 Anthony DePalma, 'Canada Accuses 47 of Misconduct in Bosnia,' *New York Times*, 18 January 1997, A6.

15 Steven Erlanger, 'The Ugliest American,' *New York Times Magazine*, 2 April 2000, 52–6.

16 Matthew Fisher, 'Our Troops Aren't Out of Control,' *Toronto Sun*, 22 January 1996, 11.

17 African Rights, 'Somalia: Human Rights Abuses by the United Nations Forces,' (July 1993), 32. Retrieved from <http://www.unimondo.org/AfricanRights/html/reports.html>. 23 June 2003.

18 Ibid., 52.

19 Marco Gregoretti, 'Primo Inchiesta,' *Panorama* Magazine. Retrieved from <http://www22.mondadori.com/panorama/numeri/pan2497/mag/primo_inchiesta.html>. 23 June 2003.

20 I borrow the term 'soldier males' from Klaus Theweleit's study, *Male Fantasies*, vol. 2, *Male Bodies: Psychoanalyzing the White Terror*, trans. Erica Carter and Chris Turner, with Stephen Conway (Minneapolis: University of Minnesota Press, 1987).

21 Tracy Xavia Karner, 'Engendering Violent Men: Oral Histories of Military Masculinity,' in *Masculinities and Violence*, ed. L.H. Booker (London: Sage, 1998), 228.

22 Ibid., 224–5.

23 Sandra Whitworth, 'The Ugly Unasked Questions about Somalia,' *Canadian Military*, 14 February 1997, A21.

24 For comments on the use of literature to understand law, see Shoshana Felman, 'Forms of Judicial Blindness, or the Evidence of What Cannot Be Seen,' *Critical Inquiry* 23 (1997), 738–88.

25 Hugh Ridley, *Images of Imperial Rule* (New York: St Martin's Press, 1983), 4.

26 Ibid., 4–5.

27 Ibid., 9.

28 Ibid., 71, 104.

29 Abouall Farmanfarmalian suggests that the United States engaged in the Gulf War to reaffirm its manhood, a 'desire to restore a lost potency to a nation that, despite its massive and well-advertised prowess, was saturated in public humiliation.' ('Did You Measure Up? The Role of Race and Sexuality in the Gulf War,' in *Collateral Damage: The New World Order at Home and Abroad*, ed. Cynthia Peters [Boston: South End Press, 1992], 126). I would like to argue that Canadians viewed Somalia as providing a similar opportunity to restore lost potency.

30 Ridley, *Images of Imperial Rule*, 141.

31 Ibid.

32 Ibid., 141–57.
33 See Sherene Razack, introduction to *Race, Space, and the Law: Unmapping a White Settler Society*, ed. Sherene Razack (Toronto: Between the Lines, 2002).
34 Anson Rabinach and Jessica Benjamin, foreword to *Male Fantasies*, vol. 2, xviii–xix.
35 Theweleit *Male Fantasies*, vol. 2, 76.
36 Rabinach and Benjamin, foreword, xvii.
37 Theweleit, *Male Fantasies*, vol. 2, 7.
38 Rabinach and Benjamin, foreword, xx.
39 Theweleit, *Male Fantasies*, vol. 2, 241.
40 Ibid., 301–5.
41 Rasinach and Benjamin, foreword, xviii–xix.
42 Theweleit, *Male Fantasies*, vol. 2, 75.
43 Ibid., 81.
44 Ibid., 82.
45 Joanne Nagel, 'Masculinity and Nationalism: Gender and Sexuality in the Making of Nations,' *Ethnic and Racial Studies* 21, no. 2 (1998): 247.
46 Dana Nelson, *National Manhood: Capitalist Citizenship and the Imagined Fraternity of White Men* (Durham, NC: Duke University Press, 1998), 88.
47 Nagel, 'Masculinity and Nationalism,' 247.
48 Ibid., 257–8.
49 Ibid., 258–9.
50 Jonathan Rutherford, *Forever England: Reflections on Masculinity and Empire* (London: Lawrence and Wishart, 1997), 12–13.
51 Graham Dawson, 'The Blond Bedouin,' in *Manful Assertions: Masculinities in Britain since 1800*, ed. Michael Roper and John Tosh (New York: Routledge, 1991), 119.
52 Rutherford, *Forever England*, 13.
53 Ibid.
54 John Nauright, 'Colonial Manhood and Imperial Race Virility: British Responses to Post–Boer War Colonial Rugby Tours,' in *Making Men: Rugby and Masculine Identity*, ed. John Nauright and Timothy J.L. Chandler (London: Frank Cass, 1996), 126.
55 James W. Messerschmidt, 'Men Victimizing Men: The Case of Lynching, 1865–1900,' in *Masculinities and Violence*, ed. Lee H. Bowker (London: Sage, 1998), 148.
56 Ibid.
57 Euan Hague, 'Rape, Power and Masculinity: The Construction of Gender and National Identities in the War in Bosnia-Herzegovina,' in *Gender and Catastrophe*, ed. Ronit Lentin (London: Zed Books, 1997), 55–7. Emphasis added.
58 Ibid., 57.

59 Steve Niva, 'Tough and Tender: New World Order Masculinity and the Gulf War,' in *The 'Man' Question in International Relations*, ed. Marysia Zalewski and Jane Parpart (Boulder, CO: Westview Press, 1998), 111.

60 James William Gibson, *Warrior Dreams: Violence and Manhood in Post-Vietnam America* (Toronto: HarperCollins Canada, 1994).

61 Ibid., 12.

62 Ibid., 48.

63 Ibid., 39.

64 Ibid., 71.

65 Jesse Daniels, *White Lies: Race, Class, Gender, and Sexuality in White Supremacist Discourse* (New York: Routledge, 1997).

66 Ibid., 54.

67 Ibid.

68 Mark Bowden, *Black Hawk Down: A Story of Modern War* (New York: Penguin Books, 2000).

69 Ibid., 3.

70 Ibid., 4–9.

71 Ibid., 6.

72 Ibid., 10.

73 Ibid., 33.

74 Ibid., 51.

75 Anonymous soldier quoted in Donna Winslow, *The Canadian Airborne Regiment in Somalia: A Socio-Cultural Inquiry*. A Study Prepared for the Commission of Inquiry into the Deployment of Canadian Forces to Somalia (Ottawa: Minister of Public Works and Government Services, 1997), 231.

76 Commission of Inquiry into the Deployment of Canadian Forces to Somalia, 'Dishonoured Legacy: Report of the Commission of Inquiry into the Deployment of Canadian Forces to Somalia,' vol. 1, 198. Hereafter referred to as 'Commission Report.'

77 See Mary Louise Pratt, *Imperial Eyes: Travel Writing and Transculturation* (London: Routledge, 1992).

78 Theweleit, *Male Fantasies*, vol. 2, 404.

79 'Commission Report,' vol. 3, 735.

80 Ibid., 756.

81 Canadian Broadcasting Corporation, *Peace and Conflict* (63 min. video), in *Canada: Growth and Change Series* (Scarborough: Prentice-Hall Ginn Canada, 1996).

82 Jean-Paul Brodeur, *Violence and Racial Prejudice in the Context of Peacekeeping*, 86, in 'Research Studies,' *Information Legacy*.

83 'Commission Report,' vol. 3, 757.

84 Ibid., 895.

85 The local militia had already left the area and the Armed Forces were completely unopposed. *Dishonoured Legacy*, vol. 1, 233.

86 For a discussion of degenerate groups occupying anachronistic space and time see Anne McClintock, *Imperial Leather: Race, Gender, and Sexuality in the Colonial Context* (London: Routledge, 1996), 40–2.

87 Desbarats, *Somalia Cover-Up*, 2.

88 Catherine Besteman, 'Representing Violence and "Othering" Somalia,' *Cultural Anthropology* 11, no. 1 (1996), 121.

89 Ibid., 120.

90 Ibid., 122.

91 Ibid., 127.

92 Ibid., 130.

93 Canadian Armed Forces in Somalia staffed the local police station; established a local judicial system; trained local teachers, nurses, and doctors; repaired wells and destroyed ammunition, mines, and explosives; and distributed medical aid and supplies. *Dishonoured Legacy*, vol. 1, 277.

94 Colonel Serge Labbé, quoted in 'Commission Report,' vol. 1, 275.

95 Quoted in Winslow, *The Canadian Airborne Regiment in Somalia*, 237–8.

96 Ibid., 33.

97 Messerschmidt, 'Men Victimizing Men,' 131.

98 The psychology department at Queen's University undertook a study of attitudes towards diversity and equity among the Canadian Armed Forces and found that its members were only slightly less accepting of diversity and equality than was the Canadian population in general. The study was commissioned and funded by the Canadian Forces Diversity Office. See John W. Berry and Rudolf Kalin, 'Diversity and Equity in the Canadian Forces.' (paper presented at the Second Biennial Equal opportunity Research Symposium, Defense Equal Opportunity Management Institute, Patrick Air Force Base, Melbourne, Florida, 2–4 December 1997).

99 Messerschmidt, 'Men Victimizing Men,' 31.

100 'Commission Report,' vol. 1, 27.

101 *Dishonoured Legacy*, vol. 2, 527–539.

102 Theweleit, *Male Fantasies*, vol. 2, 319.

103 Rutherford, *Forever England*, 27–30.

104 Richard C. Trexler, *Sex and Conquest: Gendered Violence, Political Order, and the European Conquest of the Americas* (Cambridge: Polity Press, 1995), 17.

105 Ibid., 18–19.

106 Metropolitan Desk, 'Excerpts from Final Arguments in Officers' Trial,' *New York Times*, 3 June 1999, B6.

107 Nagel, 'Masculinity and Nationalism,' 258.

108 Three Canadian soldiers allegedly tried to sodomize with a beer bottle a young fellow soldier. Les Whittington, 'Three Soldiers Accused of Hazing,' *Toronto Star*, 15 July 2000, A6.

109 John Colebourn, 'Disturbing New Troop Photos Found,' *Toronto Star*, 10 October 1996, A13.

110 Theweleit, *Male Fantasies*, vol. 2, 233.

111 Patricia Vettel-Becker, 'Destruction and Delight: World War II Combat Photography and the Aesthetic Inscription of Masculine Identity,' *Men and Masculinities* 5, no. 1 (2002), 87.

112 Ibid.

113 'Commission Report,' vol. 4, 896.

114 Quoted in Winslow, *The Canadian Airborne Regiment in Somalia*, 137.

115 Ibid., 189.

116 *Dishonoured Legacy*, vol. 1, 232. See also Captain Purnelle's testimony in 'Commission Report,' vol. 2, 619.

117 *Dishonoured Legacy*, vol. 1, 233–5.

118 'Commission Report,' vol. 3, 896.

119 Quoted in Winslow, *The Canadian Airborne Regiment in Somalia*, 230.

120 Ibid., 247.

121 Ibid., 251.

122 'Commission Report,' vol. 5, 1069.

123 Quoted in Winslow, *The Canadian Airborne Regiment in Somalia*, 255.

124 African Rights, 'Somalia: Human rights Abuses by the United Nations Forces,' 29.

125 'Commission Report,' vol. 1, 288.

126 For example, in an interview with Master Warrant Officer Bernier, on 22 June 1993, Major Vanderveer discussed the problem of looting, noting that 'initially ... there'd be one to two [intrusion or intrusion attempts] a day, until we got the wire beefed up and then it reduced to maybe I think about three or four a week. It just sort of gradually decrease[d] as we got more and more defensive stores out.' See Major Vanderveer, 'Transcript of Audiotape of Major Vanderveer's Interview held at CFB Petawawa, Ontario 22 June 1993,' Doc. No. DND295930, Control No. 901367, Document Book No.48S, Tab 03, March 04 Incident, Evidence Logs 69–71, 'Exhibits and Documents,' *Information Legacy*.

127 Note that the commissioners never comment on the language of this order. vol. 1, 295.

128 Lieutenant Colonel Mathieu, Public Hearing Transcripts, vol. 169, 34836 (20 February 1997), 'Hearings Transcripts,' *Information Legacy*.

129 Testimony of Corporal Noonan, Public Hearing Transcripts, vol. 121, 24303 (29 October 1996), 'Hearings Transcripts,' *Information Legacy*.

130 Lieutenant Colonel-Mathieu, Public Hearing Transcripts, vol. 169, 34824
(20 February 1997), 'Hearing Transcripts,' *Information Legacy*.

131 Ibid., vol. 169, 34838 and 34880.

132 Ibid., vol. 169, 34883.

133 Ibid., vol. 169, 34908.

134 Ibid.

135 Lieutenan Colonel Mathieu, Public Hearing Transcripts, vol. 170, 35057
(21 February 1997), 'Hearings Transcripts,' *Information Legacy*.

136 'Transcript of audiotape or Lieutenant Colonel Mathieu's interview held at Belet
Huen, Somalia, May 8, 1993,' Doc. No. DND 295602, Control No. 002022,
Document Book No. 48AA, Tab 01, March 4 Incident, Evidence Log 92,
'Exhibits and Documents,' *Information Legacy*.

137 Lieutenant Colonel Mathieu, Public Hearing Transcripts, vol. 170, 34999
(21 February 1997), 'Hearing Transcripts,' *Information Legacy*.

138 Ibid., vol. 170, 35031.

139 Ibid., vol. 170, 35006.

140 Ibid., Lieutenant Colonel Mathieu, Public Hearing Transcripts, vol. 171, 35352
(24 February 1997), 'Hearings Transcripts,' *Information Legacy*.

141 Testimony of Captain P.W. Hope, General Court Martial of Lieutenant Colonel
Mathieu, Transcripts, vol. 1, 97 (2 June 1994), 'General Courts Martials,' *Information Legacy*.

142 Ibid., vol. 1, 98.

143 Testimony of R.D. Mackay, General Court Martial of Lieutenant Colonel
Mathieu, vol. 1, 151 (2 June 1994), 'General Courts Martials,' *Information
Legacy*.

144 Testimony of Major C. Magee, General Court Martial of Lieutenant Colonel
Mathieu, Transcripts, vol. 2, 288–9 (3 June 1994), 'General Courts Martials,'
Information Legacy.

145 Ibid., vol. 2, 303 (6 June 1994).

146 Testimony of Lieutenant A.A. Larrett, General Court Martial of Lieutenant
Colonel-Mathieu, Transcipts, vol. 2, 364 (6 June 1994), and Testimony of Major
B. Vanderveer, General Court Martial of Lieutenant Colonel Mathieu, Transcipts, vol. 4, 665–70 (5 February 1996), 'General Courts Martials,' *Information
Legacy*.

147 Lieutenant Colonel Mathieu, Public Hearing Transcripts, vol. 170, 34931
(21 February 1997), 'Hearing Transcripts,' *Information Legacy*.

148 Ibid., vol. 170, 34933 (21 February 1997), 'Hearing Transcripts,' *Information
Legacy*.

149 Lieutenant Colonel Mathieu, Public Hearing Transcripts, vol. 168, 34663
(19 February 1997), 'Hearings Transcripts,' *Information Legacy*.

150 Prosecutor Major C.E. Thomas, General Court Martial of J.M. Rainville, Tran-
    scripts, vol. 7, 1374 (1 October 1994), 'Hearings Transcripts,' *Information Legacy.*
151 Canadian Press, 'Captain West Unpublished for Brutality,' *Toronto Star,* 28 Feb-
    ruary 1996, A5.
152 Lieutenant Colonel-Mathieu, Public Hearing Transcripts, vol. 168, p 34655
    (19 February 1997), 'Hearing Transcripts,' *Information Legacy.*
153 Ibid., vol. 163, 34614.
154 Ibid., vol. 168, 34645.
155 'Commission Report,' vol. 3, 735.
156 *Dishonoured Legacy,* vol. 1, 296.
157 *Dishonoured Legacy,* vol. 4, 1093. Indeed, the Inquiry did not believe the story
    that the two men had breached the wire of the compound. Olad Abdulle Moha-
    mud, one of the Somalis interviewed about the incident, tells of his first encoun-
    ter on 4 March with Hamdare, the survivor of the shooting. Mohamud, himself a
    patient in the hospital, claims that when Hamdare was admitted to the hospital,
    he told Mohamud of how they had been shot, his companion killed, and both
    their bodies dragged back and forth over the barbed-wire fence to make it look as
    though they had crossed it. Mohamud says that Hamdare's body was covered in
    numerous deep cuts. Hamdare retells this account in his own words as well.
    Muhumed Warsarne Elmi, one of the first relatives to be alerted to Aruush's
    death – in addition to speaking to the character of Aruush and that Aruush left
    behind a wife and two infant children – tells of how he (Elmi) went to the site of
    the shooting, and counted the steps from the fence to the first signs of blood
    where Aruush was shot. It was 150 steps away from the perimeter. The second
    stains of blood were very near to the first. Regarding the fence, he claims, 'The
    other day, when were bringing back witnesses, we found that they (Canadians)
    moved their own fence to a further place which covered those spots. They moved
    it further than the spot where he was when the first gunshot hit him and where
    his blood trail was located.' All quotations from Transcript of First videotape
    made in Belet Huen, Somalia, 1 July 1995. Control No. 901212, DND343877,
    Vol. 46, Tab 02.
158 Estimates of what constitutes 'close range' vary. Corporal Dostie, who had been in
    the watch tower on 4 March, said it was about five to ten feet. Corporal Dostie
    also used the phrase 'at point blank range.' Corporal Roch Leclerc (also in the
    watch tower) told Corporal Chabot after the shooting that he was 'close,' and
    Chabot interpreted this as anywhere between ten and twenty-five meters. 'Com-
    mission Reports,' vol. 5, The March 4th Incident.
159 'On 1 June 93, during a non-cautioned interview with the military police, MCpl
    Countway admitted that he had shot Mr. Aruush on the ground while in a "push
    up" posture. This admission fundamentally contradicted the previous claim that

Mr. Aruush was hit by an initial series of rounds, got up, fled and was fatally shot while fleeing. MCpl Countway's revised version tends to support Major Armstrong's belief that Mr Aruush was shot, went down, and was "dispatched" while on the ground.' Written Submission on Behalf of Major Buonamici, Section 3 The 4 Mar 93 Shooting, point 19. *Information Legacy.*

160 Abdi Hamdare, Transcript of First videotape made in Belet Huen, Somalia, 1 July 1995. Control No. 901212, DND 343877, Vol. 46, Tab. 02.

161 Ibid.

162 Sergeant Thomas Riley Ashman, 'Voluntary Statement of Sergeant Ashman,' 28 April 1993, Doc. No. DND294287, Control No. 000761, Document Book No. 48F, Tab 04, March 04 Incident, Evidence Logs 24–37, 'Exhibits and Documents,' *Information Legacy.*

163 Major Russell R. Brown, 'Voluntary Statement of Major Russell Brown,' 26 April 1993, Doc. No. DND 294261, Control No. 000762, Document Book No. 48E, Tab 11, March 04 Incident, Evidence Logs 8–23, 'Exhibits and Documents,' *Information Legacy.*

164 Personal notes of Master Corporal Butler, 5 March 1993, Doc. No. DND294256, Control No. 000763, Document Book No. 48E, Tab 09, March 04 Incident, Evidence Logs 8–23, 'Exhibits and Documents,' *Information Legacy.*

165 Ibid.

166 Peter Worthington and Kyle Brown, *Scapegoat: How the Army Betrayed Kyle Brown* (Toronto: Seal Books, 1997), 103.

167 Master Corporal Leclerc, 'Transcript of Audiotape of Master Corporeal Leclerc held at CFB Valcartier on 14 May 1993,' Doc. No. DND019865, Control No. 002017, 'Exhibits and Documents,' *Information Legacy.*

168 Testimony of Captain J.M. Rainville, General Court Martial of Captain J.M. Rainville, Transcripts, vol. 6, 1045 (26 September 1994), 'Hearings Transcripts,' *Information Legacy.*

169 *Dishonoured Legacy*, vol. 1, 297.

170 Theweleit, *Male Fantasies*, vol. 2, 274.

171 Captain J.M. Rainville, Public Hearing Transcripts, vol. 145, 39524 (15 January 1997). 'Hearing Transcripts,' *Information Legacy.*

172 Testimony of Captain J.M. Rainville, General Court Martial of Captain J.M. Rainville, Transcripts vol. 6, 1169 (26 September 1994), 'General Courts Martials,' *Information Legacy.*

173 Ibid., vol. 6, 1120.

174 Ibid., vol. 6, 1161.

175 Ibid., vol. 6, 1117.

176 Captain J.M. Rainville, Public Hearing Transcripts, vol. 146, 29837–9 (16 January 1997), 'Hearings Transcripts,' *Information Legacy.*

177 Captain J.M. Rainville, Public Hearing Transcripts, vol. 145, 29520 (15 January 1997), 'Hearings Transcripts,' *Information Legacy*.

178 Ibid., vol. 145, 29472.

179 Mr James Shields, Public Hearing Transcripts, vol. 146, 29751 (16 January 1997), 'Hearings Transcripts,' *Information Legacy*.

180 Testimony of Captain J.M. Rainville, General Court Martial of Captain J.M. Rainville, Transcripts vol. 6, 1165 (26 September 1994), 'General Courts Martials,' *Information Legacy*.

181 Captain J.M. Rainville, Public Hearing Transcripts, vol. 146, 29624 (16 January 1997), 'General Courts Martials,' *Information Legacy*.

182 Ibid., vol. 146, 29836.

183 Ibid., vol. 145, 29852 (15 January 1997).

184 Defence lawyer, Ronald P. Picard, General Court Martial of Captain J.M. Rainville, Transcripts vol. 6, 1216 (27 September 1994), 'General Courts Martials,' *Information Legacy*.

185 'Letter from Armstrong to Mrs. Armstrong 03/13/93,' Doc. No. DND296317, Control No. 901295, Document Book No. 48AB, Tab 05, March 04 Incident, Evidence Logs 93–97, 'Exhibits and Documents,' *Information Legacy*.

186 Captain J.M. Rainville, Public Hearing Transcripts, vol. 146, 29582 (14 January 1997), 'Hearing Transcripts,' *Information Legacy*.

187 Ibid., vol. 145, 29582 (15 January 1997).

188 Major Barry Armstrong, 'Voluntary Statement of Major Armstrong, 25 April 1993,' Doc. No.289336, Control No. 000760, Document Book No. 48B, Tab 23, March 04 Incident, 'Exhibits and Documents,' *Information Legacy*.

189 Anthony Wilson-Smith, 'Maclean's Honor Roll 1997: Barry and Jennifer Armstrong,' *Maclean's*, 22 December 1997, 50–1.

190 Lieutenant Colonel Mathieu, Public Hearing Transcripts, vol. 170, 35078 (21 February 1997), 'Hearings Transcripts,' *Information Legacy*.

191 Transcript of audiotape of Lieutenant Colonel Mathieu's interview, held at Belet Huen, Somalia, 5 May 1993, Doc. No. DND020081, Control No. 002021, 'Exhibits and Documents,' *Information Legacy*.

192 Ibid.

193 Ibid.

194 Ibid.

195 Ibid.

196 Ibid.

197 Lieutenant Colonel Mathieu, Public Hearing Transcripts, vol. 171, 35205 (24 February 1997), 'Hearings Transcripts,' *Information Legacy*.

198 Written Submission on behalf of Major Buonamici to the Commission of Inquiry into the Deployment of Canadian Forces to Somalia; Section 4: Delayed Military Police Investigation, point #10, 'Written Submissions,' *Information Legacy*.

199 Ibid., points #48 and #49.
200 'Major Buonamici to DG Secur,' 24 April 1993, Doc. No. DND020770, Control No.002177, Document Book No. 48AF, Tab 05, In-Theatre March 04, Other Related Documents, 'Exhibits and Documents,' *Information Legacy*.
201 'Briefing note for the Assistant Deputy Minister (Personnel) to appraise Adm of the results of a meeting held Nov. 17, 1994 between the Commandant, NDMC, and Major Barry Armstrong,' Doc. No. DND415499, Control No. 001712, Document Book No. 60G, Tab 01A, In-Theatre and Post-Deployment Briefing Notes, 'Exhibits and Documents,' *Information Legacy*.
202 Officier Defenseur Lieutenant Colonel D. Couture, General Court Martial of Lieutenant Colonel Mathieu, Transcipts, vol. 5, 937 (21 June 1994), 'General Courts Martials,' *Information Legacy*.
203 Quoted in Winslow, *The Canadian Airborne Regiment in Somalia*, 49.
204 Theweleit, *Male Fantasies*, vol. 2, 40.
205 Ibid., 42.
206 Anthony Paul Farley, 'The Black Body as Fetish Object,' *Oregon Law Review* 76 (1997), 472.
207 Laura Robinson has written of the masculinity of hockey players who find it necessary to degrade women and children, the latter being new or younger hockey recruits. See Laura Robinson, *Crossing the Line: Violence and Sexual Assault in Canada's National Sport* (Toronto: McClelland and Stewart, 1998), 65–97.
208 Theweleit, *Male Fantasies*, vol. 2, 207–8.
209 *Dishonoured Legacy*, vol. 2, 661.
210 'GCM Pte Brown Sitrep #28 – 281700 28 February 1994,' Doc. No. DND015521, Control No. 000801, Document Book No. 47, Tab A28, In-Theatre General Courts Martial Sitreps, 'Exhibits and Documents,' *Information Legacy*.
211 Sargeant Gresty, 'Transcription of military interview with MWO Dowd,' June 8/9, 1993, Doc. No. DND315683, Control No. 901114, Document Book No. 38N, Tab 02E, In-Theatre and Post-Deployment March 16 Incident: Evidence Logs 178–9, 'Exhibits and Documents,' *Information Legacy*.
212 Theweleit, *Male Bodies*, 303.
213 Browning, *Ordinary Men*, 189.
214 Jean-Paul Sartre, preface to The *Wretched of the Earth* by Frantz Fanon (New York: Grove Press, 1963), 14.

Chapter 3. 'Outwhiting the White Guys?'

  1 Abouall Farmanfarmalian, 'Did You Measure Up? The Role of Race and Sexuality in the Gulf War,' in *Collateral Damage: The New World Order at Home and Abroad*, ed. C. Peters (Boston: South End Press, 1992), 135.

2 Stephen Bindman, 'Graphic Photos Key Evidence in Court Martial,' *Ottawa Citizen*, 6 November 1994, A4.
3 Defence counsel Mr Patrick F.D. McCann, General Court Martial of Private E.K. Brown, Transcripts, vol. 9, p 1772 (7 March 1994), 'General Courts Martials,' in Commission of Inquiry into the Deployment of Canadian Forces to Somalia, *Information Legacy: A Compendium of Source Material/Commisison of Inquiry into the Deployment of Canadian Forces to Somalia* (Ottawa: Minister of Public Works and Government Services Canada, 1997). Hereafter referred to as *Information Legacy*.
4 Anthony Chen, 'Lives at the Center of the Periphery, Lives at the Periphery of the Center: Chinese American Masculinities and Bargaining with Hegemony,' *Gender and Society* 13, no. 5 (1999), 586.
5 Erving Goffman quoted in Chen, 'Lives at the Center of the Periphery ... ,' 587.
6 Frantz Fanon, *The Wretched of the Earth* (New York: Grove Press, 1963), 41.
7 Testimony of Brigadier General Beno, 'Board of Inquiry Canadian Airborne Regiment Battle Group,' Transcripts, vol. 4, 1033–40 (22 May 1993), 'de Faye Inquiry,' *Information Legacy*.
8 Testimony of Major Anthony Seward, General Court Martial of Major Anthony Seward, Transcripts, vol. 4, 639 (25 May 1994), 'General Courts Martials,' *Information Legacy*.
9 Ibid.
10 Ibid., vol. 4, 646.
11 Ibid., vol. 4, 697.
12 Ibid., vol. 4, 673.
13 Ibid., vol. 4, 674.
14 Ibid., vol. 4, 676.
15 Prosecutor Lieutenant Colonel J.S.T. Pitzul, General Court Martial of Major Anthony Seward, Transcripts, vol. 4, 752. (26 May, 1994), 'General Courts Martials,' *Information Legacy*.
16 Testimony of Sergeant J.K. Hillier, General Court Martial Private E.K. Brown, Transcripts, vol. 4, 791 (18 February 1994), 'General Courts Martials,' *Information Legacy*.
17 Judge Advocate Lieutenant Colonel A. Menard (paraphrasing Sergeant Boland), General Court Martial of Sergeant Boland, Transcripts, vol. 2, 388 (29 April 1994), 'General Courts Martials,' *Information Legacy*.
18 Testimony of Sergeant Boland, General Court Martial of Sergeant Boland, Transcripts, vol. 2, 280 (27 April 1994), 'General Courts Martials,' *Information Legacy*.
19 Defending officer Major K.A. Lindstein closing address, General Court Martial of Captain M. Sox, Transcripts, vol. 4, 861 (15 March 1995), 'General Courts Martials,' *Information Legacy*.
20 Ibid., vol. 4, 761.

21 Prosecutor Major B.C. Mayo, General Court Martial of Sergeant Boland, vol. 1, 36 (25 April 1994), 'General Courts Martials,' *Information Legacy*.
22 Testimony of Private E.K. Brown, General Court Martial of Private E.K. Brown, Transcripts, vol. 9, 1631 (3 March 1994), 'General Courts Martials,' *Information Legacy*.
23 Defence counsel Mr. Patrick F.D. McCann, General Court Martial of Private E.K. Brown, Transcripts, vol. 9, 1632 (3 March 1994), 'General Courts Martials,' *Information Legacy*.
24 See, for example, Alan Thompson, 'More Somalia Abuses Detailed,' *Toronto Star*, 10 September 1996, A1–A9.
25 Judge Advocate Lieutenant – Colonel A. Ménard, General Court Martial Sergeant Boland, Transcripts, vol. 1, 149 (1 December 1993), 'General Courts Martials,' *Information Legacy*.
26 Testimony of Lieutenant-Colonel P.G. Kenward, General Court Martial Sergeant Boland, Transcripts, vol. 1, 154 (27 April 1994), 'General Courts Martials,' *Information Legacy*.
27 Ibid., vol. 1, 155.
28 Ibid., vol. 1, 157.
29 Testimony of Major A.G. Seward, General Court Martial of Sergeant Boland, vol. 1, 205–7 (27 April 1994), 'General Courts Martials,' *Information Legacy*.
30 Testimony of Captain Walsh, General Court Marital of Sergeant Boland, vol. 2, 254 (27 April 1994), 'General Courts Martials,' *Information Legacy*.
31 Defence counsel Mr Rodney G. Sellar, General Court Martial Sergeant Boland, vol. 2, 355 (29 April 1994), 'General Courts Martials,' *Information Legacy*.
32 Ibid., vol. 2, 356.
33 Ibid., vol. 2, 358.
34 Testimony of Private M.A. Boland, General Court Martial of Major Seward, Transcripts, vol. 3, 445 (18 May 1994), 'General Courts Martials,' *Information Legacy*. See also M. Hanlon, 'RCMP Investigate Deaths of Saskatoon Aboriginals,' *Toronto Star*, 17 February 2000, A3.
35 Defence counsel Mr. Rodney G. Sellar, General Court Martial of Sergeant Boland, Transcripts, vol. 2, 362 (29 April 1994), 'General Courts Martials,' *Information Legacy*.
36 Prosecutor Major B.C. Mayo (paraphrasing Sergeant Boland), General Court Martial of Sergeant Boland, Transcripts, vol. 1, 38 (25 April 1994), 'General Court Martials,' *Information Legacy*.
37 Ibid., vol. 1, 39.
38 These details were confirmed in several trials. See for example, General Court Martial of Sergeant Boland, Transcripts, vol. 1, 37–40 (25 April 1994), 'General Courts Martials,' *Information Legacy*.

39 David Pugliese, 'Anatomy of a Cover-Up,' *Ottawa Citizen*, 21 June 1997, B3.

40 Peter Worthington and Kyle Brown, *Scapegoat: How the Army Betrayed Kyle Brown* (Toronto: Seal Books, 1997), 270.

41 Testimony of Master Corporal J.H.M. Giasson, General Court Martial of Private E.K. Brown, Transcripts, vol. 7, 1331 (28 February 1994), 'General Courts Martials,' *Information Legacy.*

42 Defence counsel Mr E.L. Greenspan, General Court Martial of Private Brockle-bank, Transcripts, vol. 5, 826 (27 October 1994),'General Courts Martials,' *Information Legacy.*

43 Testimony of Corporal B.J. MacDonald, General Court Martial of Captain M. Sox, Transcripts, vol. 2, 434 (27 February 1995), 'General Courts Martials,' *Information Legacy.*

44 Ibid.

45 Testimony of Corporal B.J. MacDonald, General Court Martial of Private E.K. Brown, Transcripts, vol. 6, 1224 (24 February 1994), 'General Courts Martials,' *Information Legacy.*

46 Testimony of Corporal B.J. MacDonald, Court Martial of Captain M. Sox, Transcripts, vol. 2, 438 (27 February 1995), 'General Courts Martials,' *Information Legacy.*

47 Testimony of Corporal B.J. MacDonald, General Court Martial of Private E.K. Brown, Transcripts, vol. 6, 1228 (24 February 1994), 'General Courts Martials,' *Information Legacy.*

48 Judge Advocate Lieutenant Colonel A. Ménard (parphrasing Sergeant Campbell), General Court Martial of Captain M. Sox, Transcripts, vol. 4, 862 (15 March 1995), 'General Courts Martials,' *Information Legacy.*

49 Master Corporal R.E. Campbell, Voluntary Statement to Military Police, 27 March 1993, Doc. No. 014930, Control No. 900967, Document Book No. 38D, Tab 13, March 16 Incident, In-Theatre and Post-Deployment, Evidence Logs 18-42, 'Evidence and Documents,' *Information Legacy.* Campbell's rank changed from master corporal to sergeant by the time he testified at Brown's court martial in 1994.

50 Newswire, 'Moaning Termed Nothing Unusual,' *Victoria Times Colonist*, 20 January 1995, 1.

51 Situation Report referring to Corporal Bibby's account of what he heard Master Corporal Alarie say during the March 16 incident, February 23 1994, Doc. No. DND015497, Control No. 000796, Document Book No. 47, Tab A23, In-Theatre General Courts Martial PTE Brown, Sitrep #23, 231800, 'Evidence and Documents,' *Information Legacy.*

52 Ibid.

53 Judge Advocate Lieutenant Colonel A. Ménard (parphrasing Sergeant Campbell),

General Court Martial of Captain M. Sox, Transcripts, vol. 4, 861 (15 March 1995), 'General Courts Martials,' *Information Legacy*.

54 Ibid.
55 Testimony of Private D.J. Brocklebank, General Court Martial of Private Brocklebank, Transcripts, vol. 4, 649 (25 October 1994), 'General Courts Martials,' *Information Legacy*.
56 Ibid., vol. 4, 677.
57 Sunday Report, on *The National*, CBC Television, 15 January 1995.
58 Assistant Prosecutor Major D.K. Abbott, General Court Martial of Private Brocklebank, Transcripts, vol. 5, 768 (27 October 1994), 'General Courts Martials,' *Information Legacy*.
59 Assistant Prosecuter Major D.K. Abbot, General Court Martial of Private Brocklebank, Transcripts, vol. 5, 752 (27 October 1994), 'General Courts Martials,' *Information Legacy*.
60 Defence counsel E.L. Greenspan,General Court Martial of Private Brocklebank, Transcripts, vol. 5, 795 (27 October 1994), 'General Courts Martials,' *Information Legacy*.
61 Ibid., vol. 5, 805.
62 Ibid., vol. 5, 806.
63 Ibid., vol. 5, 809.
64 Ibid.
65 Ibid., vol. 5, 831.
66 Ibid., vol. 5, 821.
67 Ibid., vol. 5, 825.
68 Ibid.
69 Testimony of Private E.K. Brown, General Court Martial of Captain M. Sox, Transcripts, vol. 3, 545 (6 March 1995), 'General Courts Martials,' *Information Legacy*.
70 Prosecutor Major B.C. Mayo, General Court Martial of Sergeant Boland, Transcripts, vol. 2, 343 (29 April 1994), 'General Courts Martials,' *Information Legacy*.
71 Defending officer Major J. Dunn closing address, General Court Martial of Captain M. Sox, Transcripts, vol. 4, 760 (3 March 1995), 'General Courts Martials,' *Information Legacy*.
72 Judge Advocate Lieutenant Colonel A. Menard (paraphrasing Master Corporal Haines) at General Court Martial of Sergeant Boland, Transcripts, vol. 2, 390 (29 April 1994), 'General Courts Martials,' *Information Legacy*.
73 Judge Advocate Lieutenant Colonel A. Menard (paraphrasing Sergeant Lloyd), General Court Martial of Sergeant Boland, Transcripts, vol. 2, 390 (29 April 1994), 'General Courts Martials,' *Information Legacy*.
74 Jean-Paul Brodeur, *Violence and Racial Prejudice in the Context of Peacekeeping*. A

study prepared for the Commission of Inquiry into the Deployment of Canadian Forces to Somalia (Ottawa: Minister of Public Works and Government Services Canada, 1997), 63.

75 Jonathan Glover, *Humanity: A Moral History of the Twentieth Century* (London: Pimlico, 2001), 59.

76 Ibid.

77 Ibid., 60.

78 Fanon, *The Wretched of the Earth*, 52.

79 Brodeur, *Violence and Racial Prejudice*, 190.

80 Warren Cariou, *Lake of the Prairies: A Story of Belonging* (Toronto: Doubleday Canada, 2002), 205.

81 Ibid., 208. See also Canadian Press, 'Hate Mail Shakes Soldier's Parents,' *Hamilton Spectator*, 29 November 1994, A2.

82 Cariou, *Lake of the Prairies*, 210.

83 Tony Hall, 'Who Silenced Clayton Matchee? We Did,' *Canadian Forum*, April 1997, 5–6.

84 Ibid., 6.

85 Testimony of Commander Jenkins, Public Hearings Transcripts, Commission of Inquiry into the Deployment of Canadian Forces in Somalia, Transcripts, vol. 14, 2553 (2 November 1995), 'Hearings Transcripts,' *Information Legacy*.

86 Karen D. Pyke, 'Class-Based Masculinities: The Interdependence of Gender, Class and Interpersonal Power,' *Gender and Society* 10, no. 5 (1996), 532.

87 Ibid., 545. See also Nancy Ehrenreich, 'Subordination and Symbiosis: Mechanisms of Mutual Support between Subordinating Systems,' *UMKC Law Review* 71, no. 2 (2003), 251–324.

88 Pyke, 'Class-Based Masculinities,' 532.

89 See Ehrenreich, 'Subordination and Symbiosis,' and Angela P. Harris, 'Gender, Violence, Race and Criminal Justice,' *Stanford Law Review* 52 (2000), 777–808.

90 Chen, 'Lives at the Center of the Periphery ...,' 586.

91 Ibid.

92 See James Messerschmidt, 'Men Victimizing Men: The Case of Lynching, 1865–1900,' in *Masculinities and Violence*, ed. L.H. Bowker (London: Sage, 1998), 125–51.

93 Harris, 'Gender, Violence, Race and Criminal Justice,' 797.

94 Ibid., 798.

95 Brodeur, *Violence and Racial Prejudice*, 154.

96 Laura Miller and Charles Moskos, 'Humanitarians or Warriors? Race, Gender, and Combat Status in Operation Restore Hope,' *Armed Forces and Society* 21, no. 4 (1995), 618.

97 Ibid., 621.

98 Ibid., 626.

99 Ibid., 629.

100 Testimony of Major A.G. Seward, General Court Martial of Sergeant Gresty, Transcripts, vol. 4, 588 (6 April 1994), 'General Court Martials,' *Information Legacy.*

101 Testimony of Sergeant Boland, General Court Martial Sergeant Boland, Transcripts, vol. 2, 262 (27 April 1994), 'General Court Martials,' *Information Legacy.*

102 Testimony of Master Corporal J.H.M. Giasson, General Court Martial of Private E.K. Brown, Transcripts, vol. 7, 1337 (25 February 1994), 'General Court Martials,' *Information Legacy.*

103 Peter Cheney, 'Death and Dishonour,' *Toronto Star*, 16 July 1994, B2.

104 Ibid.

105 Brodeur, *Violence and Racial Prejudice*, 159.

106 Testimony of Corporal B.J. MacDonald, General Court Martial of Private E.K. Brown, Transcripts, vol. 6, 1232 (24 February 1994), 'General Courts Martials,' *Information Legacy.*

107 Worthington and Brown, *Scapegoat*, 87.

108 Testimony of Mrs. Karen Turner, General Court Martial of Private E.K. Brown, Transcripts, vol. 11, 2031 (16 March 1994), 'General Court Martials,' *Information Legacy.*

109 Ibid.

110 Testimony of Corporal B.J. MacDonald, General Court Martial of Private E.K. Brown, Transcripts, vol. 7, 1435 (28 February 1994), 'General Court Martials,' *Information Legacy.*

111 Testimony of Private D.J. Brocklebank, General Court Martial of D.J. Brocklebank, Transcripts, vol. 4, 685 (25 October 1994), 'General Court Martials,' *Information Legacy.*

112 Richard Wright, *Native Son* (New York: HarperCollins, 1993), 437.

113 Ibid., 447.

114 Ibid.

115 Ibid., 446.

116 Ibid., 451.

117 Peter Worthington, 'Private Brown: He Was Little More than a Witness,' *Saturday Night*, September 1994, 30.

118 Defence counsel, Mr Patrick F.D. McCann, General Court Martial of Private E.K. Brown, Transcripts, vol. 7, 1441 (28 February 1994), 'General Court Martials,' *Information Legacy.*

119 Judge Advocate Lieutenant Colonel J.S.T. Pitzul, General Court Martial of Private E.K. Brown, Transcripts, vol. 7, p. 1449 (28 February 1994), 'General Court Martials,' *Information Legacy.*

120 Testimony of Private E.K. Brown, General Court Martial of Private E.K. Brown, Transcripts, vol. 7, 1644 (3 March 1994), 'General Court Martials,' *Information Legacy.*

121 Ibid., vol. 9, 1645 (3 March 1994).

122 Ibid., vol. 9, 1647.

123 Ibid., vol. 9, 1657.

124 Ibid., vol. 9, 1682.

125 Ibid., vol. 9, 1654.

126 Defence counsel, Mr Patrick F.D. McCan,General Court Martial Private E.K. Brown, Transcripts, vol. 9, 1782 (7 March 1994), 'General Court Martials,' *Information Legacy.*

127 Ibid., vol. 9, 1811.

128 Ibid., vol. 9, 1813.

129 Ibid., vol. 9, 1777.

130 Testimony of Private E.K. Brown, General Court Martial Private E.K. Brown, Transcripts, vol. 9, 1625 (4 March 1994), 'General Court Martials,' *Information Legacy.*

131 Defence counsel, Mr Patrick F.D. McCann, General Court Martial Private E.K. Brown, Transcripts, vol. 9, 1776 (7 March, 1994), 'General Court Martials,' *Information Legacy.*

132 Worthington and Brown, *Scapegoat,* 87.

133 Miller and Moskos, 'Humanitarians or Warriors?' 623.

134 Ibid.

Chapter 4. Bad Apples and a Nation Wronged

1 Toni Morrison, 'The Official Story: Dead Man Golfing,' in *Birth of a Nation'hood: Gaze, Script, and Spectacle in the O.J. Simpson Case,* ed. Toni Morrison and Claudia Brodsky (New York: Pantheon Books, 1997), xvi.

2 Blake Brooker, *Somalia Yellow.* Based on a performance of the play by Denise Clarke. Calgary, Alberta, April 2002. Production draft script, scene 6.

3 Ibid.

4 Morrison, 'The Official Story,' xvi.

5 See Patricia Williams, *The Alchemy of Race and Rights: Diary of A Law Professor* (Cambridge, MA: Harvard University Press, 1991).

6 See Raymond Williams, 'Structures of Feeling,' in *Marxism and Literature* (New York: Oxford University Press, 1977), 132–3.

7 Lauren Berlant, *The Queen of America Goes to Washington City* (Durham, NC: Duke University Press, 1997), 10.

8 John R. Butler, 'Somalia and the Imperial Savage: Continuities in the Rhetoric of War,' *Western Journal of Communication* 66, no. 1 (Winter 2002), 1–24.

9 See, for example, the following headlines in the following issues of *Maclean's*: Mary Nemeth, 'Somalia: City of Slaughter,' 14 January 1991, front cover; 'Violence and Famine Stalk Drought-Ravaged Somalia as Aid Begins to Flow,' 7 September 1992, front cover; Bruce Wallace, 'Cry of a Dying People,' 7 September 1992, 20; 'National Beyond Hope: The World May Have Waited Too Long to Save Somalians from a Holocaust of War and Famine,' 7 September 1992, front cover; 'Somalia: The Cavalry Charges: The UN Chooses Force to End Somalia's Agony,' 14 December 1992, front cover; Rae Corelli, 'Deliverance: U.S. Marines Land in Somalia,' 21 December 1992, 12–15. See also Canadian Press, 'Mercredi Links Tragedies to Poverty,' *Calgary Herald*, 25 March 1993, A20; Canadian Press, 'Chief Fears Wave of Teen Suicide,' *Ottawa Citizen*, 28 March 1993, A5; and Brian Maracle, 'Crazywater: The Cycle of Native Alcoholism Must Be Exposed If It Is to Be Broken,' *Ottawa Citizen*, 29 March 1993, A9.

10 Butler, 'Somalia and the Imperial Savage,' 5.

11 For example, Eric Shackleton, 'Canadian Peacekeepers Shoot Two Somali Intruders,' *Kitchener-Waterloo Record*, 5 March 1993, A4.

12 Canadian Press, 'Canadians Kill Man Guarding Aid in Somalia,' *Toronto Star*, 18 March 1993, A20.

13 Paul Watson, 'Tense Vigil in Somalia,' *Toronto Star*, 21 March 1993, F1.

14 See Robert Lewis, 'Duplicity and Cowardice,' *Maclean's*, 14 July 1997, 2.

15 See Geoffery York, 'Military Admits Error in Handling Somali's Death,' *Globe and Mail*, 15 April 1993, A8.

16 Mr Peter Vita, Counsel for Attorney General of Canada, 'Notice of Application for Standing,' Public Hearing Transcripts, vol. 31, 5972 (20 December 1995), 'Hearings Transcripts,' *Information Legacy*.

17 Douglas L. Bland, *National Defence Headquarters: Centre for Decision*, Chap. 6, 'A System in Trouble,' esp. section 'A Problem of Ethics.' 'Research Studies,' in Commission of Inquiry into the Deployment of Canadian Forces to Somalia, *Information Legacy: A Compendium of Source Material/Commission of Inquiry into the Deployment of Canadian Forces to Somalia* (Ottawa: Minister of Public Works and Government Services Canada, 1997). Hereafter referred to as *Information Legacy*.

18 Morrison,'The Official Story,' xvi.

19 See Canadian Press, 'Canada's Shame,' *Toronto Star*, 8 November 1994, A1, A3.

20 See James Travers, 'A Soldier's Snapshot of Brutality,' *Ottawa Citizen*, 8 November 1994, A1.

21 *Canada A.M.*, Canadian Television Network, 17 November 1994.

22 Dirk Meissner, 'MP Out of Touch on Racism Opinions,' *Victoria Times Colonist*, 21 January 1995, 1.

23 See Jeff Sallot, 'Airborne in Danger of Being Disbanded. Hazing on Video "Horrible," PM Says,' *Globe and Mail*, 20 January 1995, A1, A22.

24 Deborah Harrison, a sociology professor at Brock University, quoted in Joe Chidley, 'Bonding and Brutality,' *Maclean's*, 30 January 1995, 18.

25 See Jeff Sallot, 'Airborne Leadership Held Culpable,' *Globe and Mail*, 21 January 1995, A4; Canadian Press, 'Ex-Soldiers Fault Airborne Leaders,' *Winnipeg Free Press*, 21 January 1995, A5.

26 See Canadian Press, 'Morale in Military Suffering, Study Says,' *Victoria Times Colonist*, 30 January 1995, 1; Jeff Sallot, 'Morale Plummets Among Soldiers. Many Use Food Banks, Take Extra Jobs to Make Ends Meet, Report Says,' *Globe and Mail*, 28 January 1995, A1.

27 See Allan Thompson, 'The Military Scandal that Simply Refuses to Die,' *Toronto Star*, 28 January 1996, C1.

28 Linda Goyette, 'Somalia Inquiry Must Plunge Ahead,' *Edmonton Journal*, 7 April 1996, F8.

29 See Allan Thompson, 'The Plight of the General,' *Toronto Star*, 20 April 1996, C1.

30 Rex Murphy, 'Commentary,' *The National Magazine*, CBC Television, 11 September 1996.

31 See 'Canada Notes: Somalia: Part 2,' *Maclean's*, 31 March 1997, 35.

32 See Matthew Fisher, 'Our Troops Aren't Out of Control,' *Toronto Sun*, 22 January 1996, A11.

33 See Charles Gordon, 'Why the Somalia Report Failed to Shock,' *Maclean's*, 28 July 1997, 7.

34 See Rosie DiManno, 'Military Cover-up Outrages Us More Than Somali Deaths,' *Toronto Star*, 7 October 1996, A7.

35 David Matas, co-counsel for B'nai Brith Canada, Public Hearing Transcripts, vol. 184, 37656 (7 April 1997), 'Hearings Transcripts,' *Information Legacy*.

36 'Letter, Cdr. Jenkins,' 4 February 1993, Doc. No. DND129697, Control No. 002307, Document Book No. 8, Tab, 2, Racism, 'Exhibits and Documents,' *Information Legacy*.

37 Karen Mock, interview with author, 13 April 2000, Toronto, Ontario.

38 Mr Marvin Kurz, Counsel for B'nai Brith Canada, Public Hearing Transcripts, vol. 5P, 776P (22 June 1995). 'Hearings Transcripts,' *Information Legacy*.

39 Hal Joffe, Counsel for Canadian Jewish Congress, Pubic Hearing Transcripts, vol., 4P, 659P (21 June 1995), 'Hearings Transcripts,' *Information Legacy*.

40 Written submission on behalf of the Canadian Jewish Congress (14 June 1995), 14, 'Written Submissions,' *Information Legacy*.

41 Mr Marvin Kurz, Counsel for B'nai Brith Canada, Public Hearing Transcripts, vol. 5P, 812P (22 June 1995).

42 Ibid., vol. 5P, 769P.

43 Ibid., vol. 5P, 784P.

44 Dr Karen Mock, Counsel for B'nai Brith Canada, Public Hearing Transcripts, vol. 5P, 794P (22 June 1995), 'Hearings Transcripts,' *Information Legacy*.

45 Testimony of Corporal Christopher Robin, Public Hearing Transcripts, vol. 6, 1045 (12 October 1995), 'Hearings Transcripts,' *Information Legacy*.

46 Ibid., vol. 6, 1050.

47 Ibid., vol. 6, 1064.

48 Testimony of Captain Patrick Koch, Public Hearing Transcripts, vol. 23, 4234 (28 November 1995), 'Hearings Transcripts,' *Information Legacy*.

49 Testimony of Major Anthony Seward, Public Hearing Transcripts, vol. 32, 6085 (15 January 1996), 'Hearings Transcripts,' *Information Legacy*.

50 Testimony of Sergeant Major (Ret.) Clarence Jardine, Public Hearing Transcripts, vol. 106, 21135 (20 September 1996), 'Hearings Transcripts,' *Information Legacy*.

51 Testimony of Commander Paul Jenkins, Public Hearing Transcripts, vol. 14, 2636 (2 November 1995), 'Hearings Transcripts,' *Information Legacy*.

52 Testimony of Sergeant Major (Ret.) Clarence Jardine, Public Hearing Transcripts, vol. 106, 21136 (20 September 1996); Testimony of Master Warrant Bradley Ross Mills, Public Hearing Transcripts, vol., 23, 4372–3 (29 November 1995), 'Hearings Transcripts,' *Information Legacy*.

53 Testimony of Sergeant Major (Ret.) Clarence Jardine, Public Hearing Transcripts, vol. 25, 4664 (11 December 1995), 'Hearings Transcripts,' *Information Legacy*.

54 Mr Marvin Kurz, Counsel for B'nai Brith Canada, Public Hearing Transcripts, vol. 184, 37669 (7 June 1997). 'Hearings Transcripts,' *Information Legacy*.

55 Briefing note to the Minister, 'Colonel Watt to the Minister,' Document No. NS042167, Control No. 019394, Document Book 72D, Tab 08P, Post-Deployment Racism Document, 'Exhibits and Documents,' *Information Legacy*.

56 Testimony of Mr Robert Fowler (former Deputy Minister), Public Hearing Transcripts, vol., 51, 10237 (22 February 1996), 'Hearings Transcripts,' *Information Legacy*.

57 Testimony of Commander Paul Jenkins, Public Hearing Transcripts, vol. 6, 1242 (12 October 1995); and Mr Marvin Kurz, Counsel for B'nai Brith Canada, Public Hearing Transcripts, vol. 5P, 812P (22 June 1995), 'Hearings Transcripts,' *Information Legacy*.

58 Patrick F.D. McCann, 'Written Submission on Behalf of Kyle Brown. (Section 4. Reference to Racism),' 'Written Submissions,' *Information Legacy*.

59 The Honourable Gilles Letourneau, Chairman, Public Hearing Transcripts, vol. 5P, 815P (22 June 1995), 'Hearings Transcripts,' *Information Legacy*.

60 Mr Rubin Friedman, Counsel B'nai Brith Canada, Public Hearing Transcripts, vol, 5P, 816P (22 June 1995), 'Hearings Transcripts,' *Information Legacy*.

61 Dr Karen Mock, Counsel B'nai Brith Canada, Public Hearing Transcripts, vol, 5P, 817P (22 June 1995), 'Hearings Transcripts,' *Information Legacy*.

62 Julian N. Falconer, Urban Alliance on Race Relations, Public Hearing Transcripts, vol. 1P, 49P (24 May 1995), 'Hearings Transcripts,' *Information Legacy*.

63 Ibid., vol. 1P, 63P.

64 Ibid., vol. 3P, 571 (20 June 1995).

65 Ibid., vol. 3P, 571, 576P.

66 Ibid., vol. 3P, 579P.

67 Ibid., vol. 3P, 586P.

68 Commissioner Desbarats in response to Julian Falconer, Public Hearing Transcripts, vol. 3P, 607P, (20 June 1995), 'Hearings Transcripts,' *Information Legacy*.

69 Michelle Williams, 'Written Submission on Behalf of the African Canadian Legal Clinic' (4 April 1997), 4.

70 Ibid., 13.

71 Ibid., 22.

72 Michelle Williams, 'Written "Supplementary Submissions" on Behalf of the African Canadian Legal Clinic' (6 June 1997), 2.

73 Ibid., 6.

74 Ibid.

75 Ibid., 7.

76 Ibid., 10.

77 Ibid.

78 Ibid.

79 Ahmad Hashi, interview with author, Ottawa, Ontario, 14 January 1999.

80 Abdullahi Godah Barre, interview with author, Ottawa, Ontario, 23 September 1999,' and Hashi, interview.

81 Isaac O. Sechere, on behalf of Somali Canadian Organizations, Public Hearing Transcripts, vol. 1P, 150 (24 May 1995), 'Hearing Transcripts,' *Information Legacy*.

82 Godah Barre, interview.

83 Isaac Sechere suggested that the demand for better compensation for the families of Belet Huen was seen by many participating in the Inquiry as simply greediness on the part of Somalis. For a presentation of the views of COSCO, see *Notice of Application for Standing*, submitted by Isaac O. Sechere on behalf of the Coalition of Somali Canadian Organizations, Public Hearings Transcripts, vol. 1P 138P (24 May 1995), 'Hearings Transcripts,' *Information Legacy*.

84 Isaac O. Sechere, Coalition of Somali Canadian Organizations, Public Hearing Transcripts, vol. 4P, 728P (21 June 1995), 'Hearings Transcripts,' *Information Legacy*.

85 Commissioner Robert C. Rutherford, Public Hearing Transcripts, vol. 4P, 747P (21 June 1995), 'Hearings Transcripts,' *Information Legacy*.

86 Ibid., vol. 4P, 750P.

87 Isaac Sechere, interview with author, Ottawa, Ontario, 3 March 1999.

88 Major Barry Armstrong, 'Voluntary Statement of Major Barry Armstrong,' 25 April 1993, Doc. No. DND294226, Control No. 000760, Document Book No. 48E, Tab 02, March 4 Incident, Evidence Logs 8–23, 'Exhibits and Documents,' *Information Legacy*.

89 See Sherene Razack, 'Simple Logic: Race, the Identity Documents Rule and the Story of a Nation Besieged and Betrayed,' in *Journal of Law and Social Policy*, 15 (2000), 183–209.

90 Gilles Letourneau, 'Statement of the Terms of Reference' (3 August 1995), 12, 'History of the Commission,' *Information Legacy*.

91 Edward Said, *Culture and Imperialism* (New York: Alfred A. Knopf, 1993).

92 Sherene Razack, *Looking White People in the Eye: Gender, Race and Culture in Courtrooms and Classrooms* (Toronto: University of Toronto Press, 1998).

93 Catherine Besteman, 'Representing Violence and "Othering" Somalia,' *Cultural Anthropology* 11, no. 1 (1996), 120–33; and Butler, 'Somalia and the Imperial Savage.'

94 Butler, 'Somalia and the Imperial Savage.'

95 Testimony of Ken Menkhaus, Public Hearing Transcripts, vol. 7, 1270 (23 October 1995), 'Hearings Transcripts,' *Information Legacy*.

96 Ibid., vol. 7, 1273.

97 Ibid., vol. 7, 1276.

98 Ibid., vol. 7, 1306.

99 Ibid., vol. 7, 1307.

100 Ibid.

101 Ibid., vol. 7, 1311.

102 Ibid., vol. 7, 1345.

103 Jean-Paul Brodeur, *Violence and Racial Prejudice in the Context of Peacekeeping*. A Study Prepared for the Commission of Inquiry into the Deployment of Canadian Forces to Somalia (Ottawa: Minister of Public Works and Government Services Canada, 1997), xix.

104 Ibid., 22–5.

105 Donna Winslow, *The Canadian Airborne Regiment in Somalia: A Socio-Cultural Inquiry*. A Study Prepared for the Commission of Inquiry into the Deployment of Canadian Forces to Somalia (Ottawa: Minister of Public Works and Government Services, 1997), i.

106 Ibid., 15.

107 Ibid., 16.

108 Ibid., 35.

109 Williams, 'Written Submission on Behalf of the African Canadian Legal Clinic,' 52.

110 Dr Karen Mock, Counsel for B'nai Brith Canada, Public Hearing Transcripts, vol. 5P, 794P (22 June 1995).

111 Winslow, *The Canadian Airborne Regiment in Somalia*, 85.
112 Ibid., 98.
113 Ibid., 140.
114 Williams, 'Written Submission on Behalf of the African Canadian Legal Clinic,' 37.
115 Winslow, *The Canadian Airborne Regiment in Somalia*, 240.
116 Commission of Inquiry into the Deployment of Canadian Forces to Somalia, 'Dishonoured Legacy: The Lessons of the Somalia Affair – Report of the Commission of Inquiry into the Deployment of Canadian Forces to Somalia,' vol. 1, 329. Hereafter referred to as 'Commission Report.'
117 Ibid., vol. 1, 257–8.
118 Winslow's analysis represents the more liberal line taken by the Inquiry in that it does not entirely deny that the violence occurs. In more conservative accounts, for example, historian David Bercuson, the violence is naturalized as a result of the corrupt military leadership, the limited funding of the military, a few bad apples as well as the terrible heat of Somalia and the villainy of its population. Bercuson argues that the men had to end up 'hating' Somalis under these conditions. While this view was shared by Winslow and the Inquiry, Bercuson stresses that the answer to this kind of problem is a better fighting army. David Bercuson, *Significant Incident: Canada's Army, the Airborne, and the Murder in Somalia* (Toronto: McClelland and Stewart, 1996).
119 'Commission Report,' vol. 1, 662.
120 Ibid., vol. 5, 1411.
121 Ibid., vol. 1, 457.
122 Ibid., vol. 1, xxx.
123 Ibid., vol. 5, 1146.
124 Ibid., vol. 5, 1125–6.
125 Ibid., vol. 1, xxix.
126 Ibid., vol. 5, 1093.
127 Ibid., vol. 5, 1342.
128 Ibid., vol. 1, xxxii.
129 Ibid., vol. 1, xxxi.
130 Ibid., vol. 5, 1439.
131 Said, *Culture and Imperialism*, 9.
132 Ibid., 22.
133 'Commission Report,' vol. 1, xxix.
134 Said, *Culture and Imperialism*, 4.
135 Ibid., 52.
136 Mary Louise Pratt, *Imperial Eyes: Travel Writing and Transculturation* (London: Routledge, 1992), 56–7.

137 Peter Desbarats, *Somalia Cover-Up: A Commissioner's Journal* (Toronto: McClelland and Stewart, 1997), 3.
138 Ibid., 12.
139 Ibid., 15.
140 Ibid., 28–9.
141 Ibid., 139.
142 Ibid., 40.
143 Ibid., 23.
144 Ibid., 27.
145 Ibid., 184.
146 Ibid, 133.
147 Peter Schmalz writes of a number of treaties in reference to which the Saugeen protested that their land was seized illegally and threats made to drive them off their land, in order to make way for American speculators and poverty stricken British settlers. The colonial government forced Aboriginal peoples into dependency through such measures. See Peter Schmalz, *The History of the Saugeen Indians* (Ottawa: Ontario Historical Society, 1977).
148 Desbarats, *Somalia Cover-Up*, 147.
149 Ibid., 148.
150 Anne duCille, 'The Occult of True Black Womanhood: Critical Demeanor and Black Feminist Studies,' *Signs: Journal of Women in Culture and Society* 19, no. 3 (1994), 620.
151 So much do these five figures haunt his imagination, that in Desbarats's public reading promoting the book at the University of Toronto, these figures are assigned a prominence they do not have in the printed text. Desbarats chose to read excerpts in which Black figures appear (untitled Panel presentation, audiotape, Ontario Institute for Studies in Education University of Toronto, Toronto, September 1997).
152 Desbarats, *Somalia Cover-Up*, 25.
153 duCille, 'The Occult of Black Womanhood,' 614.
154 Desbarats, *Somalia Cover-Up*, 87.
155 Ibid.
156 Ibid., 68–9.
157 I am grateful to Bonita Lawrence for suggesting this interpretation.
158 Desbarats, *Somalia Cover-Up*, 51.
159 Ibid., 41–2.
160 Simon Watney, 'Missionary Positions: AIDS, "Africa" and Race,' in *Out There: Marginalization and Contemporary Cultures*, ed. Russell Ferguson, Martha Gever, Trinh T. Minh-ha, and Cornel West (New York New: Museum of Contemporary Art and Boston: MIT Press, 1990), 89–106.

161 Desbarats, *Somalia Cover-Up*, 206.
162 Peter Desbarats, 'Somalia: The Long-Term Effects,' in *Canada and the New World Order: Facing the Millennium*, ed. Michael J. Tucker, Raymond B. Blake, and P.E. Bryden (Toronto: Irwin Publications, 2000), 33–43.
163 Ibid.
164 Women's Caucus for Gender Justice, 'Peacekeeping Watch: Documenting Human Rights Violations Committed by UN Peacekeepers.' Retrieved from <http://www.iccwomen.org/pkwatch>. 23 June 3003.
165 'Affidavit of Abdullahi Godah Barre.' Appendix to Coalition of Somali Canadian Organizations, Discussed in COSCO's 'Notice of Application for Standing,' Public Hearing Transcripts, vol. 1P, 144–55P (24 May 1995), 'Hearings and Transcripts,' *Information Legacy*.
166 See Anthony Paul Farley, 'The Black Body as Fetish Object,' *Oregon Law Review* 76 (1997), 493.
167 See Ann Laura Stoler, *Race and the Education of Desire: Foucault's History of Sexuality and the Colonial Order of Things* (Durham, NC: Duke University Press, 1995), 65.
168 Desbarats relates his view of the legal process of an inquiry as involving impartial commissioners who critically examine testimony, lawyers who dig out the truth without violating rights or unfair practices, and outside lawyers who sort out fraudulent witnesses. Desbarats, *Somalia Cover-Up*, 139.
169 Bonnie Honig suggests the 'denationalization of democracy' is necessary in this age of transnational relations. See Bonnie Honig, 'How Foreignness "Solves" Democracy's Problems,' *Social Text* 56, no. 16.3 (1998), 18.
170 Liisa Malkii, 'Speechless Emissaries: Refugees, Humanitarianism, and Dehistoricization,' *Cultural Anthropology* 11, no. 3 (1996), 398.
171 Reuters, 'Raw Desire for Power Fed Rwandan Genocide,' *Toronto Star*, 1 April 1999, A17.
172 Commissione Governativa d'Inchiesta, *Relazione Conclusiva sui fatti di Somalia* (Rome: Ministro della Difesa, 8 August 1997), 9.
173 Amnesty International Report, 'Italy: A Briefing for the UN Committee Against Torture' (May 1999). Retrieved from <www.web.amnesty.org/ai.nsf/index/EUR300021999>. 23 June 2003.
174 Amnesty International Report, 'Belgium: January–December 1997,' *Annual Report 1998*. Retrieved from <http://www.amnesty.org/ailib/aireport/ar98/eur14.htm>. 23 June 2003.
175 Amnesty International Report, 'Concerns in Europe: January–June 1998' (September 1998). Retrieved from <http://web.amnesty.org/ai.nsf/Index/EUR010021998?OpenDocument&of=COUNTRIES\BELGIUM>. 23 June 2003.

176 Ibid.

177 Stephen Bindman, "'I'm Just Asking for the Truth:" Matchee's Wife Wants Answers about Her Husband's "Suicide" Attempt and the Role an Anti-Malaria Drug Played in Somalia,' *Ottawa Citizen*, 22 June 1998, A5.

178 Craig Wong, 'Ex-soldier in Court Over Death of Somali,' *Toronto Star*, 24 July 2002, A17.

179 'The Nightmare Drug,' *the fifth estate*, CBC Television, 16 October 2002. Host Hana Gartner. Transcript provided by Bowdens Fulfillment Services, Toronto Ontario.

180 David Akin, 'Worse Than the Disease,' *Globe and Mail*, 14 September 2002, F7; William Walker, 'Pilot Acted Oddly on Night of Bombing, U.S. Court Told,' *Toronto Star*, 16 January 2003, A1, A11.

Conclusion: Acting Morally in the New World Order

1 Romeo Dallaire, 'A Good Man in Hell.' Interviewed by Ted Koppel (12 June 2002). United States Holocaust Memorial Museum, Washington, DC. Retrieved from <http://www.ushmm.org/conscience/events/dallaire/dallaire.php>. 23 June 2003.

2 President George W. Bush, 'Speech to the 2002 Graduating Class at the United States Military Academy,' 1 June 2002, West Point, New York. Retrieved from <http://www.ashbrook.org/articles/bush_02-06-01.html>. 23 June 2003.

3 Ibid.

4 Dr James Orbinski, CBC Radio, *Ideas* 'Taking a Stand: The Ethics of Intervention,' *Ideas*, CBC Radio, 19 April 2002. Program Transcript.

5 Ibid.

6 Bush, 'Speech to the 2002 Graduating Class.'

7 Ibid.

8 Adam Hochschild, *King Leopold's Ghost: A Story of Greed, Terror, and Heroism in Colonial Africa* (New York: Mariner Books, Houghton Mifflin Company, 1999).

9 Cited in George L. Mosse, *Toward the Final Solution: A History of European Racism* (Madison, WI: University of Wisconsin Press, 1985), 205.

10 Bush, 'Speech to the 2002 Graduating Class.'

11 Mosse, *Toward the Final Solution*, xv.

12 Linda Polman, *We Did Nothing: Why the Truth Doesn't Always Come Out When the UN Goes In*, trans. Rob Bland (London: Viking Books, 2003) 8. Originally published in Dutch as *'k Zag twee beren* (Amsterdam: Atlas, 1997).

13 David Theo Goldberg, *Racist Culture: Philosophy and the Politics of Meaning* (Cambridge, MA: Blackwell, 1993), 148.

14 Mosse, *Toward the Final Solution*, xxvi.

15 Edward Said, *The Question of Palestine* (1979; reprint, New York: Vintage Books, 1992, 15–18. In November 1917, the British government (represented by Lord Balfour) in the form of a letter to Lord Rothschild (who represented Zionist interests) undertook to 'view with favour' the establishment in Palestine of a national home for the Jewish people. Palestine was Balfour's to dispose of as he saw fit, in the interests of modernity. Said quotes Balfour: 'The four great powers are committed to Zionism and Zionism, be it right or wrong, good or bad, is rooted in age-long tradition, in present needs, in future hopes, *of far profounder import than the desire and prejudice of the 700,000 Arabs who now inhabit that ancient land. In my opinion that is right* (17, note omitted).

16 Mosse, *Toward the Final Solution*, xxvi.

17 Ibid., 191.

18 Hannah Arendt, *On the Origins of Totalitarianism* (New York: Harcourt, Brace, Jovanovich Publishers, 1973).

19 Hannah Arendt, *Eichmann in Jerusalem: A Report on the Banality of Evil* (New York: Viking Press, 1963), 253.

20 Dana R. Villa, *Politics, Philosophy, Terror: Essays on the Thought of Hannah Arendt* (Princeton, NS: Princeton University Press, 1999), 40.

21 Ibid., 45.

22 Wayne Allen, 'Hannah Arendt's Foundation for a Metaphysics of Evil,' *Southern Journal of Philosophy* 38, no. 2 (2000), 185.

23 Ibid., 186.

24 Arendt, *On the Origins of Totalitarianism*, 134.

25 Villa, *Politics, Philosophy, Terror*, 15.

26 Ibid., 13, note omitted (refers to Arendt). Emphasis added.

27 Ibid., 34.

28 Ibid., 16.

29 Ibid.

30 Ibid., 18.

31 Ibid., 20.

32 Ibid., 21.

33 Ibid., 36.

34 Arendt, *On the Origins of Totalitarianism*, 199. Emphasis added.

35 See, for example, the catalogue of laws and policies affecting the civil liberties of immigrants in 'Timeline: Under Homeland Security,' *Colourlines* 6, no. 1 (2003), 18–19. Retrieved from <http://www.arc.org/C_Lines/CLArchive/timeline.shtml>. 23 June 2003.

36 Ian Buruma, 'Revolution from Above,' review of *Terror and Liberalism* by Paul Berman, *New York Review of Books*, 1 May 2003, 4.

37 Peg Birmingham makes this point with respect to Eichmann in 'Holes of Oblivion: The Banality of Radical Evil,' *Hypatia* 18, no.1 (2003), 88.

38 Anthony Farley, 'The Poetics of Colorlined Space,' in *Crossroads, Directions, and a New Critical Race Theory*, eds. Francisco Valdes, Jerome McKristal Culp, and Angela Harris (Philadelphia: Temple University Press, 2002), 100.

39 Ibid., 103.

40 I am grateful to Gada Mahrouse for observing this dynamic in operation when I gave public talks on peacekeeping.

41 Jean-Paul Brodeur, *Violence and Racial Prejudice in the Context of Peacekeeping*. A Study Prepared for the Commission of Inquiry into the Deployment of Canadian Forces to Somalia (Ottawa: Minister of Public Works and Government Service, 1997), 129.

42 Ibid., 105–9.

43 Helen Silbiger, 'Letter to the Editor,' *Toronto Star*, 23 May 2003, A27.

44 There are examples of these self-congratulatory notes in the press practically every day. For example, 'We're Nice – and Getting Nicer,' by Oakland Ross, *Toronto Star*, 17 May 2003, A3.

45 Robert Fulford, 'Canada's Anti-racism Industry Never Quits,' *National Post*, 11 January 2003.

46 Charlotte Delbo, *Auschwitz and After*, trans. Rosette C. Lamont (New Haven: Yale University Press, 1995).

47 Jennifer L. Geddes, 'Banal Evil and Useless Knowledge: Hannah Arendt and Charlotte Delbo on Evil after the Holocaust,' *Hypatia* 18, no. 1 (2003), 113.

48 Susan Sontag, *Regarding the Pain of Others* (New York: Farrar, Straus, and Giroux, 2003), 41, 83, 85.

Bibliography

Books/Periodicals/Reports

Achebe, Chinua. 'An Image of Africa: Racism in Conrad's Heart of Darkness.' In *Hope and Impediments: Selected Essays, 1965–1987*, 1–2. London: Heinemann, 1988.

Adler, Jeffrey S. '"The Negro Would Be More Than an Angel to Withstand Such Treatment": African American Homicide in Chicago, 1875–1910.' In *Lethal Imagination: Violence and Brutality in American History*, edited by Micahel A. Bellesiles, 295–314. New York: New York University Press, 1999.

Alcoff, Linda Martin. 'Philosophy and Racial Identity.' *Radical Philosophy* 75 (1996): 5–14.

Allen, Wayne. 'Hannah Arendt's Foundation for a Metaphysics of Evil.' *Southern Journal of Philosophy* 38, no. 2 (2000): 183–206.

Amnesty International Report. 'Belgium: January–December 1997.' *Annual Report 1998*. [On-line.] Amnesty International. <http://www.amnesty.org/ailib/aireport/ar98/eur14.htm>. 23 June 2003.

– 'Concerns in Europe: January–June 1998.' September 1998. [On-line.] Amnesty International. <http://web.amnesty.org/ai.nsf/Index/EUR010021998?OpenDocument&of=COUNTRIES\BELGIUM>. 23 June 2003.

– 'Italy: A Briefing for the UN Committee Against Torture.' May 1999. [On-line.] Amnesty International. <http://www.web.amnesty.org/ai.nsf/index/EUR300021999>. 23 June 2003.

Anderson, Benedict. *Imagined Communities: Reflections on the Origin and Spread of Nationalisms*. London: Verso Press, 1983.

Anderson, Kay. 'Engendering Race Research: Unsettling the Self-Other Dichotomy.' In *Body Space*, edited by N. Duncan, 197–211. New York: Routledge, 1998.

– *Vancouver's Chinatown: Racial Discourse in Canada, 1875–1980*. Montreal: McGill-Queen's University Press, 1991.

Anidjar, Gil. Introduction to *Acts of Religion*, edited by Jacques Derrida and Gil Anidjar, 1–39. New York: Routledge, 2002.

Annan, Kofi. *The Causes of Conflict and the Promotion of Durable Peace and Sustainable Development in Africa: Report of the Secretary–General.* April 1998. [On-line.] United Nations. <http://www.un.org/ecosocdev/geninfo/afrec/sgreport/report.htm>. 23 June 2003.

Arendt, Hannah. *Eichmann in Jerusalem: A Report on the Banality of Evil.* New York: Viking Press, 1963.

– *On the Origins of Totalitarianism.* New York: Harcourt, Brace, Jovanovich Publishers, 1973.

Bannerji, Himani. 'On the Dark Side of the Nation: Politics of Multiculturalism and the State of Canada.' *Journal of Canadian Studies* 31, no. 3 (1996): 103–28.

Beck, E.M., and Stewart E. Tolnay. 'When Race Didn't Matter: Black and White Mob Violence against Their Own Color.' In *Under Sentence of Death: Lynching in the South*, edited by W. Fitzhugh Brundage, 134–54. Chapel Hill: University of North Carolina Press, 1998.

Bederman, Gail. *Manliness and Civilization: A Cultural History of Gender and Race in the United States, 1880–1917.* Chicago: University of Chicago Press, 1995.

Bendersky, Joseph. 'The Disappearance of Blonds: Immigration, Race and the Reemergence of "Thinking White."' *Telos* 104 (1995): 135–58.

Bercuson, David. *Significant Incident: Canada's Army, the Airborne, and the Murder in Somalia.* Toronto: McClelland and Stewart, 1996.

Berger, Carl. 'The True North Strong and Free.' In *Nationalism in Canada*, edited by P. Russell, 3–26. Toronto: McGraw-Hill, 1966.

Berlant, Lauren. *The Anatomy of National Fantasy: Hawthorne, Utopia and Everyday Life.* Chicago: University of Chicago Press, 1991.

– *The Queen of America Goes to Washington City.* Durham, NC: Duke University Press, 1997.

– 'The Subject of True Feeling: Pain, Privacy, and Politics.' In *Feminist Consequences: Theory for the New Century*, edited by Elisabeth Bronfen and Misha Kavka, 126–60. New York: Columbia University Press, 2001.

Berry, John W., and Rudolf Kalin. 'Diversity and Equity in the Canadian Forces.' Paper presented at the Second Biennial Equal Opportunity Research Symposium, Defense Equal Opportunity Management Institute, Patrick Air Force Base, Melbourne, Florida. 2–4 December 1997.

Besteman, Catherine. 'Representing Violence and "Othering" Somalia.' *Cultural Anthropology* 11, no. 1 (1996): 120–33.

Bhabha, Homi. 'A Good Judge of Character: Men, Metaphors, and the Common Culture.' In *Race-ing Justice, Engendering Power: Essays on Anita Hill, Clarence Thomas, and the Construction of Social Reality*, edited by Toni Morrison, 232–50. New York: Pantheon Books, 1992.

– *Nation and Narration.* London: Routledge, 1990.

Birmingham, Peg. 'Holes of Oblivion: The Banality of Radical Evil.' *Hypatia* 18, no. 1 (2003): 88–103.

Bissondath, Neil. *Selling Illusions.* Toronto: Penguin Books, 1994.

Boggs, Carl. 'Overview: Globalization and the New Militarism.' *New Political Science* 24, no. 1 (2002): 9–20.

Bosniak, Linda S. 'Opposing Prop. 187: Undocumented Immigrants and the National Imagination.' *Connecticut Law Review* 28, no. 3 (1996): 555–619.

Bové, Paul. 'Discourse.' In *Critical Terms for Literary Study,* edited by F. Lentricchia and T. McLaughlin, 50–65. Chicago: University of Chicago Press, 1995.

Bowden, Mark. *Black Hawk Down: A Story of Modern War.* New York: Penguin Books, 2000.

Breckenridge, Keith. 'The Allure of Violence: Men, Race and Masculinity on the South African Gold Mines, 1900–1950.' *Journal of Southern African Studies* 24, no. 4 (1998): 669–93.

Brodeur, Jean-Paul. *Violence and Racial Prejudice in the Context of Peacekeeping.* A Study Prepared for the Commission of Inquiry into the Deployment of Canadian Forces to Somalia. Ottawa: Minister of Public Works and Government Services Canada, 1997.

Brooker, Blake. *Somalia Yellow.* Based on a performance by Denise Clarke. Performed by the One Yellow Rabbit Ensemble. Calgary, Alberta. April 2002.

Brouwer, Andrew. *What's in a Name? Identity Documents and Convention Refugees.* Ottawa: Caledon Institute of Social Policy, 1999.

Brown, Kathleen M. *Good Wives, Nasty Wenches, and Anxious Patriarchs: Gender, Race, and Power in Colonial Virginia.* Chapel Hill: University of North Carolina Press, 1996.

Browning, Christopher R. *Ordinary Men: Reserve Police Battalion 101 and the Final Solution in Poland.* New York: HarperCollins, 1992.

Bucholtz, Mary. 'You da Man: Narrating the Racial Other in the Production of White Masculinity.' *Journal of Sociolinguistics* 4 (1999): 443–60.

Bufkin, Jana L. 'Bias Crime as Gendered Behavior.' *Social Justice* 26, no. 1 (1999): 155–76.

Buruma, Ian. 'Revolution from Above.' Review of *Terror and Liberalism*, by Paul Berman. *New York Review of Books*, 1 May 2003, 4.

Butler, John R. 'Somalia and the Imperial Savage: Continuities in the Rhetoric of War.' *Western Journal of Communication* 66, no. 1 (2002): 1–24.

Cariou, Warren. *Lake of the Prairies: A Story of Belonging.* Toronto: Doubleday, 2002.

Chambers, Iain. 'Narratives of Nationalism: Being "British."' In *Space and Place: Theories of Identity and Location*, edited by E. Carter, J. Donald, and J. Squires, 145–64. London: Lawrence and Wishart, 1993.

Chatterjee, Partha. 'Beyond the Nation? Or Within?' *Social Text* 56, no. 16.3 (1998): 57–69.

Chen, Anthony. 'Lives at the Center of the Periphery, Lives at the Periphery of the

Center: Chinese American Masculinities and Bargaining with Hegemony.' *Gender and Society* 13, no. 5 (1999): 584–607.

Ching-Liang Low, Gail. 'His Stories? Narratives and Images of Imperialism.' In *Space and Place: Theories of Identity and Location*, edited by E. Carter, J. Donald, and J. Squires, 187–220. London: Lawrence and Wishart, 1993.

Chomsky, Noam. *The New Military Humanism: Lessons from Kosovo*. Vancouver: New Star Books, 1999.

– *Rogue States: The Rule of Force in World Affairs*. Cambridge, MA: South End Press, 2000.

Chopra, Jarat. 'Introducing Peace-Maintenance.' In *The Politics of Peace-Maintenance*, edited by Jarat Chopra, 1–18. London: Lynne Rienner Publishers, 1998.

Clark, Walter. 'Failed Visions and Uncertain Mandates in Somalia.' In *Learning from Somalia: The Lessons of Armed Humanitarian Intervention*, ed. Walter Clark and Jeffery Herbst, 3–19. Boulder, CO: Westview Press, 1997.

Clarke, George Elliot. 'White Like Canada.' *Transition* 73 (1998):103.

Cohen, Andrew. *While Canada Slept: How We Lost Our Place in the World*. Toronto: McClelland and Stewart, 2003.

Collard, Nathalie. 'Contre le multiculturalisme.' *L'actualité* 8, no. 49 (1994): 6.

Conrad, Joseph. *The Heart of Darkness*. 1901. Reprint, New York: Harper and Row, 1966.

Coulon, Jocelyn. *Soldiers of Diplomacy: The United Nations, Peacekeeping, and the New World Order*. Toronto: University of Toronto Press, 1998.

Courtemanche, Gil. *A Sunday at the Pool in Kigali*. Translated by Patricia Claxton. Toronto: Alfred A. Knopf, 2003.

Crosby, Marcia. 'Construction of the Imaginary Indian.' In *Vancouver Anthology: The Institutional Politics of Art*, edited by Stan Douglas, 267–91.Vancouver: Talonbooks, 1989.

Culhane, Dara. *The Pleasure of the Crown*. Vancouver: Talon Books, 1998.

Daniels, Jessie. *White Lies: Race, Class, Gender, and Sexuality in White Supremacist Discourse*. New York: Routledge, 1997.

Da Silva, Denise Ferreira. 'Towards a Critique of the Socio-Logos of Justice: The Analytics of Raciality and the Production of Universality.' *Social Identities* 7, no. 3 (2001): 421–54.

Dawson, Graham. 'The Blond Bedouin.' In *Manful Assertions: Masculinities in Britain since 1800*, edited by Michael Roper and John Tosh, 113–44. New York: Routledge, 1991.

Debrix, Francois. *Re-Envisioning Peacekeeping: The United Nations and the Mobilization of Ideology*. Minneapolis: University of Minnesota Press, 1999.

Delbo, Charlotte. *Auschwitz and After*. Translated by Rosette C. Lamont. New Haven: Yale University Press, 1995.

Delgado, Richard, and Jean Stefancic. 'Cosmopolitan Inside Out: International Norms and the Struggle for Civil Rights and Local Justice.' *Connecticut Law Review* 27, no. 3 (1995): 773–88.

Desbarats, Peter. 'Somalia: The Long-Term Effects.' In *Canada and the New World Order: Facing the Millennium*, edited by Michael J. Tucker, Raymond B. Blake, and P.E. Bryden, 33–43. Toronto: Irwin, 2000.

– *Somalia Cover-Up: A Commissioner's Journal*. Toronto: McClelland and Stewart, 1997.

Du Bois, W.E.B. *The Souls of Black Folk*. 1903. Reprint, New York: Fawcett Publications, 1962.

duCille, Anne. 'The Occult of True Black Womanhood: Critical Demeanor and Black Feminist Studies.' *Signs: Journal of Women in Culture and Society* 19, no. 3 (1994): 591–629.

Dyer, Richard. *White*. New York: Routledge, 1997.

Ehrenreich, Nancy. 'Subordination and Symbiosis: Mechanisms of Mutual Support between Subordinating Systems.' *UMKC Law Review* 71, no. 2 (2003): 251–324.

Enloe, Cynthia. *The Morning After: Sexual Politics at the End of the Cold War*. Berkeley: University of California Press, 1993.

– 'Nationalism and Masculinity.' In *Bananas, Beaches, and Bases: Making Feminist Sense of International Politics*, 42–64. London: Pandora, 1989.

Fanon, Frantz. *The Wretched of the Earth*. New York: Grove, 1963.

Farley, Anthony Paul. 'The Black Body as Fetish Object.' *Oregon Law Review* 76 (1997): 457–535.

– 'The Poetics of Colorlined Space.' In *Crossroads, Directions, and a New Critical Race Theory*, edited by Francisco Valdes, Jerome McKristal Culp, and Angela Harris, 97–158. Philadelphia: Temple University Press, 2002.

Farmanfarmalian, Abouall. 'Did You Measure Up? The Role of Race and Sexuality in the Gulf War.' In *Collateral Damage: The New World Order at Home and Abroad*, edited by C. Peters, 111–38. Boston: South End Press, 1992.

Faulkner, William. *Absalom, Absalom!* New York: Random House, 1951.

Fellows, Mary Louise, and Sherene Razack. 'The Race to Innocence: Confronting Hierarchical Relations among Women.' *Journal of Gender, Race and Justice* 1, no. 2 (1998): 335–52.

Felman, Shoshana. 'Forms of Judicial Blindness, or the Evidence of What Cannot Be Seen.' *Critical Inquiry* 23 (1997): 738–88.

Ferber, Abby L. *White Man Falling: Race, Gender and White Supremacy*. New York: Rowman and Littlefield Publishers, 1998.

Fogel, Stanley. 'Decolonizing Canadian Literature: The Deconstructive Paradigm.' In *Unequal Partners: A Comparative Analysis of Relations between Austria and the Federal*

Republic of Germany and between Canada and the United States, edited by Harald von Riekhoff and Hanspeter Neuhold, 231–40. Boulder, CO: Westview Press, 1993.

Franco, Jere. 'Bringing Them in Alive: Selective Service and Native Americans.' *Journal of Ethnic Studies* 18, no.3 (1990): 1–27.

Galloway, Donald. 'Liberalism, Globalism, and Immigration.' *Queen's Law Journal* 18, no. 2 (1993): 266–9.

Geddes, Jennifer L. 'Banal Evil and Useless Knowledge: Hannah Arendt and Charlotte Delbo on Evil after the Holocaust.' *Hypatia* 18, no. 1 (2003): 104–15.

Gibson, James William. *Warrior Dreams: Violence and Manhood in Post-Vietnam America*. Toronto: HarperCollins 1994.

Glover, Jonathan. *Humanity: A Moral History of the Twentieth Century*. London: Pimlico, 2001.

Goldberg, David. *Racist Culture: Philosophy and the Politics of Meaning*. Cambridge, MA: Blackwell, 1993.

Goldhagen, Daniel Jonah. *Hitler's Willing Executioners: Ordinary Germans and the Holocaust*. New York: Alfred A. Knopf, 1996.

Goodey, Jo. 'Understanding Racism and Masculinity.' *International Journal of the Sociology of Law* 26, no. 4 (1998): 393–418.

Goodhand, Jonathan, and David Hulme. 'From Wars to Complex Political Emergencies: Understanding Conflict and Peace-building in the New World Disorder.' *Third World Quarterly* 20, no. 1 (1999): 13–26.

Gordon, Donald. 'Canada as Peacekeeper.' In *Canada's Role as a Middle Power: Papers Given at the Third Annual Banff Conference on World Development*, edited by J. King Gordon, 51–66. Toronto: Canadian Institute of International Affairs, 1965.

Granatstein, J.L. 'Peacekeeping: Did Canada Make a Difference? And What Difference Did Peacekeeping Make to Canada?' In *Making a Difference? Canada's Foreign Policy in a Changing World Order*, edited by John English and Norman Hillman, 222–36. Toronto: Lester Publishing, 1992.

– *Canada and the New World Order: Facing the Millennium*. Toronto: Irwin Publishing, 2000.

Granatstein, J.L., and David J. Bercuson. *War and Peacekeeping: From South Africa to the Gulf – Canada's Limited Wars*. Toronto: Key Porter Books, 1991.

Grewal, Inderpal. 'On the New Global Feminism and the Family of Nations: Dilemmas of Transnational Feminist Practice.' In *Talking Visions: Multicultural Feminism in a Transnational Age*, edited by Ella Shohat, 501–30. Cambridge: MIT Press, 1998.

– 'The Postcolonial, Ethnic Studies, and the Diaspora: The Contexts of Ethnic Immigrant/Migrant Studies.' *Socialist Studies* 24, no. 4 (1994): 45–74.

Guillot, Phillipe. 'France, Peacekeeping and Humanitarian Intervention.' *International Peacekeeping* 1, no. 1 (1994): 30–43.

Hague, Euan. 'Rape, Power and Masculinity: The Construction of Gender and
    National Identities in the War in Bosnia-Herzegovina.' In *Gender and Catastrophe*,
    edited by Ronit Lentin, 50–63. London: Zed Books, 1997.
Harris, Angela P. 'Gender, Violence, Race and Criminal Justice.' *Stanford Law Review*
    52 (2000): 777–808.
Hayes, Geoffrey. 'Canada as a Middle Power: The Case of Peacekeeping.' In *Niche
    Diplomacy: Middle Powers after the Cold War*, edited by Andrew Cooper, 73–89. New
    York: St Martin's Press, 1997.
Hochschild, Adam. *King Leopold's Ghost: A Story of Greed, Terror, and Heroism in Colo-
    nial Africa*. New York: Mariner Books, Houghton Mifflin Company, 1999.
Holm, Tom. 'Culture, Ceremonialism and Stress: American Indian Veterans and the
    Vietnam War.' *Armed Forces and Society* 12, no. 2 (1986): 237–51.
Honig, Bonnie. 'How Foreignness "Solves" Democracy's Problems.' *Social Text* 56, no.
    16.3 (1998): 1–28.
Hooper, Charlotte. 'Masculinist Practices and Gender Politics: The Operation of
    Multiple Masculinities in International Relations.' In *The 'Man' Question in Interna-
    tional Relations*, edited by Marysia Zalewski and Jane Parpart, 275–88. Boulder,
    CO: Westview Press, 1998.
Howe, Herbert M. *Ambiguous Order: Military Forces in African States*. London: Lynne
    Rienner Publishers, 2001.
Hudson, Anna. 'September 11, 2002 Handout.' Distributed by Propeller Gallery,
    Toronto. [On-line.] Propeller Gallery. <www.propellerctr.com>. 23 June 2003.
Hughson, John. 'The Boys Are Back in Town: Soccer Support and the Social Repro-
    duction of Masculinity.' *Journal of Sport and Social Issues* 24, no. 1 (2000): 8–23.
Ignatieff, Michael. *Blood and Belonging: Journeys into the New Nationalism*. Toronto:
    Penguin, 1993.
– *Virtual War: Kosovo and Beyond*. New York: Henry Holt, 2000.
Indra, Doreen, ed. *Engendering Forced Migration: Theory and Practice*. New York:
    Berghahn Books, 1999.
Jacubowski, Lisa. *Immigration and the Legalization of Racism*. Halifax: Fernwood Pub-
    lishing, 1997.
Jamieson, Ruth, Nigel South, and Ian Taylor. 'Economic Liberalization and Cross-
    Border Crime: The North American Free Trade Area and Canada's Border with the
    U.S.A. Part 11.' *International Journal of the Sociology of Law* 26, no. 3 (1998): 285–319.
Johnson, Paul. 'The United Nations Should Foster Self-Government in Africa.' In
    Interventionism, edited by Paul A. Winters, 88–93. San Diego: Greenhaven Press,
    1995.
Karner, Tracy Xavia. 'Engendering Violent Men: Oral Histories of Military Masculin-
    ity.' In *Masculinities and Violence*, edited by Lee H. Bowker, 197–254. London: Sage,
    1998.

214 Bibliography

Kobayashi, Audrey. 'Challenging the National Dream: Gender Persecution and Canadian Immigration Law.' In *Nationalism, Racism and the Rule of Law*, edited by Peter Fitzpatrick, 61–73. Aldershot: Dartmouth Publishing, 1995.

Krause, Keith. 'Canadian Defence and Security, Policy in a Changing Global Context.' *Canadian Defence Quarterly/Revue Canadien de Defense* 23, no.4 (1994): 6–12.

Legault Alfred, in collaboration with Manon Tessier. *Canada and Peacekeeping: Three Major Debates*. Clementsport, NS: Canadian Peacekeeping Press, 1999.

Lehmann, Ingrid. 'Peacekeeping, Public Perceptions and the Need for Consent.' *Canadian Defence Quarterly* 25, no. 2 (1995): 17–19.

Létourneau, Gilles. *Dishonoured Legacy: The Lessons of the Somalia Affair*. 5 Volumes. In Commission of Inquiry into the Deployment of Canadian Forces to Somalia, *Information Legacy: A Compendium of Source Material/Commission of Inquiry into the Deployment of Canadian Forces to Somalia*. Ottawa: Minister of Public Works and Government Services Canada, 1997.

Litz, Brett T. 'The Psychological Demands of Peacekeeping for Military Personnel.' *Clinical Quarterly* 6, no. 1 (Winter 1996). [On-line.] The National Center for Post-Traumatic Stress Disorder. <http://www.ncptsd.org/publications/cq/v6/n1/litz.html>. 23 June 2003.

Litz, Brett T., Lynda A. King, Daniel W. King, Susan Orsillo, and Matthew J Friedman. 'Warriors as Peacekeepers: Features of the Somalia Experience and PTSD.' *Journal of Consulting and Clinical Psychology* 65, no. 6 (1997): 1001–10.

Loomis, Dan G. *The Somalia Affair: Reflections on Peacemaking and Peacekeeping*. Rev. ed. Ottawa: DGL Publications, 1997.

Lowe, Lisa. *Immigrant Acts*. Durham, NC: Duke University Press, 1996.

MacLaren, Roy. *Canadians on the Nile, 1882–1898*. Vancouver: University of British Columbia Press, 1978.

Malkii, Liisa. 'Speechless Emissaries: Refugees, Humanitarianism, and Dehistoricization.' *Cultural Anthropology* 11, no. 3 (1996): 377–404.

Mamdani, Mahmood. *When Victims Become Killers: Colonialism, Nativism, and the Genocide in Rwanda*. Princeton, NJ: Princeton University Press, 2001.

Marin, André. 'Systemic Treatment of Canadian Forces Members with Post- Traumatic Stress Disorder.' Special Reports (Ottawa: Government of Canada, 2001). [On-line.] Ombudsman: National Defences and Canadian Forces. <http://www.ombudsman.forces.gc.ca/reports/mceachern_e.htm>. 23 June 2003.

Martin, Pierre, and Michel Fortmann. 'Canadian Public Opinion and Peacekeeping in a Turbulent World.' *International Journal* 50 (1995): 370–99.

McClintock, Anne. *Imperial Leather: Race, Gender, and Sexuality in the Colonial Context*. New York: Routledge, 1996.

McNulty, Mel. 'France's Role in Rwanda and External Military Intervention: A Double Discrediting.' *International Peacekeeping* 4, no. 3 (1997): 24–44.

McRae, Rob, and Don Hubert, eds. *Human Security and the New Diplomacy: Protecting People, Promoting Peace*. Montreal: McGill-Queen's University Press, 2001.

Mehlum, Lars, and Lars Weisaeth. 'Predictors of Posttraumatic Stress Reactions in Norwegian U.N. Peacekeepers seven Years after Service.' *Journal of Traumatic Stress* 15, no. 1 (2002): 17–26.

Messerschmidt, James W. *Crime as Structured Action: Gender, Race, Class, and Crime in the Making*. London: Sage, 1997.

– 'Varieties of "Real Men."' In *Gender Violence: Interdisciplinary Perspectives*, edited by Laura L. O'Toole and Jessica R. Schiffman, 92–109. New York: New York University Press, 1997.

– 'Men Victimizing Men: The Case of Lynching, 1865–1900.' In *Masculinities and Violence*, ed. Lee H. Bowker, 125–51. London: Sage, 1998.

Messner, Michael A. *Politics of Masculinities: Men in Movements*. London: Sage, 1997.

Michalowski, Helen. 'The Army Will Make a 'Man' Out of You.' In *A Certain Terror: Heterosexism, Militarism, Violence and Change*, edited by Richard Cleaver and Patricia Myers, 154–61. Chicago: American Friends Service Committee, 1993.

Mikki, Roy. *Broken Entries: Race, Subjectivity, Writing*. Toronto: Mercury Press, 1998.

Miller, Laura, and Charles Moskos. 'Humanitarians or Warriors?" Race, Gender, and Combat Status in Operation Restore Hope.' *Armed Forces and Society* 21, no. 4 (1995): 615–37.

Milner, Marc. 'Defence Policy for a New Century: Report of the University of New Brunswick Workshop on the Defence Review.' *Canadian Defence Quarterly* 23, no. 4 (1994): 17–22.

Morell, Robert. 'Of Boys and Men: Masculinity and Gender in Southern African Studies.' *Journal of Southern African Studies* 24, no. 4 (1998): 605–30.

Morrison, Toni. 'The Official Story: Dead Man Golfing.' In *Birth of a Nation'hood: Gaze, Script, and Spectacle in the O.J. Simpson Case*, edited by Toni Morrison and Claudia Brodsky Lacour, vii–xxvii. New York: Pantheon Books, 1997.

Mortimer, Edward. 'Under What Circumstances Should the U.N. Intervene Militarily in a "Domestic" Crisis?' In *Peacemaking and Peacekeeping for the New Century*, edited by Olawa A. Otunnu and Michael W. Doyle, 111–44. Lanham, MD: Rowman and Littlefield, 1998.

Mosse, George L. *Toward the Final Solution: A History of European Racism*. Madison: University of Wisconsin Press, 1985.

Murray, Yxta Maya. 'The Latino- Crisis of Citizenship.' *U.C. Davis Law Review* 31, no. 2 (1998): 503–17.

Nagel, Joanne. 'Masculinity and Nationalism: Gender and Sexuality in the Making of Nations.' *Ethnic and Racial Studies* 21, no. 2 (1998): 247–51.

Nauright, John. 'Colonial Manhood and Imperial Race Virility: British Responses to Post–Boer War Colonial Rugby Tours.' In *Making Men: Rugby and Masculine Iden-*

tity, edited by John Nauright and Timothy J.L. Chandler, 121–39. London: Frank Cass, 1996.

Neal, Sarah. 'Embodying Black Madness, Embodying White Femininity: Populist (Re)Presentations and Public Policy – The Case of Christopher Clunis and Jayne Zito.' *Sociological Research Online* 3, no. 4. <http://www.socresonline.org.uk/socresonline/3/4/6/html>. 23 June, 2003.

Nelson, Dana. *National Manhood: Capitalist Citizenship and the Imagined Fraternity of White Men*. Durham, NC: Duke University Press, 1998.

Niva, Steve. 'Tough and Tender: New World Order Masculinity and the Gulf War.' In *The 'Man' Question in International Relations*, edited by Marysia Zalewski and Jane Parpart, 109–28. Boulder, CO: Westview Press, 1998.

Off, Carol. *The Lion, the Fox, and the Eagle: A Story of Generals and Justice in Rwanda and Yugoslavia*. Toronto: Random House, 2000.

Passey, G. 'Psychological Consequences of Canadian U.N. Peacekeeping Duties in Croatia and Bosnia 1992–93.' Paper presented at the Fourth European Conference on Traumatic Stress, Paris, France, May 1995.

Pease, Bob. *Recreating Men: Postmodern Masculinity Politics*. London: Sage Publications, 2000.

Pieterse, Jan Nederveen. 'Sociology of Humanitarian Intervention: Bosnia, Rwanda and Somalia Compared.' In *World Orders in the Making: Humanitarian Intervention and Beyond*, edited by Jan Nederveen Pieterse, 71–94. New York: St Martin's Press, 1998.

Polman, Linda. *We Did Nothing. Why the Truth Doesn't Always Come Out When the UN Goes In*. Translated by Rob Bland. Toronto: Viking, 2003.

Pratt, Mary Louise. *Imperial Eyes: Travel Writing and Transculturation*. London: Routledge, 1992.

Pred, Alan. 'Memory and the Cultural Reworking of Crisis: Racisms and the Current Moment of Danger in Sweden, or Wanting It Like Before.' *Environment and Planning D: Society and Space* 16 (1998): 635–64.

Prunier, Gerard. 'The Experience of European Armies in Operation Restore Hope.' In *Learning from Somalia: The Lessons of Armed Humanitarian Intervention*, edited by Walter Clarke and Jeffery Herbst, 135–47. Boulder, CO: Westview Press, 1997.

Pyke, Karen D. 'Class-Based Masculinities: The Interdependence of Gender, Class and Interpersonal Power.' *Gender and Society* 10, no. 5 (1996): 527–49.

Rabinbach, Anson, and Jessica Benjamin. Foreword to *Male Fantasies*, Vol. 2: *Male Bodies: Psychoanalyzing the White Terror*, by Klaus Theweleit. Translated by Erica Carter and Chris Turner. Minneapolis: University of Minnesota Press, 1989.

Razack, Sherene H. 'From the "Clean Snows of Petawawa:" The Violence of Canadian Peacekeepers in Somalia.' *Cultural Anthropology* 15, no. 1 (2000): 127–63.

– 'Gendered Racial Violence and Spatialized Justice: The Murder of Pamela George.' In *Race, Space, and the Law: Unmapping a White Settler Society*, edited by S. Razack, 121–56. Toronto: Between the Lines, 2002.

- *Looking White People in the Eye: Gender, Race, and Culture in Courtrooms and Classrooms.* Toronto: University of Toronto Press, 1998.
- 'Making Canada White: Law and the Policing of Bodies of Colour in the 1990s.' *Canadian Journal of Law and Society* 14, no. 1 (1999): 159–84.
- '"Outwhiting the White Guys": Men of Colour and Peacekeeping Violence.' *UMKC Law Review* 71, no. 2 (2002): 331–53.
- '"Simple Logic": Race, the Identity Documents Rule and the Story of a Nation Besieged and Betrayed.' *Journal of Law and Social Policy* 15 (2000): 181–209.
- 'A Violent Culture or Culturalized Violence: Narratives of Sexual Violence Against South Asian Women.' *Studies in Practical Philosophy* 3, no. 1 (2003): 80–109.
- ed. *Race, Space, and the Law: Unmapping a White Settler Society.* Toronto: Between the Lines, 2002.
- Reid-Pharr, Robert. 'Tearing the Goat's Flesh: Homosexuality, Abjection and the Production of a Late Twentieth-Century Black Masculinity.' *Studies in the Novel* 28, no. 3 (1996): 372–94.
- Ridley, Hugh. *Images of Imperial Rule.* New York: St Martin's Press, 1983.
- Robinson, Laura. *Crossing the Line: Violence and Sexual Assault in Canada's National Sport.* Toronto: McClelland and Stewart, 1998.
- Robinson, W.G. 'Illegal Immigrants in Canada: Recent Developments.' *International Migration Review* 18, no. 3 (1984): 480.
- Rosaldo, Renato. 'Imperialist Nostalgia.' *Representations* 26 (1989): 107–22.
- Ross, Marlon. 'In Search of Black Men's Masculinities.' *Feminist Studies* 24, no. 3 (1998): 599–626.
- Ruddick, Sue. 'Constructing Difference in Public Spaces: Race, Class, and Gender As Interlocking Systems.' *Urban Geography* 17, no. 2 (1996): 132–51.
- Rutherford, Jonathan. *Forever England: Reflections on Masculinity and Empire.* London: Lawrence and Wishart, 1997.
- Said, Edward. *Culture and Imperialism.* New York: Alfred Knopf, 1993.
- *The Question of Palestine.* New York: Vintage Books, 1992.
- Sassen, Saskia. *Globalization and Its Discontents: Essays on the New Mobility of People and Money.* New York: New York University Press, 1998.
- 'Whose City Is It? Globalization and the Formation of New Claims.' *Public Culture* 8 (1996): 216–17.
- Savran, David. *Taking It Like a Man: White Masculinity, Masochism, and Contemporary American Culture.* Princeton, NJ: Princeton University Press, 1998.
- Sayers, Derek. 'British Reaction to the Amritsar Massacre, 1919–1920.' *Past and Present* (1991): 130–64.
- Schmalz, Peter S. *The History of the Saugeen Indians.* Ottawa: Ontario Historical Society, 1977.
- Shapiro, Michael J. *Cinematic Political Thought: Narrating Race, Nation and Gender.* New York: New York University Press, 1999.

Shepherd, Ben. *A War of Nerves: Soldiers and Psychiatrists in the Twentieth Century.* Cambridge: Harvard University Press, 2001.

Shields, Robert. *Places on the Margins: Alternative Geographies of Modernity.* London: Routledge, 1991.

Sinha, Mrinalini. 'Giving Masculinity a History: Some Contributions from the Historiography of Colonial India.' *Gender and History* 11, no. 3 (1999): 445–60.

Slotkin, Richard. *Gunfighter Nation: The Myth of the Frontier in Twentieth-Century America.* New York: Atheneum, 1992.

– *Regeneration through Violence: The Mythology of the American Frontier, 1600–1860.* Middletown, CT: Wesleyan University Press, 1973.

Smouts, Marie-Claude. 'The Political Aspects of Peace-Keeping Operations.' In *United Nations Peacekeeping Operations: A Guide to French Policies*, edited by Brigitte Stern, translated by David Boyle, 7–39. Paris: United Nations University, 1998.

Sontag, Susan. *Regarding the Pain of Others.* New York: Farrar, Straus, and Giroux, 2003.

Stoler, Ann Laura. *Race and the Education of Desire: Foucault's History of Sexuality and the Colonial Order of Things.* Durham, NC: Duke University Press, 1995.

Stasiulus, Daiva, and Radha Jhappan. 'The Fractious Politics of a Settler Society: Canada.' In *Unsettling Settler Societies: Articulation of Gender, Race, Ethnicity and Class*, edited by D. Stasiulus and Nira Yuval-Davis, 95–131. London: Sage, 1995.

Swyngedouw, Marc. 'The "Threatening Immigrant" in Flanders, 1930–1980: Redrawing the Social Space.' *New Community* 21, no. 3 (1995): 325–40.

Tal, Kali. *Worlds of Hurt: Reading the Literatures of Trauma.* New York: Cambridge University Press, 1996.

Theweleit, Klaus. *Male Fantasies.* Vol. 1. *Women, Floods, Bodies, History.* Translated by Stephen Conway in collaboration with Erica Carter and Chris Turner. Foreword by Barbara Ehrenreich. Minneapolis: University of Minnesota Press, 1987.

– *Male Fantasies.* Vol. 2. *Male Bodies: Psychoanalyzing the White Terror.* Translated by Erica Carter and Chris Turner in collaboration with Stephen Conway. Minneapolis: University of Minnesota Press, 1987.

Thobani, Sunera. 'Nationalizing Citizens, Bordering Immigrant Women: Globalization and the Racialization of Citizenship in Late Twentieth-Century Canada.' Ph.D. diss., Simon Fraser University, 1999.

Trexler, Richard C. *Sex and Conquest: Gendered Violence, Political Order, and the European Conquest of the Americas.* Cambridge, UK: Polity Press, 1995.

Tripodi, Paolo. 'Mogadishu versus the World.' *The Colonial Legacy in Somalia: Rome and Mogadishu – From Colonial Administration to Operation Restore Hope*, 138–65. New York: St Martin's Press, 1999.

Uebel, Michael. 'Men in Color: Introducing Race and the Subject of Masculinities.' In *Race and the Subject of Masculinities*, edited by Harry Stecopoulos and Michael Uebel, 1–14. Durham, NC: Duke University Press, 1997.

van Dijk, Teun. *Elite Discourse and Racism*. Newbury Park, CA: Sage, 1993.

Vettel-Becker, Patricia. 'Destruction and Delight: World War II Combat Photography and the Aesthetic Inscription of Masculine Identity." *Men and Masculinities* 5, no. 1 (200): 80–102.

Villa, Dana R. *Politics, Philosophy, Terror: Essays on the Thought of Hannah Arendt*. Princeton, NJ: Princeton University Press, 1999.

Watney, Simon. 'Missionary Positions: AIDS, "Africa," and Race.' In *Out There: Marginalization and Contemporary Cultures*, edited by Russell Ferguson, Martha Gever, Trinh T. Minh-ha, and Cornel West, 89–106. New York: New Museum of Contemporary Art; Cambridge: MIT Press, 1990.

Weisaeth, Lars. 'Armed Conflicts.' In *International Responses to Traumatic Stress: Humanitarian, Human Rights, Justice, Peace, and Development Contributions, Collaborative Actions, and Future Initiatives*, edited by Yael Danieli, Nigel S. Rodley, and Lars Weisaeth, 257–82. Amityville, NY: Baywood Publishing, 1996.

– 'Preventive Intervention.' Paper presented at the North American Treaty Organization Conference, 1994.

Williams, Patricia. *The Alchemy of Race and Rights: Diary of a Law Professor*. Cambridge: Harvard University Press, 1991.

Williams, Raymond. 'Structures of Feeling.' In *Marxism and Literature*, 128–35. New York: Oxford University Press, 1977.

Wilson, Richard A. 'Reconciliation and Revenge in Post-Apartheid South Africa: Rethinking Legal Pluralism and Human Rights.' *Current Anthropology* 41, no. 1 (2000): 75–99.

Winslow, Donna. *The Canadian Airborne Regiment in Somalia: A Socio-Cultural Inquiry*. A Study Prepared for the Commission of Inquiry into the Deployment of Canadian Forces to Somalia. Ottawa: Minister of Public Works and Government Services Canada, 1997.

Wirick, Gregory. 'Canada, Peacekeeping and the United Nations.' In *Canada among Nations, 1992–1993: A New World Order*, edited by Fen Osler Hampson and Christopher Maule, 94–114. Ottawa: Carleton University Press, 1992.

Women's Caucus for Gender Justice. 'Peacekeeping Watch: Documenting Human Rights Violations Committed by UN Peacekeepers.' [On-line.] Women's Caucus for Gender Justice. <http://www.iccwomen.org/pkwatch/>. 23 June 2003.

Worthington, Peter, and Kyle Brown. *Scapegoat: How the Army Betrayed Kyle Brown*. Toronto: Seal Books, 1997.

Wright, Richard. *Native Son*. New York: HarperCollins, 1993.

Zack-Williams, Tunde, Diane Frost, and Alex Thomson, eds. *Africa in Crisis: New Challenges and Possibilities*. London: Pluto Press, 2002.

Zalewski, Marysia, and Jane Parpart, eds. *The 'Man' Question in International Relations*. Boulder, CO: Westview Press, 1998.

Zimmerman, Patricia R. *States of Emergency: Documentaries, Wars, Democracies.* Mineapolis: University of Minnesota Press, 2000.

Zinn, Maxine Baca. 'Chicano Men and Masculinity.' In *Men's Lives,* edited by Michael Kimmel and Michael Messner, 25–34. Toronto: Allyn and Bacon, 1998.

Zwick, Jim. ed., *Anti-Imperialism in the United States, 1898–1935.* [On-line.] BoondocksNet.com. <http://www.boondocksnet.com/ai/>. 16 February 2003.

News Articles

African Rights. 'Somalia: Human Rights Abuses by the United Nations Forces.' July 1993. [On-line.] African Rights. <http://www.unimondo.org/AfricanRights/html/reports.html>. 23 June 2003.

Akin, David. 'Worse Than the Disease,' *Globe and Mail,* 14 September 2002, F7.

Associated Press. '3 U.N. Soldiers Die in Somali Ambush.' *New York Times,* 3 July 1993, A3.

Bellett, Gerry. 'Traumatized Former Peacekeepers Will Be Offered Counselling in BC.' *Vancouver Sun,* 7 July 2000, B5.

Billet, Francois. 'Au secours du general Dallaire.' *La Presse,* 9 July 2000, A15.

Bindman, Stephen. 'Graphic Photos Key Evidence in Court Martial.' *Ottawa Citizen,* 6 November 1994, A4.

– "'I'm Just Asking for the Truth": Clayton Matchee's Wife Wants Answers about Her Husband's "Suicide" Attempt and the Role an Anti-Malaria Drug Played in Somalia.' *Ottawa Citizen,* 22 June 1998, A5.

Bissonnette, Lise. 'Ayatollah, danger.' *Le Devoir,* 12 December 1994, A6.

Bissoondath, Neil. 'Don't Call Me Ethnic: I Am Canadian.' *Saturday Night,* October 1994, 22.

'Canada Notes: Somalia: Part 2.' *Maclean's,* 31 March 1997, 35.

Canadian Press. 'Canada's Shame.' *Toronto Star,* 8 November 1994, A1, A3.

– 'Canadians Kill Man Guarding Aid in Somalia.' *Toronto Star,* 18 March 1993, A20.

– 'Captain Went Unpublished for Brutality.' *Toronto Star,* 28 February 1996, A5.

– 'Chief Fears Wave of Teen Suicide.' *Ottawa Citizen,* 28 March 1993, A5.

– 'Ex-Soldiers Fault Airborne Leaders.' *Winnipeg Free Press,* 21 January 1995, A5.

– 'Hate Mail Shakes Soldier's Parents.' *Hamilton Spectator,* 29 November 1994, A2.

– 'Mercredi Links Tragedies to Poverty.' *Calgary Herald,* 25 March 1993, A20.

– 'Morale in Military Suffering, Study Says.' *Times Colonist* (Victoria), 30 January 1995, 1.

Cheney, Peter. 'The Gung-ho Regiment That Met Disaster in Somalia.' *Toronto Star,* 15 January 1994, A1.

– 'Death and Dishonour.' *Toronto Star,* 16 July 1994, B2.

Chidley, Joe. 'Bonding and Brutality.' *Maclean's,* 30 January 1995, 18.

Claridge, Thomas. 'Jail Term Urged for Consultant to "Refugees."' *Globe and Mail*, 13 January 1989, A15.

Colebourn, John. 'Disturbing New Troop Photos Found.' *Toronto Star*, 10 October 1996, A13.

Corelli, Rae. 'Deliverance: U.S. Marines Land in Somalia.' *Maclean's*, 21 December 1992, 12–15.

Coulon, Jocelyn. 'Massacre de Casques bleus au Rwanda.' *Le Devoir*, 6 December, 1997, A5.

Crossette, Barbara. 'The World Expected Peace. It Found a New Brutality.' *New York Times*, 24 January 1999.

Delacourt, Susan. 'Immigration Deal for Portuguese Off.' *Globe and Mail*, 1 August 1990, A7.

DePalma, Anthony. 'Canada Accuses 47 of Misconduct in Bosnia.' *New York Times*, 18 January 1997, A6.

DiManno, Rosie. 'Military Cover-Up Outrages Us More Than Somali Deaths.' *Toronto Star*, 7 October 1996, A7.

Edwards, Peter. 'Ipperwash Officer's Defence Was Flawed, Court Told.' *Toronto Star*, 16 September 1999, A5.

Erlanger, Steven. 'The Ugliest American.' *New York Times Magazine*, 2 April 2000, 52–6.

Escobar, Juan. 'New Law to Curb Refugees Violates Two Rights Charters, Lawyer Asserts.' *Globe and Mail*, 28 January 1989, A12.

Escobar, Pepe. 'The New Imperialism.' *Asia Times*, 6 November 2001. [On-line.] Asia Times. <http://www.atimes.com/c-asia/ck06aG01.html>. 23 June 2003.

Evenson, Brad, with files from Ron Corbett. 'Broken Dallaire, Haunted by Rwanda, Lies Drunk in Park.' *National Post*, 29 June 2000, A1, A8.

Fisher, Matthew. 'Our Troops Aren't Out of Control.' *Toronto Sun*, 22 January 1996, A11.

Foss, Krista. 'Military on Guard for Signs of Stress as Soldiers Return.' *Globe and Mail*, 31 July 2002, A5.

Fraser, Graham. 'In Support of Canada's Role on World Stage.' *Toronto Star*, 17 September 2000, A11.

Fulford, Robert. 'Canada's Anti-Racism Industry Never Quits.' *National Post*, 11 January 2003, A16.

Giguere, Monique. 'Le général Dallaire ne va pas mieux.' *Le Soleil*, 14 October 2000, A19.

Giroux, Raymond. 'A l'assaut des marchands d'illusion.' *Le Soleil*, 21 November 1994, A14.

Gordon, Charles. 'Why the Somalia Report Failed to Shock.' *Maclean's*, 28 July 1997, 7.

Goyette, Linda. 'Somalia Inquiry Must Plunge Ahead.' *Edmonton Journal*, 7 April 1996, F8.

Greenaway, Norma. '"Bankrupt" Forces Need $2B: Dallaire.' *Ottawa Citizen*, 14 November 2002, A5.

Gregoretti, Marco. 'Primo Inchiesta.' *Panorama* Magazine. [On-line.] Panorama. <http://www22.mondadori.com/panorama/numeri/pan2497/mag/primo_inchiesta.html>. 23 June 2003.

Hall, Tony. 'Who Silenced Clayton Matchee? We Did.' *Canadian Forum*, April 1997, 5–6.

Hanlon, M. 'RCMP Investigate Deaths of Saskatoon Aboriginals.' *Toronto Star*, 17 February 2000, A3.

Hoover, Travis. Review of *The Last Just Man*, *Capsule Review*, 30 April 2002. [On-line.] Filk Freak Central. <http://www.filmfreakcentral.net/hotdocs/hdapr30capsules.htm#just>. 23 June 2003.

Howard, Robert. 'Dallaire: U.S. Troops a Liability.' *Hamilton Spectator*, 17 March 2001, D4.

Ignatieff, Michael. 'A Bungling UN Undermines Itself.' *New York Times*, 15 May 2000, A25.

Joseph, Clifton. 'On Your Mark, Get Set! Go Multiculti!' *This Magazine*, 5 January 1995, 24–7.

Kenna, Kathleen. 'Canucks "Ultimate Boy Scouts" - and Other U.S. Theories: 500 Academics in U.S. Puzzle Over Elusive Canadian.' *Toronto Star*, 18 November 1999, A14.

Koch, George. 'The Cross.' *Saturday Night*, September 1996.

Lachance, Lise. 'Chronique d'un massacre annonce.' *Le Soleil*, 11 November 2000, D13.

Leblanc, Gerald. 'La Grande Illusion,' *La Presse*, 30 October 1994, B1.

Lewis, Robert. 'Duplicity and Cowardice.' *Maclean's*, 14 July 1997, 2.

Lipovenko, Dorothy. 'Refugee Law Satisfies Charter, Judge Rules.' *Globe and Mail*, 5 January 1989, A4.

Lorch, Donatella. 'Marines Begin Somali Shooting Inquiry.' *New York Times International*, 5 March 1993, A6, and 7 April 1993, A6.

Malarek, Victor. 'Church Council Files Suit Challenging Refugee Law.' *Globe and Mail*, 4 January 1989, A1.

Maracle, Brian. 'Crazywater: The Cycle of Native Alcoholism Must Be Exposed If It Is to Be Broken.' *Ottawa Citizen*, 29 March 1993, A9.

Meissner, Dirk. 'MP Out of Touch on Racism Opinions.' *Times Colonist* (Victoria), 21 January 1995, 1.

Metropolitan Desk. 'Excerpts from Final Arguments in Officers' Trial.' *New York Times*, 3 June 1999, B6.

Murphy, Dean E. 'Old War Words Raise Academic Ire.' *Toronto Star*, 15 January 2003, A2.

Nemeth, Mary. 'Somalia: City of Slaughter.' *Maclean's*, 14 January 1991, 28.

Newswire. 'Moaning Termed Nothing Unusual.' *Times Colonist* (Victoria), 20 January, 1995, 1.

Phillip, Nourbese M. 'Signifying Nothing.' *Border/Lines Magazine* 36/37 (1995): 4.

O'Reilly, Finbarr. 'Price of Waging Peace: Roméo Dallaire's Collapse Symbolizes a New Type of Stress Afflicting Soldiers.' *National Post*, 15 July 2000, B1, B5.

Panetta, Alexander. 'Soldiers Sue Military Over Stress Syndrome.' *Toronto Star*, 27 May 2003, A24.

Pollet, Rene. 'Italy Reopens Somalia Inquiry.' *Globe and Mail*, 29 August 1997, A1.

Porzio, Giovanni. 'Somalia. Gli italiani torturavano i prigionieri: ecco le prove.' *L'Eco-mancia*, 6 June 1997. Reproduced in *Panorama magazine*. [On-line.] L'Eco Manc-ina. <http://www.ecomancina.com/somalia1.html>. 23 June 2003.

Pugliese, David. 'Anatomy of a Cover-Up.' *Ottawa Citizen*, 21 June 1997, B3.

– 'Military Scandals Plagues Italy, Belgium.' *Halifax Daily News*, 23 June 1997, 18.

Reuters. 'Raw Desire for Power Fed Rwandan Genocide: Study.' *Toronto Star*, 1 April 1999, A17.

Ross, Oakland. 'We're Nice – and Getting Nicer.' *Toronto Star*, 17 May 2003, A3.

Sallot, Jeff. 'Airborne in Danger of Being Disbanded. Hazing on Video "Horrible," PM says.' *Globe and Mail*, 20 January 1995, A1, A22.

– 'Airborne Leadership Held Culpable.' *Globe and Mail*, 21 January 1995, A4.

– 'Morale Plummets among Soldiers. Many Use Food Banks, Take Extra Jobs to Make Ends Meet, Report Says.' *Globe and Mail*, 28 January 1995, A1.

Shackleton, Eric. 'Canadian Peacekeepers Shoot Two Somali Intruders.' *Kitchener-Waterloo Record*, 5 March 1993, A4.

Steyn, Mark. 'What the Afghans Need Is Colonizing.' *National Post*, 9 October 2001.

Thompson, Allan. 'Army Chief Is Recalled for Drinking in Kosovo.' *Toronto Star*, 2 October 1999, A1.

– 'Chaplain in Somali Affair Keeps Job.' *Toronto Star*, 30 August 1999, A1, A16.

– 'The Military Scandal that Simply Refuses to Die.' *Toronto Star*, 28 January 1996, C1.

– 'More Somalia Abuses Detailed.' *Toronto Star*, 10 September 1996, A1, A9.

– 'Nightmare of the Generals.' *Toronto Star*, 5 October 1997, A14.

– 'Officer Guilty of Assault.' *Toronto Star*, 9 June 1999, A22.

– 'Parents of Slain Teen Sue.' *Toronto Star*, 9 June 1999, A6.

– 'The Plight of the General.' *Toronto Star*, 20 April 1996, C1.

– 'Raw Desire for Power Fed Rwandan Genocide: Study.' *Toronto Star*, 1 April 1999, A17.

– 'War Wounds.' *Toronto Star*, 15 December 2001, K1–2.

Thompson, Allan, and Sonia Verma. 'Investigator Linked to Somalia Furor.' *Toronto Star*, 29 August 1999. A1, A6.

'Timeless: Under Homeland Security.' *Colorlines* 6, no. 1 (2003), 18–19. [On-line.] Applied Research Center. <http://www.arc.org/C Lines/CLArchive/timeline. shtml>. 23 June 2003.

'Torture in Somalia condonnato Ercole.' *La Republica*, 13 April 2000. [On-line.] La Republica. <http://www.republica.it/online/cronaca/somalia/ercole/ercole.html>. 23 June 2003.

Travers, James. 'A Soldier's Snapshot of Brutality.' *Ottawa Citizen*, 8 November 1994, A1.

Walker, William. 'Activists Demand Entry Law Changes.' *Toronto Star*, 7 January 1999, A1, A26.

– 'Canada Puts Off Entry Law Shake-Up.' *Toronto Star*, 6 January 1999, A1, A23.

– 'Frum No Longer One of the President's Men.' *Toronto Star*, 26 February 2002, A11.

– 'Pilot Acted Oddly on Night of Bombing, U.S. Court Told.' *Toronto Star*, 16 January 2003, A1, A11.

Wallace, Bruce. 'Cry of Dying People.' *Maclean's*, 7 September 1992, 20.

Watson, Paul. 'Tense Vigil in Somalia.' *Toronto Star*, 21 March 1993, F1.

Webb-Proctor, Gary. 'New Refugee Process Violates Rights of Claimants, Lawyer Says.' *Globe and Mail*, 7 January 1989, A13.

Whittington, Les. 'Three Soldiers Accused of Hazing.' *Toronto Star*, 15 July 2000, A6.

Whitworth, Sandra. 'The Ugly Unasked Questions about Somalia.' *Canadian Military*, 14 February 1997, A21.

Wilson-Smith, Anthony. 'Maclean's Honor Roll 1997: Barry and Jennifer Armstrong.' *Maclean's*, 22 December 1997, 50–1.

Wong, Craig. 'Ex-Soldier in Court over Death of Somali.' *Toronto Star*, 24 July 2002, A17.

Wood, David. 'Suspect Showed Signs of Gulf War Syndrome.' *Toronto Star*, 25 October 2002, A6.

Worthington, Peter. 'Chaplain Left in DND Chill.' *Toronto Sun*, 9 July 1996, 11.

– 'Editorial: Turning Grief into a Growth Industry.' *Toronto Sun*, 11 May 1999, 17.

– 'Private Brown: He Was Little More Than a Witness.' *Saturday Night*, September 1994, 30.

– 'Seeking Equality but Creating Racism.' *Toronto Sun*, 27 September 1994, 11.

York, Geoffrey. 'Military Admits Error in Handling Somali's Death.' *Globe and Mail*, 15 April 1993, A8.

Films, Documentaries, News Segments

Apocalypse Now [motion picture]. Directed and produced by Francis Ford Coppola. Los Angeles: Paramount Studios. 153 min.

Canadian Broadcasting Corporation. *Peace and Conflict: A Video Series for High Schools.* Scarborough: Prentice-Hall Ginn Canada, 1997.

Dying to Tell the Story. Toronto: Turner Original Productions, 1998. Aired on *The Passionate Eye, CBC Newsworld,* 31 January 1999, 18 April 1999, and 23 July 2000.

Orbinski, James. 'Taking a Stand: The Ethics of Intervention,' *Ideas.* CBC Radio. 19 April 2002. Program Transcript.

The Last Just Man [documentary video]. Directed by Steven Silver. Produced by Barna-Alper Productions, Toronto, 2001. 70 min.

'The Nightmare Drug,' *the fifth estate.* CBC Television 16 October 2002. Host Hana Gartner. Transcript provided by Bowdens Fulfillment Services, Toronto, Ontario.

The Somalia Affair. Directed by Christine Nielsen. Toronto: Barna-Alper Productions, 2002.

The Unseen Scars: Post Traumatic Stress Disorder. CBC Television, *This Magazine,* 25 November 1998. [On-line.] CBC TV. <http://www.tv.cbc.ca/national/pgminfo/ptsd/wounds.html>. 23 June 2003.

Witness the Evil [video]. Produced by the Department of National Defence, 1998. 30 min.

Interviews, Presentations

Bansie, Rohan. Interview with author. Ottawa, 22 September 1999.

Barre, Abdullahi Godah. Interview with author. Ottawa, 23 September 1999.

Dallaire, Roméo. 'Broken Soldier: A Peacekeeper's Nightmare: Interview with Romeo Dallaire.' Interview by Ted Koppel, ABC News, *Nightline,* 7 February 2001. [On-line.] ABC News. <http://www. abcnews.go.com/sections/nightline/nightline/transcripts/nl010207_trans.html>. 23 June 2003.

– 'Death and Duty Interview with Roméo D'Allaire.' Interviewed by Brian Stewart. CBC Television, *This Magazine,* 3 July 2000. [On-line.] CBC TV. <http://www.cbc.ca/news/national/magazine/dallaire/index.html>. 23 June 2003.

– 'A Good Man in Hell.' Interview by Ted Koppel. 12 June 2002. United States Holocaust Memorial Museum, Washington DC. [On-line.] USHMM. <http://www.ushmm.org/conscience/events/dallaire/dallaire.php>. 23 June 2003.

Desbarats, Peter. Untitled Panel Presentation. Audiotape. Ontario Institute for Studies in Education/University of Toronto, Toronto, September 1997.

Hashi, Ahmad. Interview with author. Ottawa, 14 January 1999.

Mock, Karen. Interview with author. Toronto, 13 April 2000.

Purnelle, Corporal. Interview. 'Somalie-armée canadienne.' *Le Point.* Radio-Canada. 7 February 1996.

Rainville, Michel. Interview. 'Somalie-armée canadienne.' *Le Point.* Radio-Canada. 7 February 1996.

Sechere, Isaac. Interview with author. Ottawa, 3 March 1999.

Williams, Michelle. 'Written Submission on Behalf of the African Canadian Legal
    Clinic.' 4 April 1997.
– 'Written "Supplementary Submission" on Behalf of the African Canadian Legal
    Clinic.' 6 June 1997.
– Interview with author. Toronto, 6 October 1999.

Presidential Speeches

Bush, President George W. State of the Union Address. 29 January 2002. [On-line.]
    Ashbrook Center for Public Affairs, Ashland University. <http://www.ashbrook.
    org/articles/bush_02-01-29.html>. 23 June 2003.
– 'Speech to the 2002 Graduating Class at the United States Military Academy,'
    1 June 2002. West Point, New York. [On-line.] Ashbrook Center for Public
    Affairs, Ashland University. <http://www.ashbrook.org/articles/bush_02-06-
    01.html>. 23 June 2003.

Government Documents

Canadian Forces. 'Haiti – Board of Inquiry into Leadership Relationships with the
    Military Police and Events Surrounding Mistreatment of Haitian Detainees.' *Final
    Report.* Ottawa: Department of National Defence, April 1999.
Citizenship and Immigration Canada. 'News Release 1997–05: Lucienne Robillard
    Announces the Introduction of the Undocumented Convention Refugee in Canada
    Class.' 22 January 1997.
– 'Regulations Amending the Immigration Regulations, 1978 and Making a Related
    Amendment: Regulatory Impact Analysis Statement.' *Canada Gazette, Part 1.*
    12 December 1998. Ottawa: Public Works and Government Services Canada.
Commission of Inquiry into the Deployment of Canadian Forces to Somalia. *Informa-
    tion Legacy: A Compendium of Source Material/Commission of Inquiry into the Deploy-
    ment of Canadian Forces to Somalia. Héritage documentaire: recueil des ressources/
    Commission d'enquête sur le dééploiement des Forces canadiennes en Somalie* [CD-
    ROM]. Ottawa: Minister of Public Works and Government Services Canada,
    Canadian Government Publishing, 1997.
Commissione Governativa d'Inchiesta. *Relazione Conclusiva sui fatti di Somalia.* Rome:
    Ministro della Difesa, 8 August 1997.

Index